BELIEVABLE

Kelly Brake

DEDICATION

This book is dedicated to Lenora: my faith partner, my wife, and my best friend. Without her faith and friendship, the stories in this book would never have unfolded. She has been my greatest encouragement, and a witness with me of the resurrection evidences of Jesus Christ that have unfolded before us again and again.

Though told in the first person, these are not the stories of one person's faith. This story has many individual moments, but without the partnership of a marriage and family that were dedicated to seeking first the kingdom of God, none of what follows would have unfolded. Without Lenora's faith and hearing ear for the voice of the Lord, I would never have had the courage to live the life that God has graciously allowed us to live. I would not have had the confidence to write this book, nor the determination to press forward in ministry during the difficult seasons of life.

For all of this and more, I am forever grateful to God for granting me the very best wife and friend that a man could ever dream to have.

Let us keep dreaming my beloved, for our best is yet to come!

INTRODUCTION

At times when we look back at 37 years of God's faithful intervention and provision, the life we have lived seems almost like a dream. We recount a story from our past and look at one another smiling, confirming to ourselves once again that it happened exactly as we remembered it. The facts are not fogged by the emotion of the moment or by the passage of time. God really and truly intervened in supernatural ways over and over again, until eventually, early on in our journey, we began to realize that the supernatural was God's intended pattern of life for those who have chosen to place their trust in Him.

We are only mid-way thorough our adventure, yet already there is plenty to tell. More importantly, the story of God's miracles and His Spirit's leading need to be told, for His glory and as a signal fire for those who are just now launching their own journey. My last protest against writing was "why would anyone want to read our story?" God's answer was compelling: "It's not your story...it's MY story; and I want it to be told."

Today's generation is looking for that which is authentic. They have no heart for hype or exaggeration. There is a justifiable demand and hunger to know whether or not a dynamic life of faith and adventure is still available and relevant in a fast changing 21st century world. The stories that follow are not romanticized embellishments of vague recollections. Nearly 30 years of journaling, 365 days of every year, have preserved the record for such a time as this.

Over the years, the response to reports of our experiences has often been a single word of surprise or astonishment, and most often that single word has been **"unbelievable"**! This does not come from a skeptical heart, but rather it is a reflexive response in a world where we are conditioned to **not** see or expect the supernatural intervention of God. If something is "unbelievable" or "incredible" (another frequent response), then it is thought to be that which cannot normally be believed. It shows us that believing something which we normally cannot see has become difficult for much of the church world. We have become as Thomas, who found the reports of a risen Savior to be "not credible", such that only a personal encounter and visual proof would change his mind.

And so we have titled this story of our journey with the single word, **BELIEVABLE**. We long to bury those tendencies of our human nature that always rush to doubt, suspicion, and a disassembling of every reported move of God's power. We ask God's grace to remain as little children, ever in wonderment at the effortless display of His promises.

As you read along with our journey, may His story cause a fresh faith to arise in your heart, and may you grab tenaciously to the promise of abundant and supernatural living for your own family and future. God is no respecter of persons. What He has done for others, He desires to do for you!

- KELLY BRAKE

ACKNOWLEDGEMENT AND THANKS

Our three children grew up in anything but an ordinary home. The particular path that we have followed required much sacrifice from every member of the family. God in His goodness compensated with many adventures around the world that other children might never imagine, yet the stability of a typical American childhood with its schooling, sports programs, proms and predictability was something we were unable to provide.

In spite of all the twists and turns, our daughter and two sons have been among our greatest friends. They have never held us back from the field for fear of what might go wrong. The love and honor that they extend toward us now in their early 30's are among the greatest joys we could ever know. We are deeply thankful to Melissa, Omar, and Jonathan for taking the journey with us and becoming in their own unique lives our very favorite stories. Now we have our son in law Derek, our daughter in law Lynn, and our grandchildren living the adventure as well. The best is yet to come!

I am so grateful for the many members of the body of Christ who have over the years encouraged and confirmed the calling to write. This book has been slow in coming, but you persevered and believed in us, prodded and prophesied, and at last a fruit is born from your willingness to be God's voice of conviction and affirmation. Somehow I feel that the cumulative years of friendly reminders were all meant to culminate at such a time as this.

Kelita Deems has been a gift from God in our writing endeavors, a direct answer to a prayer in 2014 when I asked God to give us someone who could help us complete what we were unable to complete on our own. On our way to Florida we stopped to preach at the Rock Family Worship Center in Parkersburg, West

Virginia. Having no idea of our plans to publish, Kelita felt to call and offer her services in bringing us through to a final printed product if God had perchance given us an assignment to write. Her help was invaluable in the printing of our first book, the marriage devotional 40 WEEKS. Once again she has proven a God sent resource with her encouragement, servant's heart, and production expertise. Whatever blessing others may derive from BELIEVABLE is directly connected to Kelita's own willingness to hear the voice of the Holy Spirit and align herself with the purposes of God.

TABLE OF CONTENTS

1 ARRESTED BY AN ANGEL

In 1981 we were not particularly interested in a supernatural life. I'm not even sure that we ever used the word in our vocabulary at that time. All that mattered then was that we were two teenagers falling crazy in love in between our studies and work at our Bible College in Nyack, New York.

We didn't exactly hit it off when we first began preaching together. In September of 1980 we were assigned to the same street ministry team targeting Manhattan's Lower East Side. It was my first time out, and at 17 years old I was proud as a peacock to have been entrusted with the safety of four college girls who obviously, in my mind, would have been swallowed up without my protection by the perils that lurked in darkened alleys as we sauntered up and down the streets of the Bowery and Chinatown.

We actually had some great successes that night, the highlight being when three elderly Italian men bowed their heads and prayed to receive Jesus as Savior. I was flying high as I introduced each of my team to those we attempted to talk with. "Rhonda" was fairly quiet much of that evening. I had introduced her by name a number of times, but I could tell she was not dazzled by my leadership. As the evening was wrapping up and we were loading up into the van to head home, I politely said "it was very nice to meet you Rhonda".....except that I was not anticipating her curt reply: "By the way, my name is Lenora, **NOT** Rhonda!".

My response, unspoken but thought, was immediate and adamant: "Actually, I could care less what your name is!" Lenora whirled away from the proud peacock, and I whirled away from her indifference toward my team leadership skills.

A few months later we found ourselves working side by side in the college cafeteria. Offenses were long gone, and suddenly "Rhonda" was the prettiest girl in the room. The peacock's feathers as well had been clipped, as he furiously scrubbed and sweated over the pot washing sink, trying to earn some pocket money so that he could gather the courage to ask Lenora out to dinner.

That first date was one we still laugh about. Lenora, wanting to be ladylike, left half of her steak on her plate. And I, having paid good money for that steak, was tolerating no such waste. I leaned over and asked, "are you going to finish that?," and when I was certain that she was abandoning this gleaming piece of cow which had cost me 7 hours of pot washing, I reached across the table with my fork and transferred it to my side.

To my sorrow, I have since come to know that that was the first and last steak Lenora would ever sacrifice at the altar of my excessive craving for beef.

We were made for each other by Divine design, and after that first date, unbeknownst to me, Lenora had heard from God and began planning her wedding. It took me another month of fun outings before I too realized that so much sooner than I had ever imagined, God had brought me together with the girl I would spend my life with.

In those days, we were both determined and destined for foreign mission service, having been called to such as kids. In those earliest weeks we envisioned a traditional and typical life of ministry service, 40 years in one nation, reaching the unreached, and retiring after a job well done.

But God had other plans, and quickly began to show us another way.

It was early Spring of 1981, just after we had begun dating. We walked together late at night down Houston Street in New York, charged with retrieving the 15 passenger van that had been parked several blocks from our host church.

I could see in the distance a man lying on the sidewalk, and my inclination was to sidestep a situation that I could not likely resolve. The sight of a hopelessly intoxicated homeless person was all too common on the streets. We were on a schedule and had to get our team back before curfew. But there was no blocking out his words as we came closer: "Please....can you help me?"

I looked up and down the street, and there was no one anywhere for blocks. The man looked and smelled horrific. As we knelt down, I asked him "what do you want us to do?" He said without hesitation, "please help me to the other side of the street." I somewhat breathed a sigh of relief as that seemed an easy assignment. I would simply take his hand and help him walk over. But there was no easy solution I soon learned. He informed me that he could not walk, and would I be willing to carry him. The man was saturated with a terrible smell, and this teenage kid from suburbia in Ohio had not signed up for this kind of duty. But something powerful was pulling at our hearts.

Lenora and I looked at each other and we knew that we had to help.

I told him to put his arms around my neck, and as I slid one arm under his legs, I realized that one limb was artificial and he was indeed incapable of rising unassisted. With my other arm under his back, I picked him up and began walking across the streets. Manhattan's streets are always busy, but I again noted that there was not a car in sight. As we carried him across, I asked him where he wanted to go? He pointed to a bench and said "put me there."

As I gently laid him down, he reached into his pocket and pulled out a dollar to pay us, which of course we refused. We did not have a great deal of experience with the addicted and homeless, but we knew enough to know that being paid for kindness was not the norm. We prayed for him and turned to retrieve our van, parked only a few dozen yards away.

Still, not one vehicle or person anywhere in sight. Less than 90 seconds passed, and we were in our van and pulling up to the bench where we had deposited our friend. Lenora and I both caught our breath and parked there in stunned silence. He was gone. We jumped out of the van and looked intensely up and down the street, all around the bench, behind every bush; we were frantic not from compassion, but because we both immediately knew that we were witnessing something impossible. Short of spontaneous combustion, that man could not have relocated himself anywhere in the vicinity within that minute our backs were turned. There was no place to hide, no place to crawl to, not even a place to run to, if indeed he could have run with one leg. There were no left belongings, no residue of odor, no sign that a human being had just been laid incapacitated upon that bench. And still, there was neither a car or person anywhere on the street.

We looked at each other quietly and gathered our thoughts. I don't know which of us dared to breathe it out first, but we both knew we had just experienced our first encounter with an angel. My theological brain began doing gymnastics to try and understand why an angel had to smell and why he only had one leg?

I've never quite been able to satisfactorily answer those questions, other than to recognize that God was desiring to test and mark us with His compassion. But a greater thing occurred, and that was the marking, for the first time, of the supernatural activity of God upon our shared ministry. We both grew up in

Christian homes and had seen God answer prayer, but this was something entirely different: a visible, undeniable, insertion by God into our view of Christian living.

It was so shocking that we told no one right away. We asked ourselves for some time afterwards, "did that really happen?" Yet we were both there, and we both knew that the laws of physics forbade any other conclusion. God had chosen to place an angel into our path. It was believable, and we believed.

We had no idea of just how far God was intending to stretch the boundaries of our belief in the years to come.

2 A COLLISION WITH ACTS CHAPTER 2

After the angel incident, our hunger for God's supernatural intervention began to stir. Our Bible College gave us an excellent foundation in the Scriptures, but our childhood training left us fairly uninformed when it came to things like healing, hearing God's voice, and interacting personally with the Holy Spirit.

I was walking across our beautiful campus lawn in Rockland County, New York, and I remember the exact spot where Fred, a Sophomore, came up and began badgering me about Acts Chapter 2. "Have you been baptized in the Holy Spirit?", was his insistent question. I explained patiently to Fred that I had been instructed in my childhood Baptist church that such things were of the devil, and I was contented with what I had, thank you very much!

"But what if there is something more that God wants for your life?" Fred's challenge began to run through my mind, for indeed I had developed a deep hunger for something more. I wanted to preach Jesus, and was gifted to do so, but why were the sick in our churches always sick, the neurotic forever neurotic, and the stories of Bible miracles just that....stories of <u>Bible</u> miracles, but not the miracles of today?

I listened as Fred patiently explained the purpose of Acts 2, that Jesus intended we have power for ministry so that we could really and truly help people to the highest degree possible. We could become the kind of witnesses that the world would believe. We could demonstrate that God is real!

I took some literature that Fred gave me, a book called <u>9:00 In The Morning</u>, and I devoured its pages. My upbringing whispered that I should run, but my spirit began to hunger for something deeper than what I had known.

Alone in my dorm prayer closet, I had determined that this would be the testing hour. I spoke frankly to God, informing Him that "I did not believe in such things as speaking in tongues or the baptism of the Holy Spirit, as everyone knows that those things were confined to the days of the Apostles"...but then I conceded to the Lord that it was possible that I was wrong....and since I did not want to miss anything He had for my life, He was more than welcome to prove to me that Fred and Acts Chapter 2 were not mutually contradictory to sound doctrine!

I opened the door just a crack...and God blew through it with a tornado! No sooner had I finished my speech, when the air came rushing out of my diaphragm and a noise unlike I had ever heard before. I knew instantly what was happening. I was speaking in a language no one had taught me, and I was in a euphoria that I did not know existed for the follower of Christ. I laughed and rejoiced and kept on going. For three days, I could barely do anything but speak in a heavenly language. I did my laundry while praying in that language. I was afraid to greet people for fear of exposure in a school that did not openly encourage such a practice. Soon after the prayer closet I made a beeline for Fred to tell him that it was real after all! I also told Lenora, and it was just a few years later during our first pastoral assignment when she too had a profound encounter with the power of God's indwelling Spirit.

Lenora and I had both been solid, born again believers for many years since childhood. We had the seal of God's Spirit in our lives, and had been reborn by His revelation of Jesus. But as we began to discover on our journey, there is a difference between "me having all of Him, and Him having all of me!" I was indeed saved, but I was not fully equipped for the task to which I had been called. We were called to do far more than quietly labor for 40 years in an unknown land. We were called to be witnesses and a demonstration of His very resurrection life. We were called to make the supernatural the norm in our natural. We were challenged to develop an intimate acquaintance with the One Who was not only a Comforter, but also an ever present Teacher Who would whisper daily and point us down extraordinary paths we could never have imagined.

Recently I tracked down Fred by means of Facebook. I needed to thank him, and I owed him a debt of gratitude I could never repay. Without Fred's boldness to tell me truth I had not known, the life that you are about to read of in this book could never have unfolded. I believe that with all my heart. Everything supernatural we have experienced has been initiated and quantified by the gracious leading of the Spirit of God.

He has become our Counselor, our Teacher, and life's most faithful Guide. He has ushered us faithfully into the quality of life that Jesus promised and died for, a life "more abundant", making us those who would have rivers of living water flowing out from their innermost being.

3 MARKED FOR SOMETHING MORE

We dove headlong into life, school, marriage, and children. We spent three more years working in lower Manhattan, preaching on the streets, loving and teaching kids in the projects while the paraphernalia of their parent's drug dealing lay a few feet away on kitchen tables and in bathtubs. God began to develop a fearlessness in us during those days, and much more importantly, a deep love for these lost souls which enabled us to feel completely at home among them. In the darkest alleys or stairwells we felt His hands all around us. People knew we loved their kids, and so the word on the streets was "don't mess with the Bible Club teachers."

Not that there weren't close calls. I remember the day a heroin addict held a knife to my belly and informed me that he was going to stab me and kill me. I had such a wave of God's love come over me as I looked into his eyes and told him, "I'm so sorry that you feel that way...but I want you to know that I love you and God loves you." He looked at me like I was crazy, and a few minutes after the incident when my heart rate became normal again, I considered that perhaps I was indeed just a little bit crazy.

We have learned that if you are going to live a supernatural life, there are many times when you will do things that people think are crazy.

We invested our money more out of emotion than inspiration back then. Perhaps thinking that we could outdo the Biblical standard, we decided that 10% wasn't a daring enough tithe, and wanting to be radical Christians, we would tithe no less than 30% of our income. But God honors the intention of the heart, and He supplied for us in so many miraculous ways. We were working two jobs each, and things were tight, but we were going to live our lives with an open hand, not always looking for a hand out.

That worked okay for a while until we ran into our first severe economic tests, and then suddenly tithing only 10% didn't seem so unspiritual after all. We had not yet learned about the difference between tithes and offerings, and we were placing ourselves under a self-created law to try and attain that radical way of living we hungered for. God graciously over time taught us about being Spirit led in our giving, and we learned that 30% was not a magic number, but the right number was actually whatever God instructed for each moment and occasion. In the years since, we've let 10% be the minimum, and then enjoyed watching Him direct the rest of our giving as He has seen fit; sometimes 20% or 30%, and in a few instances even all that we had.

He doesn't need any of it, but we know now it is all about trust, obedience, and keeping the windows of His grace and provision open over our lives so that we can increasingly be entrusted with more for the advancement of His kingdom.

A life of sowing and giving results in a life of continual open doors. We were married in June of 1983, fully intending to put college behind us and head out to conquer the world. But then came the chilling words, "**I want you to go to seminary!**" I did not want to go to seminary. I love learning, but I do not like studying and writing papers for class. I wanted to be on the streets of Manhattan or deep in some jungle reaching a lost tribe. Greek Exegesis and Hermeneutics seemed like a curse.

Lenora had graduated with her B.A. in Social Science the month before we married, and 5 months later in December I graduated with my B.A. in Biblical Studies. We were ready to go to a church, but God said "seminary!" Ugh! Well, we had an easy out because we had absolutely no money, and seminary was costly. The Pastor of Lenora's church in Coudersport, Pennsylvania, called to ask us about our plans. People were interested in supporting up and coming missionaries. We mentioned that we were thinking about seminary, but made no requests. Three days later we received a phone call from Pastor Thomas, informing us that the board of the church had determined that our entire three years of seminary training should be paid for in full.

Sometimes God pays for what you don't want. We took a deep breath and started our four year journey toward a Master of Divinity degree, three in the classroom and one year of internship. Most of the time I did not feel very divine! The Holy Spirit who had invaded me so tangibly seemed far away as I toiled in the classroom, while Lenora toiled with our babies, Melissa born the second semester of seminary, Omar born between the second and third year, and Jonathan born half way through the third and final year.

17 credit hours of class, 50 hour work weeks, and a new Brake baby every time we turned around...something had to give, and we decided to forego the standard three months internship after second year and ask for a one year assignment. It was another turning point in our destiny.

4 FIRST CHURCH BALDWIN, UNITED METHODIST

I knew I was in trouble early into my internship. It was September of 1985, and full of excitement for my year off from study, I asked the pastor if we could get to know one another by exchanging the stories of our testimonies.

He looked a bit quizzical, and then said wisely, "why don't you go first!" I launched into a long and dramatic tale of my childhood, of leading friends to Jesus, street ministry, God's calling through Brother Andrew when I was seven years old, and later through

Billy Graham when I was ten years old. It was a royal retelling and I was sure he would be dutifully impressed.

He wasn't. He cleared his throat, and then stated very matter of factly: "I was born in Jamaica, and when I was around ten years old, our family nanny told me: 'your brother is the first born and he should be a preacher, but he isn't willing to be a preacher...so you are gonna have to be the preacher!'" He concluded with a flourish, smiling as he said to me, "So here I am 55 years later - a preacher...that's my testimony."

I was crushed, and somewhat ticked off. I wanted to intern under some great anointed man of God, a fiery evangelist who could teach me all the ways of God. Instead, I found myself highly suspect of my new employer's spiritual credentials. (Let me happily report here that 31 years later, I am now well aware that this man who has since gone on into glory was a sincere servant of God - we simply had come from two very different worlds).

Two months into my assignment I called our chaplain at Alliance Theological Seminary and demanded a transfer: "This guy isn't even saved! How could the school send me here? What placement criteria does our school have?" It was not one of my more noble moments.

Thankfully Chaplain John Stevey was a wise and Godly man who informed me that I would not be transferred, and that I would need to man up and stick it out and **submit** to the leadership of the Pastor of the church to which I had been sent.

Oh, how thankful I am for the wisdom of our Chaplain! I wanted a powerful preacher to take me under his wing and inspire me, but God knew I needed a better inspiration learned only through obedience and submission to authority. So many are craving a supernatural life, but they want it without having to serve or submit to the larger body of Christ around them. They become lone rangers and self-promoters. I thank God for sparing us from such a fiasco.

Baldwin, our first Long Island assignment, became one of the most formative years of our ministry. I learned the submission and discipline of preaching 16 minute sermons. I learned to do the tasks that no one else wanted. I learned to be faithful while working a 60 hour work week for a wage of $127. And I also learned that there was a great deal more waiting for us in the realm of supernatural living. Half way through our internship, I began to sorrow and feel dry. I wanted a deeper walk and experience, not a life of 16 minute sermons and confirmation classes for kids whose sole qualification was that they were turning 12 years old.

I cried out and God answered. I don't remember how I met them, but someone connected me with a group of Pastors who met weekly for prayer: Episcopalians, Methodists, and a few from Independent churches. They were a Charismatic group of just six or seven men, and when I first walked into the living room where they met, I looked into the eyes of the most loving man I had ever met. He radiated Jesus, and as we sat to pray, I was immediately transported into a sense of God's presence unlike anything I had known before. I had enjoyed the power of God's presence in my personal life, but never had I been with a company of men to experience what can happen when a group cries out together for the presence and power of God's Spirit.

I explained my dilemma in Baldwin, our lack of fellowship, and my own experience with the Holy Spirit four years previously. I simply did not know where and how to go forward in my spiritual life. Patiently and lovingly, they asked me if I knew that I could continue praying in the Spirit and communing with the Holy Spirit whenever I wanted; I in fact did not know that, and had assumed that my initial experience was a one-time event. "Oh, not at all," they replied! "You have the right to immerse yourself in deep communion with the Holy Spirit at any time on any given day!" Well this was news to me, so when they asked if they could pray for me, I gladly assented. And once again, heaven invaded earth.

This was the turning point that sustained me through that year of internship. Every week I eagerly drove myself over to the Episcopal church and reveled in the atmosphere of heaven that attended those prayer gatherings. Those men became my mentors, and patiently answered so many of my questions. They taught me much about the ways of God's Spirit. God also used them to soften my heart concerning Long Island, for it was His plan to send us back in 1987 for a series of God encounters that would change our life forever.

5 WHICH WAY IS THE FUTURE?

Our final year of seminary was a whirlwind. Our eldest son Omar was born two months before we left Baldwin, and soon we were immersed back into classes, Lenora was pregnant with Jonathan, and Long Island was happily behind us. We were quite determined that there would be no reason to return there again. We would graduate, find a church to fulfill the two years of service required before we could be sent to the foreign field, and then we would fulfill our dream by leaving America for foreign shores. Our early dreams rotated between Lebanon, Irian Jaya, or Gabon. Unreached, foreign and far away were our only stipulations.

One day in my Church Administration class, I had a profoundly upsetting experience. The professor asked the students where they intended to serve upon graduation. One by one they began to discuss the perks and pleasantries of various parts of the country.

One wanted to go South for the weather. Another preferred the foliage of New England. Others insisted on being near a major city. Some disliked certain districts because of the local leadership, while others spoke of things like medical benefits, retirement guarantees, book allowances, and so on.

I left quiet and deep in thought. Why had not one single student spoken about finding a direction of God's choosing? The general consensus was that it did not matter all that much to God where you went, as long as you went somewhere. This view of God did not sit well with my spirit. I sensed the sorrow of the Holy Spirit inside of me, grieving for those who desired to serve yet without a dependence upon His guidance and instruction. These were good men and women who wanted to honor God...yet they had inadvertently been trained to accept a very natural way of life.

I did not know much, but I knew enough to know that Lenora and I did not want normal or natural. We did not want a predictable way of living. We wanted to be on the edge of God's great adventure. This could not be attributed to an inherent virtue, but in retrospect now we recognize that God was stirring us to desire that which was essential for the fulfillment of His call. And that call was anything but incidental or non-specific. God had a plan and a destiny for our family. He was extremely particular about the church we would be assigned to. And if we were willing to ask, He was willing to make it crystal clear.

Just two months after Jonathan was born in June of 1987, our local Superintendent asked us to consider a church assignment in Yorktown Heights, New York. We were brimming with excitement about the possibility of our very first senior position. But we were not going to guess about this matter. We told God that we knew He was a speaking God, and we needed Him to speak. Rather than go directly for an interview, the church was near enough to our seminary that we decided to simply drive over and ask God to give us an indicator. Do you know that God is able to speak loudly and clearly? No sooner had we stepped into the parking lot of that church, than a distinct heaviness was felt by both of us. We could not get out of there fast enough. It was a beautiful church building in a beautiful town in a very lovely part of the country, and I am quite sure it was filled with very beautiful Christian people. But it was **not** the place of God's choosing. We had asked the Spirit to speak, and He had spoken with clarity: "You are not permitted to go to Yorktown Heights!" Our unwillingness to even allow our names as candidates seemed presumptive and ungrateful to the District leadership, but thankfully they decided to give us another try.

A couple of years prior in 1984 we had been invited to visit one of our denomination's affiliated churches in Glen Cove, NY. I was asked to deliver the Sunday morning message as a guest student preacher. My college roommate's brother had been pastor there for several years, and now in 1987 they were preparing to leave for missionary service in Africa. The District Office asked if we would be willing to consider spending a few years pastoring this small congregation of 35 men, women, and children before our assignment to the mission field.

We were honored of course to be considered, but there was a big problem: Glen Cove was on the dreaded Long Island, just a dozen miles due north of our previous assignment in Baldwin. Even though we retained some good friendships from Baldwin (and some to this day), we did not have warm and fuzzy thoughts about living again in Nassau County, with some of the wealthiest and least needy zip codes in the USA.

Jesus came for the sick and hurting, not for Nassau County, or so we foolishly thought. We were woefully telescopic in our view of how Jesus felt about people...and He knew exactly how to cure our limited vision.

6 GETTING THE GROUND READY IN GLEN COVE

As heavy hearted as we may have felt in Yorktown Heights, to the opposite degree we began to feel an elation about Glen Cove. It was true we had a familiarity, and the North Shore of Long Island is one of the most beautiful parts of the country. But nothing less than a Divine directive would get us to agree to an extended residency.

We sat with their board one Saturday afternoon, and all was well with the world. When they asked if I knew the salary, my shrugged shoulders elicited a simultaneous cry of "Oh NO!" from the elders. They had assumed the District Office would have warned me in advance. "Fear not!", I informed them with a flash of noble faith, "It doesn't matter to us what the pay is...all we care about is being in the will of God!"

I found out not too long after that it actually **does** matter what people pay you...especially when you have three young children. A 100 year old parsonage next door to the church and $180 per week, and we were off and running! We moved in on October 8th, 1987, our first senior pastoral role and we were ready to change the world. I began to lay out the first few months of a preaching plan. We dove into every program with gusto.

We visited every shut in and senior more than they probably wanted to be visited. We led the worship, cleaned the building, taught the youth and children, led men's and women's meetings, midweek Bible study, and every other thing an aspiring young ministry couple thinks they are supposed to be doing.

The congregation slowly began to grow, by a trickle here and there, but something was missing. I counseled endlessly yet no one was changing. Our first Summer there the church faced a crisis when our prayer leader, a mother of seven children, died suddenly during family vacation. We spent all of the following year watching the youngest boy during school hours. The church went into crisis management mode, and we devoted ourselves to caring for one another as a proper community and church family.

Yet still we burned for something more. Growth, incremental salary increases, lots of loving fellowship, and a board that did not fight...these things were wonderful. We had it better than many of our classmates, whose horror stories we had been hearing from their first assignments. We were only going to be here for two years anyway, so why press in for more?

But it was God Who would not stop pressing in. He called us into prayer, and we began to seek the face of God. We began to cry out, "Holy Spirit, magnify Jesus in this place!"

Prayer began at 6:00 AM every week day, and some days we would linger for three hours or more, worshipping and seeking the presence of God. I had a lovely congregation of faithful people, but something within said there was more to this Kingdom of God, and we had only just begun to scratch the surface. It was the Fall of 1989, and after two years in Glen Cove, the date for my formal Ordination service was fast approaching. From there we would be free to move away from Long Island and fulfill our long awaited missionary dream.

7 DO YOU WANT TO BE ARTICULATE, OR ANOINTED?

I was meticulous in the preparation of my messages. Some weeks the study and careful manuscript notations would take upwards of 30 hours. I was called to preach, but I also wanted to excel at preaching. I wrote the most perfect sermons I could write, then went over them to rewrite them again.

Each Sunday I stood with my neatly typed manuscript, usually on four sheets of paper. This was before the days of owning a personal computer, so having a functional typewriter was like a treasure. I preached word for word from these notes, though no one knew it, as I had perfected the technique of reading it while maintaining good eye contact with the congregation.

God had blessed me with an abundance of passion, a gift for preaching, and an ability in the English language. I preached effectively, and there was no lack of appreciation in the people. They did not know of the anguish I went through weekly, the Saturdays of tension when the children had to "leave Daddy alone." In their innocence they had no idea that Daddy was on the verge of a nervous breakdown every Saturday night as I pounded away at the typewriter in my own strength, determined to master every word, inflection, and grammatical nuance that would make my delivery a home run the next morning.

It was early in January, 1990, and I preached that Sunday with eloquence. I caught myself in the middle of my sermon, momentarily day dreaming about an event scheduled for that afternoon. My congregation was oblivious as I raced through my manuscript and didn't miss a beat. I was preaching the holy and eternal word of God with fervor, yet my mind was a million miles away.

A well-dressed woman in her 60's was visiting that day, and she made a beeline for me after the service. "Young man, you are exceedingly articulate...you have a wonderful mastery of the English language...I so enjoyed listening to your speech."

My heart sank to the floor as a wave of humiliation swept over me. I was keenly aware that I had not put my whole heart into the message, even day dreaming during the delivery. I had become satisfied with satisfying the ears of the crowd.

Back in my room, I cried out to the Lord for forgiveness, when I suddenly heard the words that changed my life forever: **"Do you want to be articulate, or do you want to be anointed?"**

I did not really understand the meaning of the question, for I did not really understand the full meaning of the word "anointed." The Spirit began to elaborate, and again I heard the question: "Do you want to be articulate, or do you want to be anointed? Do you want to impress men, or change them? Do you want man's applause, or do you want to hear 'well done, good and faithful servant'?"

'Oh God", I cried out, "I want to be anointed!" "I want to make a difference in the lives of men; I want to preach out of the well of your Spirit, not the well of my own ability."

And then again, I heard His still small voice: **"Very well then; next Sunday, you are not to take a single piece of paper, not a single note, into the pulpit with you. I will meet you, and you will learn what it is to be anointed."**

I was immediately stricken with fear. Never mind that I might at some point have been articulate or polished. I was a manuscript preacher. I didn't just take outlines. Other than street preaching, I had never stood in a church pulpit without an entire manuscript before me. Was God asking me to go out of my mind?

And in fact, that following week, I think I almost did. In fear and trembling I studied my Bible endlessly the six days that followed. I wrote out my notes, then went over them a thousand times in my head. I was almost sick emotionally when Sunday rolled around. I'm pretty sure that the Saturday before was our worst family Saturday ever.

Slowly I walked up to the platform when the preaching moment came. I carried not a shred of paper with me. I opened my Bible...and thus commenced 40 of the most powerful minutes I have ever known. The rushing wind that had come out of me back in my dorm room closet in 1981 now came down upon my mouth with a force unlike ever before. I began to preach like a man from another world. A Holy Spirit articulation took ahold of my tongue that I absolutely on my best day could not have manufactured with my natural ability.

And the crowd knew it. Everyone there knew that something had happened to their pastor that Sunday. I was electrified and astonished in my own soul. I did not know that in preaching one could experience so intensely the present reality of God.

It was the beginning of my calling to preach with prophetic inspiration, and I have from that day never looked back. It was a full decade at least before I ever again carried a note into the pulpit. Not by preference, but by Divine mandate; not as a superior methodology over any other, but as God's chosen means for training me to hear His voice with accuracy and to rely on His ability completely. It was and still is the greatest schooling I have ever received.

I went home to my journal that day, and one can read still where I have written these words: "I'M FREE....I'M FREE....I'M FREE!" I knew it down in the deepest part of my soul that something had been unlocked which was going to take my family in a direction far different than I would have ever dared dream; not to the pulpit of one church, but to the pulpits of hundreds of churches; not to one nation, but to scores of nations; not to a crowd of 35 souls on the North Shore of Long Island, but to hundreds of thousands of souls all over the world.

God had offered me just a taste of what true Spirit empowered ministry was supposed to look like. If you had asked me at that moment, I would have said "there can't possibly be a greater glory than this!"....but Jesus had only just begun to pour out His Spirt in Glen Cove.

8 THE HEALING POWER OF JESUS

Immediately following the transformation of the preaching was an initiation into the ministry of healing. Up to that point we had not experienced any significant demonstrations of God's healing power in our own church, though Lenora had personally experienced God's healing of a painful foot condition during our seminary days. In fact, things had not gone so well when we first ventured out to pray for the sick in Glen Cove. We had a saintly church member named Mathilde Koop, a shut in who still retained her heavy German accent. Mathilde had broken her hip and was recuperating at home when I dropped by to pray for her and attempt to secure a healing miracle. It didn't go very well at all. As I began to pray fervently, Mathilde began to scream loudly, "what have you **done**...what have you **done**?! You made it worse!" I was utterly demoralized in my hopes for the healing ministry, as well as slightly paranoid of a potential lawsuit. Thankfully Mathilde was not the pastor suing type, and she did get some relief eventually (probably right after I left the house).

But the breakthrough did come, in the most unexpected way. Lenora was sitting home on the couch with an incapacitating migraine headache. She had suffered more than once with these attacks. She asked for prayer, and immediately I heard that voice that was becoming increasingly familiar, the voice of God's Spirit; only this time He was not whispering, but His words came forcefully: **"Command the headache to leave in Jesus' name!"** Neither Lenora or I were familiar with the concept of "commanding" anything. We believed strongly in prayer, and believed strongly that God answered prayer. But up to this point we had not considered the authority of the believer over darkness or disease. Jesus had commissioned his disciples to "heal the sick", but we still were of a mindset that "hoped for healing for the sick."

The instruction however left no room for half-hearted intercession. Immediately I laid my hand upon Lenora's head, and somewhat forcefully declared "I command this headache to be healed, in Jesus' name!"

Lenora became instantly wide-eyed. "It's gone...it's completely gone!", she exclaimed. For the first time as a ministry couple, we had witnessed the immediate and instantaneous power of God's healing, and thus began another revolution in our ministry journey. If God could do this for a headache, what else would He be willing to do this for? We began to pray for the church members with a new confidence and authority, and we did not have to wait long to discover that God indeed could heal headaches and so much more!

9 COUGH INTO MY HAND

Not long after this first miracle, we began to hold special times of prayer for healing. Word began to get around that God was healing people of all sorts of ailments. Chronic pain would leave instantly. Concurrent with the wave of healing came another wave, the gift of "words of knowledge" about people's conditions. We were not seeking this, it just suddenly was dropped onto our church by God's grace. The first was in a prayer meeting in our church basement, when I heard the whisper, "pain in the left knee". I was surprised, as I had never heard such before, yet I knew it was God speaking. I asked our group, "is there someone here with pain in their left knee?" Immediately one of our elders spoke up and began to tell of his condition. Once more, a confident prayer with authority was spoken, and instantly the man was healed.

Our faith began soaring. During a Sunday morning service altar call, a word came into my mind that I did not know the meaning of, and was certain I had never previously heard. Yet the word was clear: "diverticulitis". I hesitated, not wanting to make a fool of myself by pronouncing something that didn't exist; but again it clearly came to my mind… "diverticulitis". I sheepishly asked our congregation, "is there someone here who has something called diverticulitis?" I looked around pretending to be confident, but inwardly I was nervous. It only took a moment though for Jessie Wilson, our church treasurer, to shoot her hand up in the air and call out, "That's **ME** Pastor! I have diverticulitis!…the doctor just diagnosed it." I dared to ask Jessie what exactly diverticulitis was, and not being shy, she happily began to explain exactly what would happen with her digestion if she ate raspberries or nuts. I politely terminated Jessie's vivid medical description with the urgency of prayer. Jessie was immediately and permanently healed.

I don't understand all of God's ways, and have learned not to insist upon an explanation. But there are times when He stretches our faith with instructions that seem to border on the bizarre. I believe this is often to test and develop our obedience. We were in the middle of a series of special healing services. Jessie, who always had great faith for the impossible, had a friend in the hospital who was dying of lung cancer. I had been informed beforehand that they were going to attempt to bring her directly from the hospital that evening. As we worshiped, the rear door of the sanctuary opened and two men very delicately escorted in an emaciated woman who could barely stand unassisted. We stopped our worship and I asked them to bring her forward.

I already had been told the specifics, that she had advanced lung cancer, an inoperable football size tumor in one of her lungs, and that doctors were giving her just a few weeks to live. She was not a church goer, but she came at Jessie's prompting, hoping for a miracle from Jesus.

As the two men helped her forward, I heard once again the distinct voice of God, only this time I was not happy with what I heard: "Tell her to cough into your hand." I'm sure that many can relate to my immediate mortification. If there is one sound manufactured by people that I absolutely cannot abide, it is the sound of someone clearing their sinuses. I have an automatic gag reflex upon hearing such a sound. Even worse is when they cough something up. I don't want to nauseate anyone, but I am illustrating here the important link at times between God's healing and our obedience. God does not like to be put into a box, and God very much likes that we exercise our faith in His instructions as we endeavor to lead people into His grace. And as best I can figure, God wanted to teach me something yet again about the value of unquestioning obedience to His voice.

As this dying woman stood before me, I told her that Jesus loved her and could heal her of cancer. And then I told her the unthinkable: "We are going to pray, but first I want you to cough into my hand"...and then gritting my teeth, I held out to her the palm of my hand. Well, this woman had come to be healed, and bless God, if the preacher said she needed to cough, then she was going to give it the best cough she could muster! And that she did, emitting the ferocious cough of a tortured lung with all the gusto that remained in her mind and body.

The cough seemed to last a moment or two longer than I would have thought probable. I will never forget it...and I will never forget the miracle that fell upon her in that instant when her coughing ceased. An invisible rush of air surged into her lungs. With eyes wide open, she began to inhale with a prolonged breath as God forced His power into her body. She knew immediately that she was healed, and began to walk and trot with strength up and down the aisle of the church, with no one assisting her. Our people went crazy with joy, and even more so when the x-rays confirmed that no trace of her tumor remained.

Jessie just sat in the front row beaming with tears running down her face. She had told her friend that Jesus was a healer, and everything happened just exactly as she had promised. I often think of how different the story may have been, if Jessie had never thought to invite her friend to that healing service.

10 THIS TOO I WOULD NOT RECOMMEND

During this wonderful time of miracles some friends invited us to travel with them for a four day vacation on the island of Aruba. My Mom and Aunt came up to watch the kids, and off we went to paradise! Having never been to a tropical island, we were beyond excited...too excited it seems, for the day prior to returning home, I got caught up chasing an iguana over a lava rock field, and misjudged the leap between two boulders. We all heard the snap as my ankle folded over, and after yelling in pain, I began to fervently pray in the spirit for God to alleviate my misery.

Lenora and our friends helped me hobble back on one foot to our rental car, and as we began to speed back to the hotel, we passed a Pentecostal Church. "Stop there", I implored; "I'll get them to pray for my healing!" We knocked on the door, and as the warden of the church looked out suspiciously and asked what we wanted, I pleaded for the assistance of their faith. "No one is here to help you" she muttered, and summarily closed the door in my face! "Well God", I said, "please let me never do that to anyone that knocks on the door of our church!"

Back at the hotel my ankle swelled mightily, but I did not want to end up in a foreign hospital, and we were flying out the next morning anyway. They wheeled me in a wheelchair out to the plane, helped me up the steps, and I collapsed in my seat for an agonizing flight back to John F. Kennedy airport back in New York. As soon as we were home I made an emergency appointment with an orthopedist, who confirmed via x-ray that I had indeed fractured my ankle, and immediately he put me into a six week cast.

Being that healing was all the buzz at our church, everyone set themselves to pray for their pastor. I too was praying, and having seen God already do some astounding things, was fully expecting God to do the same for me. About one week after being put in a cast, I was again in prayer, and heard the voice of God: "I have healed your ankle". Hmm...this piece of information now presented me with a problem. I was in a cast for five more weeks, but I was certain that God had told me He had healed me. I supposed that the proof would be proffered after they removed the cast a month later and took another x-ray. But I was not going to be let off the hook so easily. God was interested in developing both my faith and my hearing, and so He pushed me further.

"Do you believe I have healed you?" These words rang repeatedly in my spirit. "Yes Lord, I am certain that you have touched me." And indeed, I had felt a kind of warmth in my leg after prayer and all discomfort had left as well. "If you know then that I have healed you, then cut off that cast and get about your business!."

It is good to insert here that we do not believe or promote a healing ministry where folks run out and do whatever pops into their brain. It is imperative to hear clearly from God. Jesus said "My sheep know My voice." Many have brought serious injury to others by improperly pressuring them to "prove their faith" by discarding essential medications that they were taking for a physical or emotional malady. I would never recommend cutting off a cast...but I always recommend hearing and obeying the voice of God! When Elijah had his wild contest on Mt. Carmel with the false prophets who served Ahab and Jezebel, he wasn't emotionally plunging forward with fingers crossed. He built his altar and then prayed: "Answer me O Lord, answer me...and let these people know that I have done all of these things **at Your word**!" The healing ministry must always be conducted within the parameters of God's word.

But in the case of my ankle, I knew I was hearing a clear word from God. For His own purposes in my life, He wanted me to do something I would not normally be inclined to do...just as I would not normally be inclined to tell someone to cough into my open hand (which I have never repeated). I got some tools and strong scissors and went to work on that cast, until finally I had freed my foot completely from its prison. All the while the other voices that we must wrestle with, those of doubt and accusation, were mocking and condemning my brain, as the devil whispered what an idiot I must be.

The next morning was Sunday, and when I walked in to preach without my cast, more than a few of my members were in agreement that I had indeed probably behaved like an idiot. Everyone was praying for a miracle, but let the miracle be shown when the cast came off by the doctor's hands. No one thought it was a clever idea for me to cut it off myself!

I made an appointment early that week with the doctor, and when he came into the room to see why I had returned, he was appalled at what I had done. I informed him God had healed me after prayer, and "would he please take another x-ray to confirm this fact?" Frustrated, the doctor ordered another x-ray. Some minutes later he returned to the examination room, and with some stammering, told me that the technician must have made a mistake and x-rayed the wrong ankle. I assured him that the correct ankle had indeed been x-rayed, for I was fully aware of which of my ankles had been in a cast for the past week. He looked at me soberly and I could tell his mind was racing. There was absolutely no evidence by x-ray that my ankle had ever been fractured. Furthermore, when I went back out to the waiting room, the receptionist quietly informed me that my bill was no longer due and there would be no further charges. Divine healing is good not only for the body, but for the pocket book as well!

11 HARVEY, YOU NEED TO GET UP TO THIS ALTAR NOW!

Healing miracles became frequent, and we began to realize that ours was not a unique revival, but God's desired norm for His people everywhere. In the midst of the physical miracles however, we always recognized that the greatest miracle was that of individual salvation, when a lost person came into a personal relationship with Jesus Christ.

Jessie Wilson had prayed for well over 20 years for her husband Harvey, but Harvey was immovable. A heavy drinker and a grumpy old school war veteran, Harvey had no use for going to church. But Jessie was tenacious in her faith, crying out to God in our morning prayer meetings, and determined to see her husband of nearly 50 years won over to the love of God. One day finally he consented to attend church with Jessie, perhaps more to escape her nagging than anything else.

He certainly didn't seem open. Harvey would sit and stare ahead every Sunday as I preached. He did not seem interested and his countenance let me know it. One Easter Sunday, in 1990, we were concluding a wonderful time of celebration and the altar was open for prayer as it was most Sundays. Jessie was the first one forward. She knelt at the altar rail, quietly weeping before the Lord. Harvey sat like stone.

Suddenly I heard again that familiar, and again this time, mortifying instruction: **"Command Harvey to come to the altar!"** WHAT?? Impossible! This was unthinkable, and I was pretty sure also not consistent with sound doctrine. People are supposed to willingly choose God. Eternal life is a free offer, take it or leave it. Certainly we are not supposed to strong arm a person's decision. I wrestled mightily with the voice, but He would not relent. **"Command Harvey to come to the altar!"** Over and over God spoke to my spirit, while Harvey just sat there and stared.

Finally I could take it no longer, and grabbing the microphone, I practically shouted: **"HARVEY!...you need to get up here to this altar next to your wife!"** I have learned that heaven opens up over people in the most unusual of ways. As if struck by lightning, Harvey shot to his feet and began to weep loudly. He raced to the front of the church, threw himself at the altar next to Jessie, and began to cry out to God like I had never before seen a man cry out to God. Our whole congregation was astonished, and then all began to cry tears of joy. Jessie and Harvey stayed there a good long time, weeping together before the Lord, as years of division between them melted away.

And just like that, Harvey was gloriously and permanently a follower of Jesus Christ. He never missed church again. He beamed with joy, and tears flowed easily. I still remember his wide eyed stare during one of our men's meetings, when all of us gathered around Harvey to pray for his painful left leg which was an inch shorter than his right. Every man that day, including Harvey, watched as the left leg grew forward until it equally matched the length of the right. We were not crazy people. Our congregation had men from all professions in life, including a brilliant research scientist, company executives, businessmen and laborers. But all of us were giddy after men's breakfast that day, celebrating with Harvey that Jesus is both Savior and Healer.

Harvey and Jessie are both long with the Lord now, but how eager I am to see them once again and reminisce together on the amazing grace of God.

12 OUR FIRST TASTE OF REVIVAL

It didn't take long before every seat in the pews became full on Sunday mornings, and as the testimonies began to spread, people began to stand in the foyer once all the seats were taken. People would awaken in the night with the presence of God heavy upon them, some having dreams from the Lord, and others awaking to find themselves praying in tongues for the first time. There was a tangible expectation and excitement in the members of the congregation.

We had two critical health situations for which we had long been praying. A young woman in our church had battled lupus for years, and was growing progressively weaker. We also had a 14 year old boy who had been diagnosed with a degenerative problem in his hip, which was causing great pain. The doctors had given a very grim prognosis for the boy's future mobility.

Several nights before the Easter when Harvey was saved, the young lady with lupus had a vivid dream. In the dream it was Easter Sunday, and she and the boy were at the front receiving prayer. In the dream they both were instantly healed. She called me the next day to ask what I thought, and we agreed that it may have been God indicating His desire and intention for that upcoming service. After Harvey's response to God's "forceful invitation", we spent time ministering to others at the front of the church...and the dream came to pass! Exactly as she had dreamed, God's power descended upon both together, as following the prescription of the dream, we had brought them up front together. They knew something was happening, but the medical confirmations of God's working came shortly thereafter when both went to their physicians and received the news that indeed, the afflictions were no longer to be found in their bodies.

Having never experienced this kind of revival in our childhood churches, Lenora and I were not able to fully explain why God was moving in this way, or exactly where this move would take us. People were coming to Christ, many were being healed, and the gifts of the Holy Spirit were in full operation through various members of the body. Joy absolutely overflowed each time the people gathered. When we had first arrived in the Fall of 1987, the services were 60 minutes exactly, and we were rigidly traditional in our order of service. All of that flew fast out the window as the winds of revival blew. We no longer set a time of dismissal, and the order of service changed weekly as we hungered for the Holy Spirit to be in charge.

When the Spirit of God is moving freely in a church, things previously hidden in darkness begin to surface. God began to teach us in the area of healing needed by those under spiritual oppression. The Scriptures show clearly in Luke 6:17 that Jesus' healing ministry included those who were suffering from the torment of unclean spirits. We had not learned much about this in seminary or Bible College, but we were going to have to learn fast. And one of the most important things we learned was that this ministry was not all about fireworks and shouting and dramatic exorcisms, but it was very much about the love of Jesus for broken people, and his longing to heal them all, body, soul, and spirit. Compassion was to precede any exercise of authority.

We had a sweet family in our church who were rock solid people, lovely Christians, and very gentle in their demeanor. When the revival began, it wasn't long before they came to me very alarmed to ask for our help. Their daughter had suddenly developed a rapidly deteriorating eating disorder, and was refusing all food. They had taken her for medical and psychiatric examination, but no one could persuade her to retain food. Would we come to the house and pray?

When we entered her room, immediately we sensed that this was a battle with a dark oppression that wanted to snatch away their daughter's life. Praying for direction, the thought came suddenly to check her room for any ancestral attachments; in other words, items that may have been owned by a deceased relative who may have practiced association with the demonic spirit realm. Their ethnic and cultural background made this a strong possibility. Without hesitation they pointed out the items in her room, and with their agreement to dispose of them, we then prayed over the room and for their daughter. Once again, we witnessed God's instantaneous healing. The spiritual sickness that was destroying her body, and up to that moment had been medically unstoppable, was vanquished in a flash of Divine love. She recovered fully and continued on, radiant in her faith.

When we hunger for a move of God, revival does not always come neatly. Our traditions and preferences may be set aside, and we are often unprepared for the consequences. We were not interested in finding a demon under every rock, but many hurting people on Long Island came through our doors who needed the power of Jesus' blood and name to deliver them from a torment they could not escape. Not every problem had a physical or psychological root cause. In the Bible, the root for some may have been a hidden sin, an inherited spiritual bondage, or a simple matter of spiritual warfare. The battle for the souls of people is one worth fighting, and many times our willingness to suit up in our spiritual armor is the only chance someone may have to find complete freedom.

The Holy Spirit provides all the power we could ever need for the problems of this life. Jesus won decisively through the Cross and Resurrection, but there is a battle still today for the eternity of every precious person created in the image of God. We determined that we would exercise all the faith we had for anyone who walked through our door. No one was beyond the reach of Jesus. Everything needed for abundant living was in Him.

13 A HOUSE FULL OF THE HOMELESS

One of the great dangers of revival movements is that they can quickly become self-serving and contained within the four walls of the church. People turn out in numbers for a quick boost of God's presence, but may not realize the imperative of taking their experience out into a needy world. Jesus told the disciples that they would "receive power when the Holy Spirit came upon them, and then would become His witnesses".

Power without witness is a misapplication of the gift and person of the Holy Spirit.

We were blessed shortly after arriving in Glen Cove to partner with a wonderful ministry that served the homeless population in lower Manhattan, particularly in the area of Tompkins Square Park. Teams would go in several times weekly to feed hundreds of hungry souls who would line up to receive a delicious meal. Counseling and prayer ministry were provided, as well as references for other types of social service, medical care, and even housing when possible. It was true that the majority on the streets had extreme addiction and often some form of mental illness, but it was among the "least of these" that we found some of our greatest joy in ministry.

For almost four full years our church was completely invested into caring for these people. The church garage was converted into walk in refrigerators and storage of canned goods. Our fellowship hall and kitchen were command centers for weekly food preparation. We even at times hosted holiday banquets for the homeless, driving them in from lower Manhattan, a distance of about 22 miles. On such occasions our church hall smelled to high heaven, more so from the aroma of humanity than from the delicious food. But it was a fragrance we all tolerated gladly for the privilege of showing God's love.

Zealous at times to an extreme, we weren't always wise in the use of our private space.

Our parsonage next to the church where we were raising our three children became an occasional overnight campground for someone who the ministry was endeavoring to rescue from the streets. We housed the staff in our spare bedrooms, and even staff from off the streets who had been clean from their drugs. One day I came home to find a strange woman sleeping on our couch. Lenora informed me that she was a prostitute named "Rainbow" who needed a safe place for the evening. "She has fleas, so I didn't think it best to put her in one of the bedrooms," she explained. I expressed my appreciation for her sound judgment.

It was a crazy and wonderful way of life, and we thank God for His grace that kept watch over our children even when in our zeal to be like Jesus we may have exceeded those things He was requiring of us. Those are some of our best memories of Glen Cove, and I remind myself at this stage of life to always be first in line to encourage and endorse the "out of the box" radical outreach that some who are younger dive into, rather than being the tiresome voice of endless caution about all the things that might possibly go wrong if they fail to follow the preferred methodology of their forebears.

Many of these homeless men and women had powerful experiences of encountering Jesus. Many became permanently set free and were helped into productive lives.

One Saturday we conducted an evangelistic outreach meeting in Tompkins Square Park. Bringing in a sound system and setting up on the bandshell, the plan was to serve the meal as always, and then preach the gospel and pray for the sick. Several hundred were present, and it was a beautiful day as we concluded the worship and message and then began to pray for those responding.

Scanning the crowd from the platform, my eyes fell on a man in a wheelchair a great distance away. His back was to us, and he was parked under a tree, all alone. I was certain that I heard the Lord's instruction that He wanted me to pray for this man. I sent one of our team members over to ask him if he would be willing for us to pray. I watched as he nodded his head in affirmation. When our worker took the handles of his wheelchair and wheeled him around toward our direction, my heart sank to the floor.

The man was a double amputee, with no legs...only the tattered cut offs of his jeans where his legs should have been. I felt a momentary panic attack coming on, but only for a moment, as the Lord quickly braced me with His compassion, reminding me that no one was outside of God's reach. Jesus was the one who raised the dead, opened blind eyes, and raised up the lame...all of which we would see in years to come. He had even told his disciples that "greater things than these they would do in His name."

Surely it was not too tall of an order for this same Jesus to create a missing limb.

Our context was not one of a spiritual desert. We were experiencing revival and extraordinary miracles at home in Glen

Cove. As the man was wheeled up to the base of the bandshell, I truly expected the impossible. The entire crowd became still, for no one had seen such craziness before. Even our team members were nervous, but I asked that every one of them enter into prayer. I stepped down to talk quietly with the man. He wasn't mentally ill. He wasn't dramatic. He simply had agreed to give a chance to God.

I prayed for some time, and the atmosphere was electric. God's presence was palpable to everyone, and we just **knew** that something was bound to happen. But nothing visible happened. He didn't jump up and start dancing on a new pair of legs. I knew that some of our team members were nervous that we had attempted this kind of miracle so publicly. My heart hurt for the man. I didn't want to embarrass him or make a spectacle out of his disability. We have seen others who were more concerned with fabricating melodrama than they were for the dignity of the soul in need. In one meeting I had watched a foolish preacher take off the eyeglasses of over 20 people on a prayer line, then he proceeded to stomp all their glasses to bits. None of them were healed, and he got out of town as fast as he could. I did not want to be that foolish preacher. The power of God administered wisely can be a wonderful thing, but when handled in ignorance we can bring wounds and disaster.

After praying with the man, and after he received the greater miracle of salvation through faith in Jesus, I climbed back up on the bandshell. The man with no legs was not upset - he had just been loved and given hope and had found eternal life. But I was a bit unsettled by the thought of what the crowd, and even my own teammates must surely be thinking. And then I heard the comforting and clear counsel of my Heavenly Father. He spoke to me and I have held on to His words since that day: **"Because you were willing to risk humiliation for the sake of believing in My power to heal, the day will come when your eyes will see such things as you've prayed for."** It was a settled and rock solid promise that I have never let go of. We have seen withered limbs straightened, blind eyes and deaf ears opened, people thought dead resuscitated, and others rise from their chairs...but to this day, we have not yet seen the creative miracle that would restore a person's missing limb.

Christian, is this hard for you to swallow? Why do we believe so readily in the Bible stories that we read from long ago, yet resist in our western rationalism the promise of God to do the same in this day in which we live? I know of cases where others have seen such a creative miracle, and we have more than once since then prayed for people in a similar condition. We are confident, each time we pray, that this may very well be the time that God's word and promise will come to pass before our eyes. For very deeply and strongly we do believe that "the same Spirit that raised Christ Jesus from the dead dwells also in us." God's people are not an impotent army. They are the most powerful army the world has ever seen. And without hesitation we remind ourselves always, the best is yet to come!

14 MOM & POP FORSTERLING

Teddy and Betty walked through the door of our church right in the middle of the revival. Danish immigrants who came first to Canada in the 1920's, they had already enjoyed nearly 60 years of marriage when they bounded up the front steps and into our sanctuary. They had given up on finding a local church where God moved in the ways they were accustomed to in the first decades of the 20th century after the Azusa street revival, so they quietly attended a nearby Reformed church, all the while praying for more. Someone had encouraged them to check out what was happening over in Glen Cove, one town away from their Locust Valley home.

Coming early into the Pentecostal experience as newlyweds, Teddy & Betty had the maturity with the things of God's Spirit that we needed in our wide eyed congregation. (Their legal names were Borge & Gudrun, but at their request, we called them by their Anglicized nicknames). Betty had served for some years as the librarian at a local Bible College. They had listened to all of the best preachers and theologians in the early days of the Assemblies of God and other Full Gospel groups.

Betty always said, "Brother Kelly, once you have tasted of the Holy Ghost, nothing else will satisfy". We learned that Betty was 100% correct on that subject, and have often recounted these words in the 30 years since.

They were our "miracle" couple. Nothing could keep these two down. With Teddy and Betty we learned the power of the words, "be it unto you according to your faith"...because they carried a radical, mountain moving faith. I remember one time driving down Glen Cove Road when suddenly God's crystal clear voice flashed in my mind, "go immediately to the Forsterlings!" I turned the car around, drove the 5 miles up to Locust Valley, and heard the Hallelujahs within after I rang the doorbell. Betty, always very dignified, opened the door with a flourish and said "Oh Brother Kelly, we were feeling a bit low so I asked God to send you....we knew that He would tell you to come!"

This was how the Forsterlings had lived for 60 years. They prayed often and powerfully in the spiritual language God had given them decades earlier. They never missed church; and they were constantly getting healed! Those two just could not be kept down. They had such a revelation of Divine Healing that no matter what curve ball was thrown their way, they would insist upon a rapid rebound in prayer.

I remember the urgent call from their son one day: "Please, get to the hospital as soon as possible; mom and pop have been run over by a truck." Well, the alarm was not exaggerated, for when I made it to the hospital, I found exactly that. After stopping for Roy Rogers chicken (their favorite), Teddy had pulled out into heavy traffic and directly in front of a delivery truck...which proceeded promptly to run over their tiny car.

I entered the hospital where they lay, complete with multiple fractures, severe lacerations, and various internal injuries from being crushed. They looked rather ghastly, but when I quietly walked into their room and called their names, they informed me that "we won't be staying long...so please get busy praying the prayer of faith...we need to get home as we have things to do!". By the time I said goodbye, they both were laughing and joking and praising God with all their hearts. Within a week they were back home, and missing only one Sunday, they were soon back in church, testifying to the power of God.

A greater crisis came several years later, long after we had left Glen Cove and were now pastoring a church in Hicksville, Long Island, about 30 minutes further south. Teddy, now in his late 80's, had decided to shovel heavy snow on his very long driveway. I got the urgent call that "Pop" had suffered a severe heart attack and was not expected to live - would I come? Immediately I drove to the hospital in Glen Cove, and gathered with Betty and their only son, to confer over the doctor's prognosis. They had been told to prepare for Teddy's passing. His heart was severely damaged and fast failing. There was no surgery that they could offer. I bowed my head with this great woman of God who by now had lived almost 70 years with this man she adored.

I looked into Betty's eyes to ask her what was her heart's desire, and those familiar eyes of fiery faith flashed back at me without hesitation. With tenderness and yet great resolve, Betty informed me that she wanted God to give her and Teddy 5 more years together.

Their son began protesting furiously! "Five more years! That's ridiculous! What kind of quality of life would he have? This is irresponsible!" He was heated and adamant. So I quietly tuned him out, and once more asked Betty, "is this what you really want?" "Yes Brother Kelly", she said, "I want Pop to have at least 5 more years." "Then that, Betty, is what we will ask God for", and compelling her son to take my hand, I led our little group of three in a declaration that God would grant our beloved Teddy another five quality years of life. There were no flashes of light or great sense of anointing. Just a quiet, confident prayer of faith, offered up on behalf of one who had walked boldly with the Spirit of God for nearly three quarters of her long life.

For the rest of my life, I will never forget the details of what became one of my greatest hospital visits ever on that following day. I had received no follow up phone calls, and quietly entered the elevator to the wing where Teddy was in a private room. I was almost holding my breath in hope that he had made it through the night. Well, Teddy had more than made it through the night. As I stepped around the corner, I immediately heard a loud noise coming from the end of the hallway. A few steps further, and I recognized that someone was shouting in a heavenly language. Quickening my pace, I recognized an instant later the forceful Danish accent that was booming up and down the hallway. I burst into Teddy's room to find him sitting straight up in bed, his hands held high, tears pouring down his cheeks as he worshiped Jesus with all the power that had flowed into his body that night. "Oh Pastor....Oh Brother Kelly", he cried; "God has touched me....God has healed my body....glory to God in the highest!...Hallelujah, Hallelujah!"...over and over he exclaimed, as we sang and celebrated the miracle.

After tests that morning, the doctors returned scratching their heads. Not only could they find no evidence that Teddy had had a heart attack, they also found that his heart seemed to be functioning at full strength, much like that of a young man. They were absolutely dumbfounded, and did not hesitate to attribute it to the power of prayer.

Betty of course was elated, checking her man out of the hospital just a few hours later so that he could get home to finish shoveling out the driveway!

God gave her those five more years, and even added a few extra for good measure.

Teddy died at 96 years old, strong and full of joy at the end. I had the privilege of recounting this story at his graveside service in the Locust Valley Cemetery.

And what of Betty? She was far from finished. Every Sunday that she could, well into her late 90's, she would call upon her granddaughter to drive her the half hour to Holy Spirit Church in Hicksville, where she would slowly come in on her walker and take her seat of honor. She was hungry still for the presence of God. She had tasted the Holy Spirit, and no substitutes for His moving would satisfy.

One January day, in 2013, I awoke from a vivid dream that I had while ministering in South America. In the dream I saw Betty, a beautiful young woman in her 20's, wearing a long, white dress, and with bare feet. She called to me: "Brother Kelly...watch me run in this beautiful grass...I feel so free!"; then she took off laughing as she dashed across the lush lawn. I immediately woke up and said to Lenora, "Betty must be soon going to be with the Lord". I felt a bit sad, thinking of how much I would love to be there for her funeral, but we were rarely on Long Island during that season of full time travel.

But God knew the desires of Betty's heart, and Betty's faith always seemed to pull down the grace of God. She had told her family that "Brother Kelly should preach my funeral". Just five months later, in June of 2013, we were on Long Island for a friend's wedding, and in 36 hours we were to fly out for another preaching engagement. My phone rang, and Betty's granddaughter was calling to tell me that at 103 years old, in her right mind and worshiping Jesus, Betty had gone on to join Teddy in eternity. "Are you anywhere near Long Island? It would mean the world to our family, and Nana wanted you to preside".

God does all things well. I was 10 miles away when I received that phone call. Within one hour, the funeral home and cemetery had coordinated to arrange a burial service for the following morning. We would honor this giant of the faith, then fly out directly to the West Coast. We would celebrate 103 years of Betty's life, and rejoice in the knowledge that her best days had just begun. We committed Betty into the ground next to Teddy, to await that great resurrection day soon to come. I so much am eager to race barefoot in that grass with Teddy & Betty, laughing with joy about the many adventures we had together living lives filled with the Spirit of God.

15 THE WIND BLOWS ON OUR CHILDREN

During these intense years between 1989 - 1992, God began to touch our children in unique ways. Each of them during that span prayed with us that Jesus would be Lord and Savior of their young lives, and each of them had supernatural experiences that demonstrated to us that God's hand of purpose was watching over them.

Ogunquit, Maine had become a favorite place to run off to for an overnight getaway, or even a long day off on the occasional Monday, our regular family day. Driving straight we could get there in just under five hours, and we would spend a glorious day catching starfish in the tidal pools, climbing on the rocks along the famous coastal path called The Marginal Way, and always wrapping up with tuna sandwiches, corn on the cob, and blueberry pie at The Oarweed Restaurant.

There were several long promontories of volcanic rock that jutted far out into the surf, and it was always fun to carefully make our way to the very end and daringly hang on the edges to watch the spray. One day I was out on the end with Omar and Jonathan, poking at crabs and soaking up the sun. The boys were very young at the time, and I was reveling at this precious moment of privacy and quality time with my sons. For that reason I was mildly agitated when I observed a single man turn abruptly off of the Marginal Way, and as he climbed up onto the beginnings of the promontory of rocks, he began walking as fast as possible in our direction. I was perturbed that he would invade our family moment, as there seemed a million other places he could enjoy nature's beauty without having to crowd into our personal spot. But onward he came, fast and focused, staring directly at us all the while. Now it was getting weird, especially when he walked right up to us, looked out at the ocean, then turned and spoke to me with distinct authority: **"The tide is coming in!"** He then stepped two steps back, folded his arms, and waited.

It only took a moment. Still irritated by the interruption, I glanced out at the ocean just in time to see a mammoth wave beginning to crest and heading directly for us. It seemed to be rising out of a perfectly tranquil sea. I yelled to the boys, **"RUN!"**, at which Jonathan immediately turned and began running back toward shore. But Omar stood in awe, fascinated by the wave only seconds away. In the split moment that I realized he was not turning with me, the large wave crashed down upon him.

Omar's little body was immediately dragged violently down the face of the last volcanic rock at the end of the promontory, cutting his arms and legs on the razor sharp edges. Only his head and upper body were now above water. In those moments, it was like watching a movie in slow motion. I reached down to grab his hand, one eye on him and the other on the secondary wave which was just as big as the first one. This one was likely to drag us both out into the ocean. But in that moment, a mighty hand grabbed my flailing left, while I clung to Omar with my right.

With seemingly little effort, the man who had positioned himself with folded arms now yanked us both out of the water and up onto firm footing, right as the second wave crashed over us. Omar was crying and I was shaken by the narrow escape from what had just happened. The man looked at me again as we followed stumblingly back along the rocks, assuring himself that we were safe. I watched him as he outpaced us in our rush back to the Marginal Way...and then, like the man in Manhattan 10 years earlier, he was suddenly not to be found. I scoured the beach, up and down the pathway, eager to thank him. But he was nowhere. He had only had a few moments jump on me, and I wasn't sauntering, but carrying Omar in my arms and racing to get him out of his wet clothes, with his relieved little brother now hoofing it behind us. Had this man been put there by God's hand, perhaps even an angel sent from God? A man who had absolutely no business rushing out to our location, reporting to me the tidal schedule, then folding his arms at the ready only three feet away. A man who had briefly caused me great irritation, and whom now I very much wanted to find to pour out my gratitude. But as I've learned, angels don't hang around for praise. They are sent by God to minister to His people, and to serve the purpose and destiny for which we each have been born.

This wasn't the second possible angelic encounter, but actually our third, for two years prior my own life had been saved by a well-placed guardian. I had taken the youth group to hike to the top of a high waterfall outside of Ellenville, New York. Reaching the top, we all reclined to listen to and watch the rushing river that poured over the top of the falls. Suddenly, and again out of nowhere, for we were deep in the woods and not on a hiking trail, a man came climbing up behind us, made his way to the very mouth of the falls, braced himself against a large boulder, and just stared at our group.

"What a creepy guy" I thought, muttering to a few of the kids that they should stay away from the weirdo who was crashing our party (I realize I am a bit slow at recognizing angels). For reasons I don't know, perhaps just to be daring and show off to the teens, I began walking right along the sloped rock edge just above the water line. Unfortunately I failed to observe the super slick moss growing where the rocks were wet, and in an instant my feet flew out from under me, I landed dead center in the raging current, and began sweeping out of control toward the falls.

The picture I next saw is forever frozen in my mind: as I turned in the water, my eyes wide with fear captured the picture of the "creepy stranger" braced against the boulders, right at cliff's edge, with both arms outstretched to powerfully grab me in the last possible moment before I plunged over. He hoisted me right out of the water and pulled me onto firm footing. Then the strangest thing happened: he looked me right in the eye and said, "You've lost your glasses...I'm going to look for them"...and like that, he scurried down the rock ledges we had just climbed up, never for us to see him again.

We waited, and waited, and then finally realized he was never coming back. Was I even wearing my glasses? No one else could remember that detail, but somehow, it was a pertinent fact for this random savior. But now I think it was just a good excuse to make a quick getaway. As I said above, angels don't like to hang out and explain themselves. They complete their assignment and move on to the next task. But he left his mark, not only in my heart, grateful for supernatural intervention, but in the mind of each of those teens that day, all of whom could talk of nothing else but the "totally cool angel that saved their Pastor." They knew that given our remote location, the exact timing of his arrival and positioning of his body were impossible coincidences. Our youth were learning at any early age that God's power is real, and He delights to enter into our natural world with glimpses of His supernatural world.

16 GET OUTSIDE RIGHT NOW!

We learned early as parents that only God has the power to secure the future of our children. There is a great freedom in releasing that responsibility to Him. We do our part, in nurture, provision, responsible decision making, and training, but ultimately He is a far better caretaker and guardian than we could ever be. One of His most liberating statements to us as we watched them grow was this: "I love your children more deeply than you do, and I have far more invested into their success than you ever will".

Lenora was working in the back yard of our Glen Cove parsonage, when an unexpected urgency hit her, a powerful insistence that Jonathan had to immediately come to his mother. In the loudest voice she had, she yelled with authority back into the house: "Jonathan, come out here right now!" Jonathan was only around four years old at the time, but instantly he obeyed, running to the back door to see what was troubling his mama.

Our parsonage had been built more than 100 years earlier, one of the first homes on Forest Avenue in our city. The ceilings were made from a heavy plaster and lath, and there were cracks in various places to which we had never previously given much attention. Within a moment of Jonathan appearing outside, Lenora heard a thunderous crash. Racing back into the house to see what had happened, she found that the entire ceiling over the area of the living room where Jonathan had played with his toys only moments before had collapsed to the floor. Immediately she called me and I raced over from my office in the church next door. We were both incredulous. There was a great weight of ceiling material on the exact spot where our boy had been playing. There isn't much that one says in such a moment, only to stand in amazement at the ways of our loving Heavenly Father. How grateful we were that He had been teaching us to be sensitive to the sound of His voice.

Around that same time, there was another unusual event in Jonathan's life. One morning during breakfast, I was eating my cereal at one end of the table, and Jonathan was eating his at the other end. Very nonchalantly, he looked up at me and said, "Jesus came into my room last night". Not very nonchalantly, I put down my spoon, paused for a moment to study his expression, then asked the only thing I could think to ask: "Did He say anything?" "Yes", Jonathan replied. "Well what did He say to you?", I asked in a firm parental tone, making it clear that it was his four year old obligation to dutifully file a full report with his dad. Obviously at this moment, as a Christian parent and as a Pastor who had been deeply seeking for God to reveal Himself, I was somewhat holding my breath and prepared to hang on every word that Jonathan was going to tell me.

After a moment's pause, Jonathan looked up with a bit of a smile and said, "I'm not supposed to tell". If my son didn't have my undivided attention before, he certainly had it now! Pondering my next move, and not wanting to violate whatever confidentiality agreement my boy had with his Maker, I decided to take a different line of questioning:

"Were you afraid?", I asked. Another long pause, and then came the closing line of our short exchange: "Yes...but it was a **good** afraid...not a bad afraid". Wow! My four year old had just theologically articulated the "fear of the Lord", in a way most adults I knew had never grasped. I had no further questions. I also had no trace of doubt that for whatever reason, Jesus had interacted verbally with our son. Today at 30, Jonathan no longer remembers our conversation about that God encounter. But I have cherished it dearly, reminded each time I look at him that before me stands a man who was uniquely visited by God, with a unique purpose and plan for his life, as God has for all.

God showed Himself not only as the protector of our children, but also as Baptizer. John the Baptist preached that the coming Messiah would baptize with the Holy Spirit and fire. Lenora had experienced her own encounter with God's power early in 1991 at a Ladies' Conference in Virginia, very similar to what I had experienced 10 years earlier at Nyack College. Our daughter Melissa soon after became the first of our children to be visited in this same manner by the Spirit of God.

We were on family vacation at the beach in July of 1991, and while Lenora put the kids down to bed, I decided to take a late walk along the beach. I had not been out for too long, but by the time I returned to the room, everyone but Melissa was asleep. As I opened the hotel room door, I heard the distinct sound of our daughter's voice singing, but not at all in English. I quietly walked in and toward the beds where Lenora and the boys were sound asleep. Melissa was momentarily oblivious to my presence. Sitting up in bed and with hands raised in worship, she was singing so beautifully in a language only God could understand. Not wanting to disturb her, I waited until she noticed that I had come in. I knew this was not something that Melissa had experienced before, so I asked her to tell me what had happened. "I was just singing praises to Jesus, and suddenly I started singing in a different language." That touch from God has remained on our daughter throughout her journey, carrying her ultimately to Oral Robert's University for her degree in Nursing, in and out of several nations for ministry, and finally into a God ordained marriage that is one of the more unique stories in this book.

We are forever grateful that God did not fail to include our children when He began immersing us into His revival.

17 THE DISTRICT SUPERINTENDENT COMES CALLING

We had enjoyed an amazing season of Divine intervention and presence in those years, and we dreamed of impossible dreams, dreams of filling stadiums on Long Island and leading multitudes to Jesus. Lenora and I had originally intended to stay briefly in Glen Cove and then hurry off to the nations, but the revival was going so wonderfully, who in their right mind would ever want to leave? And then came the dreaded phone call.

The District Superintendent of our denomination was on the line, informing me that he would be paying a visit that coming week. He was straightforward as to his purpose: one of our members had called him to complain that the church was becoming too charismatic with the public demonstrations of spiritual gifts and celebration. I was stunned, even more so when I learned that the person who called him was the very man who had prayed more fervently than anyone in our prayer meetings for an outpouring of God's Spirit. But as the man explained to me later, "the way things are happening here is not the way they happened in my home church…the Holy Spirit did everything there very quietly…and this is just too loud and demonstrative to be a genuine move of God!"

That was a real shocker for me. I quickly learned that the greatest opposition to revival comes from within the Christian community, not from without. Those who are lost in the world are desperate for living water, but those who are secure in the confines of the faith are often the most dogmatic about what living water is and what living water isn't.

Our Superintendent was a good and devout man, overseeing around 70 churches in our District. He was quite serious as he sat in our living room, informing me that though our denominational doctrine assented to the present use of spiritual gifts, certain of these gifts should be kept out of sight. He expressly instructed me that going forward, all prayer for healing, all prophetic words or words of knowledge, and all exercise of the gifts of tongues or interpretation were to be conducted outside of our public services.

Then, to add a bit of leverage, he informed me that if I did not consent, he would revoke my ministerial license.

As I said, he was a good and faithful man; but I knew that his own discomfort with demonstrative worship was now pushing him beyond the boundaries of his authority. Taking a deep breath, I gently replied that we were doing nothing that violated either Scripture or our denominational policy, and that what he was now asking me to do would force me as a pastor to violate the Word of God and to quench the Spirit. That is something I would not do, and if that meant losing the license given us by men, then so be it. Lenora and I were fully aware that what was happening in our church wasn't connected to a piece of paper, but was something given and licensed by God.

The conversation ended peacefully a few moments later, without him bringing up again the issue of our licensing. Perhaps, he simply was testing the waters to see how strong our convictions were, and if in fact these convictions were our own, rather than something being imposed upon us by a forceful faction of the church. At any rate he departed cordially, and we returned to pastoring God's people. There were no more complaint calls to the District office, and the man who had called initially decided to relocate his family to a more emotionally conservative church in the next county.

18 A MAN MAKES PLANS...
BUT GOD'S PURPOSE PREVAILS

I actually got along quite well with our Superintendent in the year following. We continued doing exactly what we had been doing in the church, and he never again raised the subject. He even asked me to speak that year at District Conference on the subject of contemporary worship. I don't know if he changed his views, or simply had satisfied himself that we weren't flaky or doctrinally aberrant. He is in heaven now, and I look forward to seeing him again one day, where the misunderstandings and disagreements we had on earth will be forgotten and inconsequential.

Even though the external pressure was alleviated, a great pressure began to build up inside of me. There had originally been seven openly charismatic pastors in our district, but six of them had relocated to districts where they felt more accepted. I began to feel terribly alone, and even though we had many wonderful men in our district, I was not finding empathy in regard to the distinctive ways the Holy Spirit was working with us.

One day God spoke something that changed the entire course of our life: **"What I have called you to do cannot be fulfilled within the structure of your organization. It is time for you to step out by faith into the purpose for which I created you"**. In these words, God did not put down or bad mouth in any way my colleagues, or the organization I was working with. They were and continue to be some of the most wonderful Christian people I know, and we have many friends among them to this day. Lenora and I weren't any better than anyone else. We weren't more spiritual, or called to do something more noble. We were simply called to do something different than what would have been possible were we to remain.

In September of 1991, I sat in my Superintendent's New Jersey office and willingly surrendered my denominational credentials, the very credentials that had almost been revoked the year prior. My leaders were kind and gracious, making every effort to find a solution whereby I could stay. But as I explained, this was not a matter of personal offense, but rather one of Divine imperative. It was true that I did not want to be the odd man out in our fellowship, but even that I would endure if it was meant to be our continued assignment. We had not taken this decision lightly. The entirety of our education had been spent in preparation with the expectation that we would become missionaries sent by our denomination's mission board. We did not know any other methodology for doing world mission outreach. We were stepping out in faith and obedience, and truthfully, it was quite frightening to go obediently into a way of life of which we knew very little.

We told our church that we had surrendered our licensing with the denomination, and thus would need to step down, but the elders promptly informed us that under no circumstances would they accept a replacement pastor and go back to the structured format of past years. In the now familiar refrain of Betty Forsterling, they had "tasted of the Holy Spirit, and nothing else would satisfy".

Incorporated 70 years prior as an "affiliated church" (a technical term used to refer to congregations that have a less formal relationship with the district), they had never legally become a fully organized church within the denomination. They had received pastors and participated in district activity, but like most churches that begin independently, they had a strong bent toward preserving their liberty.

They asked us to stay on and lead the congregation, and not having any alternative direction from the Lord, we were glad to do so. Why would we do otherwise?...God was still moving wonderfully in our services. In the naivety of our late 20's, it all seemed quite simple and neat. But we soon learned that when it comes to church property, things are rarely that simple and neat.

Notifying the District of our intentions, the District office promptly notified us of theirs: they were laying claim to the property, and we had a brief time before we must vacate the premises. I was completely shocked and unprepared. We were living in the church owned parsonage, and our church sanctuary had been built 50 years prior through the effort and giving of the local families, several of whom still attended.

The folks were ready for a fight, but God placed a clear and heavy mandate on my heart: **"You will not fight for this property by disputing against your brothers in a secular courtroom"**. It was one of the clearest instructions God had yet spoken.

He was expressly forbidding me to contest the notice to vacate. I overcame my disappointment, and considered the solution to be simple: God was great and mighty, was He not? We would simply find another building. We would start over and build bigger and grander and have a greater revival than ever before! I felt certain our folks would be thrilled with this expression of faith. They were not.

Now please know that we had one of the most wonderful boards of directors that any church could ever be blessed with. They were wonderfully spiritual men and women of prayer and faith. But I had not built that church, they had. They had sacrificed, invested, and poured their lives into that faith community. Lenora and I had been there less than five years. What God was asking of us, they did not feel He was asking of them.

Yet because of their humility and tenderness toward our pastoral leadership, they did not openly resist us. Several joined us in searching for property. They were conflicted, but willing to give it a try if those were the conditions under which we would stay.

We learned something powerful during that season: sometimes God requires something of us that He is not requiring of others. God knew that the hearts of our leadership were not fully persuaded. The weight of my personal conviction was placing them under great strain. Several of them, and rightly so, asked about the issue of the injustice of being forced out of their own property. They were absolutely correct. The denomination's office in another state did not have the legal or ethical right to evict them from their house of worship built with their resources. The fact that God forbade Lenora and I from becoming embroiled in a courtroom drama did not negate our membership's right to defend themselves against an improper intrusion upon their personal community property. And suddenly we recognized that God hadn't just called us out of our denomination. He was also calling our family out of the security of Glen Cove, our home, and every way of doing ministry we had ever known. I cried with a broken heart when I realized that this season of our life was concluding. We had prepared ourselves to give everything for revival on Long Island. But God saw a bigger picture than the one we could see or imagine. Quietly we began to pray, asking God to show us His next assignment for our ministry.

19 MIRACLES FLOW IN ECUADOR

Just 18 months prior, I was invited on my first overseas mission trip to the nation of Ecuador. Lenora had been long before that to Thailand, in 1981, for a two month college missions immersion experience. Working in the refugee camps and on the front lines with veteran missionaries had reinforced her passion and dream to follow God's call to foreign fields.

My own heart had been inspired all the way back in 1970, when my parents took me to hear Brother Andrew speaking in California of how God had used him to smuggle Bibles into the Soviet Union. "When I'm big I'm going to do something like that", was a thought I clearly remember contemplating in my little boy's mind. It is amazing to think of how early God' Spirit can begin to stir a calling into the human heart. I had just turned seven!

Now twenty years later, I was beyond excited about my first official missions outreach.

A veteran missionary to Quito had invited me to join his team. I fell absolutely in love with that nation, doing things that stretched me, such as preaching for the first time with an interpreter. I was also very anxious about what to preach...and God was merciful toward my missionary beginner's butterflies. Twice during those two weeks I had dreams the night before preaching, in which I was announcing the text for my message. When I woke up the next morning, I looked up the passages and knew what to preach! I foolishly thought this was some clever new gift I had received, and all messages would henceforth come in my sleep. It was not too be, and though it has happened 4 or 5 times over the years, every other message since then has come by virtue of being awake, walking with and waiting upon God, and hearing His voice. The Spirit filled life is not a life of laziness, and contrary to the reputation created by some within certain circles who have a bias against preparation or education, those who want to hear clearly from God should live lives of devotion, study, and prayer.

Now in January of 1992, just as Lenora and I realized God had in mind a broader calling than we could fulfill in Glen Cove, I was packing to embark on a return trip to Quito, Ecuador's beautiful capitol city 9,000 feet up in the Andes Mountains. This time I brought along our oldest son Omar, who though still under six years old, was excited about an adventure with his dad. The adventure turned out to be far more than I had ever imagined.

Our team advertised and conducted an evangelistic outreach under a large tent, and on the final night I was scheduled to preach. The goal was to pray for the sick, and I was excited about what God might do. The message I preached that night was taken from the words of Peter when Jesus asked His disciples if they too "were going to leave Him". "To whom shall we go", replied Peter... "You have the words of eternal life". The line of people that formed for healing was long, extending all the way back to the tent, and I became nervous as to how to properly pray for so many. This type of mass outreach was not something we had tackled on Long Island.

"God, please help me!", I prayed under my breath, looking at the huge crowd before us. We had promised that Jesus was a Healer, and now the hurting and hungry crowd were expecting God to deliver on His word. I heard the gentle voice of the Spirit, once again giving me His specific directive for that specific moment of ministry: "Just lay your hands upon them and declare, 'The word of Jesus heals you'." That seemed strangely simple to me; no loud prayers, no dramatic requirements; just the softly spoken word, that His word would heal them.

For two hours that night, God's power flowed, and every type of sickness vanished. A woman came to the platform, dragging her crippled foot behind her. She was well known to the church, having been severely injured 20 years prior in a car accident, her foot completely crushed and now withered. I placed my hands upon her, declared "The word of Jesus heals you", then was shaken by what happened next. She shot straight back onto the concrete platform, and her head smacked the floor so hard that everyone standing nearby heard the collision between skull & cement. She was not moving at all, but people kept coming forward. Very anxious that something terrible had happened, I nevertheless kept praying the simple prayer over each person, while glancing continuously at the woman who lay immobile at my feet. We did not have a tradition of people falling over in our Glen Cove church, and this was definitely not in my play book.

Suddenly she shot back up to her feet with a mighty shout. She began dancing and jumping all over the platform, as those in the crowd who knew her went wild with joy. Her lame foot was no longer lame. It had been completely healed into a brand new foot. She danced all over the tent that night, and the faith of the crowd began surging.

When the tally was taken, the leadership had a verifiable testimony of healing from every person who had stood in that line, save one. I was exhilarated, but also confused as to why one solitary person in all of that crowd did not receive the miracle as did so many others. But I have learned that there are aspects of the healing ministry that are mysterious and not always disclosed to our understanding. Our job is to obey Christ's commission and pray in faith for the sick. Jesus is the Healer, and His healing methods, timing, and purposes can never be put into a box.

I was so caught up in that two hour prayer line that I had no idea what had happened to Omar. When I asked where he was, one of the ushers pointed over to the edge of the platform, where he had been standing for the entire two hours watching his father pray for the sick. I was forever grateful that God had prompted me to bring my five year old boy on this journey.

Flying home a couple days later, I was deep in thought and deep in prayer. We had experienced several rich years of revival in Glen Cove, but this experience I was leaving behind in Ecuador was something far different. Ministering to mass crowds of people had stirred my heart with the memory of a time in 1973, when as a 10 year old boy I had watched a Billy Graham crusade and begun weeping at the invitation. I was overcome by the joy of seeing so many come to Christ, and in that moment I knew clearly the call of God, as I heard what was then unfamiliar, the voice of God, telling me "this is what I have called you to do with your life". I believe now that a gift of evangelism was deposited in me then, even before my supernatural encounter at Nyack, for immediately after watching that crusade, at the same time in which I was baptized (March of 1973), I began to continuously share about Jesus with my 6th grade friends and classmates...and each one I shared with summarily gave their heart to the Lord.

Heading back to Long Island, I sensed that a new chapter of our lives was about to begin. Out of the blue, I again heard God speaking: "I want you to return to this nation with your family and preach My word". Within seconds of hearing this, with my mind whirling at the concept of our entire family traveling to Ecuador, Omar tapped my arm and said: "Our family should move to Ecuador!" That may not seem all that profound to some, but the instantaneous confirmation was profound enough for me. I spent the remainder of that flight plotting on how I would work up the courage to drop this news on Lenora once I got back home. Omar and I thought it a grand idea, but I wasn't sure how this would go over with the rest of the family.

20 A SIX MONTH WHIRLWIND, AND THE PERILS OF PRESUMPTION

I should have known not to worry. Lenora had already heard clearly from the Lord. Back around the age of 10, she also had been feeling the childhood stirrings of a missionary call. Some missionaries had visited her home church, showing slides of their field. One picture stood out in particular to Lenora's mind, a slide of Mt. Cotopaxi, a 16,000 foot snow- capped volcano about one hour south of Quito, Ecuador. Feeling the tug of the Spirit on her heart, Lenora remembers thinking how wonderful it would be to one day stand on Mt. Cotopaxi. God certainly knows how to prepare us years in advance. Her dream was about to come to pass, only much sooner than either of us had imagined.

I dragged my feet for about two weeks, finally working up the courage to share what I believed God had spoken. "I already knew you were coming home with this calling - God spoke to me while you were away, and I'm ready to follow His leading"...her words thrilled my heart. In all of our years together, we have never made a major decision until we have both been in agreement and hearing the same thing in our prayer life. And neither of us wanted to embark upon such a dramatic transition unless we were both all in spiritually and emotionally. We spent the next two weeks fasting and praying to be absolutely certain. It was now time to put our plan into action.

Notifying our fellow leaders at our Glen Cove church brought both pain and promise. It was incomprehensible to them that God would call us out, when so many wonderful things had happened. In an effort to change our minds, the elders decided that if they withheld salary, we would out of financial necessity reverse course. I was crushed by their response, having hoped our missionary endeavor would be celebrated. Seeing my disappointment and hurt, they quickly reversed their decision, but I foolishly allowed pride and bitterness to cloud my thinking. When a paycheck was placed on my desk a week later, I tore it up and informed them we would get along just fine without their help.

This was incredibly stupid, demonstrating a lack of grace when grace was what they most urgently needed from their pastor. Some months later, before our family actually flew out to South America, God required me to stand in the pulpit and apologize for my actions. We have all received mercy from God, and when others stand before us needing mercy, it is a woeful thing to withhold it. God was good, and allowed my friendship with these men to continue for many years.

I am so glad that God never lapses into resentment. His mercies toward us are new every morning! With three small children and income for neither our daily bread or our future mission plans, we had to learn a whole new level of trusting in God. In spite of my error, God fulfilled His promises to be Jehovah Jireh, our Provider. One lady had only recently been attending our midweek teaching service to enjoy the word and the atmosphere of revival. The very first week we lacked a paycheck, Marilyn showed up one evening knocking at our door: "Pastor, I have no idea what your situation is, but I received a dividend check in the mail and the moment I opened it, the Holy Spirit spoke that I was to bring this for your family. I'm sure that it is meant to meet some need". She handed me an endorsed check for over $800.00. Such miracles began to happen weekly from that point onward. We had not advertised or pleaded for charity. God was simply confirming that He would be with us as always in our journey forward. One particular provision was not only huge, but also would figure prominently in God's plans for our future. A pastor I had never met, from a church I had never attended, called me to say that God had instructed him to send us $1,000 per month for three months. Little did we know that this mysterious congregation in Hicksville, Long Island would one day be our home and setting for a life changing decade of pastoral ministry.

Contacting the missionary with whom I had twice traveled to Quito, we began to lay the groundwork with the ministry network there for our family's arrival. We would be working with Ecuador's most prominent full gospel association at that time, with churches in many cities around the country. They were delighted to hear of our decision, and would welcome us gladly. A close friend who pastored a strong church on Long Island agreed to handle our finances and serve as our sending agency.

Several weeks into preparing for God's call, we also were in the middle of one of the biggest mistakes we have made in the ministry. The mistake was not in leaving our church. It was not in traveling as a family to Ecuador. But in one of the most common mistakes made when hearing from God, we committed the error of presumption concerning things God did **not** say. God told us to journey to Quito, but He did not tell us how long we would be there...and we never bothered to ask. Squeezing everything into the only concept of missions ministry we had known, we immediately assumed that if God was sending us out of the country, then Ecuador would be our new home for the remainder of our ministry life. We wrote letters telling friends and family of our destiny in South America "for the next 40 years". It seems absurd in retrospect, but we were totally sincere at the time in our desire to be obedient as career missionaries. God knew that we were operating out of the only missions paradigm we knew, and that we did not even know that other paradigms existed. He graciously provided, helped us with obtaining residency visas, and surrounded us with plenty of loving supporters who were cheering us on in our grand assignment. We would find out soon enough that He had something much different in mind when commissioning us to "declare His word in Ecuador". Our omniscient God knew that this was simply the first of scores of international outreaches He had planned for our future. But we weren't interested in hearing anything about multiple nations...it took all that we had emotionally and spiritually to get everything ready logistically and as a family without losing our grip.

Working on a slate roof as a roofer's assistant in the Summer of '92 on Long Island was hot and demanding labor, but it gave us the extra funds we needed for daily expenses before flying to the field. We also visited different churches each weekend, raising awareness of the work we would be doing, while waiting throughout the Summer for our visas to be processed. One of those Sundays we visited and preached at The Holy Spirit Christian Church in Hicksville, the congregation that had helped us some months earlier. They too committed to monthly mission support.

And what of our precious church family in Glen Cove? We did not abandon them. A wonderful friend of ours had been sharing our building for over two years, meeting Sunday afternoons with his congregation while our folks met in the mornings. We had enjoyed numerous joint services over that time period, celebrating revival together, and co-hosting many special guests and meetings. It was a natural fit for these two very similar groups to merge under one leader, and we were so delighted when God confirmed to both churches that Pastor John Burns and his wife Robin would take the helm. In August of that Summer John was officially set in as the Senior Pastor, the congregations became one, and this Summer of 2017 will mark 25 years that Pastor John has faithfully led and served the people of Community Gospel Church, the new name chosen for the two merging families. (And yes, they did go on to successfully defend their property against the unwarranted effort to dislocate them - a court case that climbed all the way up into the Federal Judicial Court, which ruled, which ruled unanimously in their favor). And as for our ongoing relationship, we have enjoyed returning to preach for our church family every year since, 33 consecutive years of ministry on the North shore of Long Island.

21 OUR FIRST HOUSING MIRACLE

From the time we first were married God had been gracious to us in the provision of housing. Our first small apartment was a highly coveted third floor nook that sat up amid the treetops in the home of Dr. Frank Farrell, one of our seminary professors. It opened up right after our honeymoon, and we were thrilled to spend our first two years there. The home we had enjoyed in Glen Cove was enormous, a 110 year old home into which we had moved with very little, but which was now filled with rooms full of excellent furnishings that we had accumulated during our time pastoring the church.

Selling items to make money for our mission was the obvious path, but an unexpected instruction came: "Sell nothing; give what you cannot take with you to families in need".

This brought a bit of consternation to some of our family and friends, for it seemed illogical to forsake such an obvious resource of finance. Others were troubled that we didn't just put things into storage, "just in case things don't work out in Ecuador...at least you will have something with which to restart your life in America". But we knew that we were heading into missionary service for the long haul, and there was no point in saddling family with the task of storing our large amount of goods.

"Where will you be living?" This was the most frequent question we were asked, and one which we could not immediately answer. I resolved to fly down to Quito ahead of time and organize our housing, but again, a very clear instruction came during prayer: **"I want you to trust Me for your housing; I am sending you, and I will prepare the way"**. I knew immediately what this meant: not only was I not to fly down and work things out like any normal and responsible husband or father might do, but I was also not to pester our future hosts about the suitability of what they were arranging. This was an excruciating test of faith for me. Lenora seemed much more composed about it, but I was very concerned about the thought of flying my entire family down to South America without any idea of where we would be spending our first night, let alone the months that were to follow. True, our colleagues in Quito had confirmed their expectation of our arrival and were waiting eagerly, but they had not spoken a word about our housing...and I was not being permitted by the Spirit to ask them!

A life of faith does not necessarily have to be radical or contradictory to logic...but it does have to follow the specific mandates of God's word, whether the written word we have in the Scriptures, or the specific words of instruction that might come by the Spirit as we wait on Him and listen for His voice. God is a speaking God, and faith comes by hearing deeply what He has said and what He is saying. The problem is that He often speaks things that are challenging to our familiarity and comfort. He leads us in ways that might not be traditional, but those pathways are designed to develop a dependence upon His provision and a loyalty to His Lordship.

Our residency visas came through in early October, and within days our tickets were purchased, our duffel bags were packed, and with great excitement we boarded our flights in New York to wing our way toward destiny. The romance of the whole project almost came crashing down during our layover in Miami, when we had to recheck into our connecting flights, hustling desperately with seven large duffel bags and multiple carry-on bags through the terminal, trying not to lose our kids, sweating profusely, and ransacked mentally by the thought that I did not know where we would be sleeping that night, or even if someone would be faithful to meet us at the airport. Something of a cold panic was trying to creep in, but I put on a brave face in front of the children. Omar already had tasted of the exotic adventure ahead, but Melissa and Jonathan were heading to Ecuador for the first time.

God demonstrated to us as He had so many times before that it always pays to trust His voice and obey His commands. A welcoming contingent was waiting at the airport, and with joy they whisked us away to an apartment they had spent months constructing within their large church facilities. Not only was a place waiting, but an entire home had been built just for us! It was small, but it had a kitchen, living room, bathroom, two bedrooms, privacy, and a full complement of furnishings. We were beside ourselves with gratitude at the faithfulness of God, the miracle meaning so much more because we had faced the test of faith, and could now enjoy the reward of passing the test. It had never occurred to our hosts to tell us they were building us a home...they were excited at the thought of surprising us. Hmm...next time save the surprise and have mercy on my administratively insistent mind!

22 IMMERSING OURSELVES IN A FOREIGN LAND

We hit the ground running and each day was a new discovery in a world that didn't work anything like what we were accustomed to on Long Island. Within the first few weeks, the church threw a big party for my 30th Birthday, Lenora's childhood dream of Mt. Cotopaxi was fulfilled as we tagged along with a group from the church, and we had the excitement of visiting Mitad Del Mundo, the "Middle of the World", where we all posed for pictures on the line that marked the Equator.

I began preaching regularly and teaching in the Bible School, my first regular class being on the topic of "The Victorious Life"...a subject of which I would need to learn far more than what I knew when I began teaching. Interpreters were always around to help me in the classroom and Lenora in the market place. Meals were sometimes traumatic, like our first lunch out in the countryside, when Melissa began to distress over the rooster foot swimming on top of her soup; or the time our neighbors appeared with a plate of marinated squid heads, the very sight of which compelled Jonathan to burst into tears because he was convinced dad would force feed this to all of us as a sign that we were a noble missionary family. Neither Jonathan or I ate the squid heads - none of us for that matter.

We battled a lot of illnesses those first two months, but prayer and perseverance kept us from excessive discouragement. Lenora became extremely ill on one occasion, a crisis that had all of the staff pleading for us to go to the hospital. We set ourselves to prayer, and within 24 hours she was on her way to full recovery.

My closest friend in Quito, the director of the Bible College and my primary interpreter, was Patricio Robelly. He had an extraordinary gift from God for the healing of the sick. Even with all we had seen on Long Island, I had never seen healing flow so easily as it did through Patricio's ministry. He was just 25 at the time, but God had begun using him in a special way from his teenage years. God knew exactly what He was doing in knitting our hearts with Patricio and his wife Elena, for we were both about to be thrown into a storm as the enemy set about to turn everything we had dreamed of upside down.

23 TROUBLE IN PARADISE

I was uncomfortable with one particular man from the beginning. He had arrived to our Ecuadorean church at the same time as my family, and his family seemed quite lovely...but there was something about him that made me worried. An Ecuadorean himself, he came with a freshly earned degree in Missiology from the USA. He had in the past been imprisoned in Quito, and the story was that he had found the Lord while there. I do not doubt that he had experienced some kind of conversion while locked away, but whatever he found there, the dynamic of it seemed to have become much diluted during his time of study.

The staff were enamored with his education, certain that he knew by virtue of his degree more than the rest of them. This grieved my heart. Lenora and I had our own post-secondary degrees, but we had well learned in Glen Cove that all the university training in the world will not help you in the ministry if you do not have the help of the Spirit of God. Jesus said, "without Me, you can do nothing". We had experienced His help as the Spirit guided us daily, and the thought of running after a man of "letters" who functioned completely independent of God's Spirit was truly frightening.

Because I was a North American and educated, this man miscalculated my beliefs and decided to take me into his confidence. I don't know what made him so careless, but one day he took me aside to inform me of his plan: he was proposing that the leadership grant him complete authority over all of the organization, including it's 20+ daughter churches in various cities; once in authority, and with financial control, he would remove Patricio Robelly, and in his own words, "the other young guys like him, with their emphasis on speaking in tongues and too much focus on the Holy Spirit." "We need to polish up this uneducated crowd" was his attitude and aim. I was mortified, but immediately recognized this foolish disclosure as a window into the schemes of the enemy. I held my tongue as he spoke, resolving to keep watch, but also certain that the absolute authority he was demanding would never be granted. After all, that would completely upend the very purposes for which we believed we had come to Quito, and I was equally certain that this was something God would never allow. I was sadly quite wrong, and also woefully unprepared for what happened next.

I sat in on a board meeting of the senior Pastoral staff over the organization, dumbfounded as not one objected to the proposal before them: "would they be willing to transfer all legal, financial, and program control over to this man" the very man who had whispered his intentions into my ears only weeks prior. I was not only confused by their passivity, but I was also wrestling with God. I did not want one of my purposes in Quito to be the exposing of another man's intentions. We had moved to the mission field to love people, preach the gospel, pray for the sick, and bring relief to the poor. Church politics and property disputes and contending with those who jostle for position were far in my rear view mirror...at least this is what I thought. I did not realize that people are the same everywhere. Ministry, in any place, will bring us face to face with the fallen nature of men. But it will also, if we desire it, bring us face to face with the grace and glory of God. What was unfolding was ugly, but an abundance of grace was going to be granted to carry us through.

I had consulted in those weeks prior with our own pastors and spiritual leadership from home, men who had worked with the ministry in Quito. They gave me no out, letting me know that if God had allowed me to be aware of this man's intentions, then I had a moral obligation to inform the Ecuadorean leadership. They had in fact just been to Quito to conduct another healing campaign in the city, and assured me of their prayers that I would "be faithful to my calling". I was heavy hearted over the seemingly unavoidable conflict.

Having voiced their collective agreement to submit themselves to this man's requests, I knew that it was my time to speak. Softly, and respectfully, I began to plead with them not to abdicate from their God given authority and responsibility. I pleaded with them not to allow anyone, simply by virtue of an advanced degree, to dismantle the emphasis on Holy Spirit dependence and anointing. And I delivered what I knew was a warning from God, that the entire organization would be put at risk if they proceeded with this transition. Their response was firm and final: "Brother Kelly, we appreciate your concern...but we trust this man. Sometimes a person thinks he "sees" a problem, but it is better to be quiet; we love your ministry here, but we are happy if you just teach and preach...don't worry about the church; everything is going to be just fine."

There was nothing more to say. They had made their unanimous decision, giving him full control over the finances and programs of the church. Within a short period of time there was talk of misappropriation as the man slipped away from Ecuador and back to the USA. The organization struggled for years to recover from the fallout. But at the end of December in 1992, I knew nothing of how these matters were going to unfold, other than knowing that it wasn't going to be good; what I did know was that my family was now in a dilemma and we urgently needed some fresh direction.

24 GOD PLEASE HELP US - WHAT DO WE DO NOW?

Within days, this newly empowered administrator made good on his word to remove Patricio from his post at the Bible College. Demotions of other anointed young men soon followed. The organization we had come to partner with as we poured our hearts into Ecuador was suddenly, after only several months in Quito, no longer a stable place for my family. We knew we could not stay, but the very thought of returning to the USA was utterly humiliating. We prayed about partnering with the young men who each as well faced starting over from scratch, but no internal witness for this came.

At the same time, some things began to make sense. A dear woman from Virginia had traveled down with the USA team in December, and approached us with what she believed was a word from God for our ministry. Confusing at the time, we now were clinging to what in our present circumstances seemed profound: "God showed me a picture of a seagull, flying over the seas; you have not been called to one nation, but to many nations, and you will be sent with God's authority to advance His kingdom from country to country". We desperately hoped that now, in this moment of huge disappointment, these words were a true promise from God.

Where to go? This was the first order of business, and God answered in amazing fashion. We knew that going back to New York was not on the table, and heading to either of our parent's homes was even less desirable. Both sets of parents were strong supporters of our ministry, but it was simply too humiliating after our long and dramatic goodbyes. We had one option that seemed possible to our minds, and that was the ministry of Calvary Pentecostal Tabernacle located in Ashland, Virginia. Calvary Camp had figured largely in the move of God we experienced on Long Island. We had first met some of their staff, including Rev. Wallace Heflin, when they held special meetings at a friend's local church, also in Glen Cove. We were powerfully impacted in these meetings, and many of our members subsequently traveled during 1990-1991 down to Virginia to enjoy Men's, Women's, and Minister's conferences. The folks in Ashland were old school Pentecostals, but they had an intimate acquaintance with the person of the Holy Spirit and His gifts. They also centered their entire organization around the Great Commission of world missions, so in these two areas of mission and anointing, we found a great deal in common and Ashland had become like a second home.

But the decision was excruciating. Because of our significant error of presumption regarding our length of tenure in Quito, I did not fully trust my own hearing. I pleaded with God to have mercy on my weakness, then proceeded to do something I had only done once previously, when I was 14. It was something that as a Pastor I would never advise anyone to do. But indeed, His mercies are new every morning, and He is compassionate during our times of weakness.

Desperately wanting to know if Calvary Camp in Ashland was the place to which we should flee, I held up my Bible, prayed "Lord, either confirm this or refute it", then opened it up and stuck my finger straight down on the page. And these were the first words that I read in Micah 4:10: **"for now you must leave the city, to**

camp in the open field". I was elated and incredibly relieved all at the same time. The directive was unmistakable. We had prayed about whether we should head to Calvary Camp, and God had graciously answered. I realize that in sharing this some might be troubled to think that it could lead others into a careless usage of Scripture, or a shallow method of discerning God's will. But remember that this is simply a retelling of a moment in which God's heart of love reached out to where we were at and communicated His plan and purpose for our life. Again, as a church leader I don't promote this methodology. It is the domain of the desperate. But God is not boxed in by what we consider to be an acceptable means of receiving Divine direction. He is near to the broken hearted, and our hearts were broken by the loss of a dream. Little did we know that the dream was far from dead, and far broader than we ever would have comprehended.

25 THE EXACTNESS OF A DAY AND A DOLLAR

With our destination determined, and no presumption this time as to how long we would be there, it was time to inform our children, pack our belongings, and figure out the logistics of our upcoming journey. We had no idea what it would cost to buy one way tickets on short notice, but I immediately checked with our friend who was managing our bank account in the USA to find out if we even had enough to get out of the country. He reported a balance of $1,801.13. I immediately cashed a check in Quito for $1,800, leaving $1.13 in the bank at home. Whatever this was going to cost, $1,800 had better cover it! The plan was to fly to Miami direct from Quito, where another dear friend would arrange a rental car so that we could drive up to his home in South Carolina. Once there, I would send an express letter to Rev. Heflin in Virginia to inquire about relocating to his ministry. Not even our parents knew that we were preparing to return.

One thing we have learned about departures in ministry is that God is very specific. There is a timing for everything, and we did not want to run chaotically out of Ecuador, but to leave peacefully and at the right moment. We prayed for instruction, and the date came with great clarity - January 16th. It was already early January, and the thought of leaving so quickly was sobering.

Trusting God's voice, I headed down to the American Airlines ticketing office, informing the agent that I needed five tickets to fly one way to Miami on January 16th. She shook her head and laughed: "I'm sorry Mr. Brake, but we are completely sold out on almost every flight over the next two weeks - this is the high holiday season you know". I asked that she please go ahead and check anyway for the 16th...as I was certain that this was the day we should travel. Checking her computer, her face suddenly showed great surprise as she looked up at me to report, "You are in luck! There must have just been a cancelation...believe it or not, there are exactly five seats still available on the 16th...and I actually am able to seat all five of you together!". She was amazed and I was rejoicing...but now it was time to find out the price: "That comes to $1,675.00."Relieved, I counted out to her the amount in American dollars; we now had remaining $75 to cover the drive up to South Carolina, and $50 for food....with just $1.13 in the bank to spare!

Despite these confirming details, our hearts were heavy as we trudged once again with our bags back to the airport in Quito. The leadership in Quito could not understand why we insisted on leaving. We knew that nothing would make sense to our supporters at home. It certainly did not even make sense to us at the time. Yes, God was leading with great specificity, but the prospect of facing an endless series of humiliating questions, the answers to which would not satisfy the majority, was simply overwhelming. God is not obligated to explain everything in the moment. Looking back 25 years later, things are abundantly clear. But in the middle of the whirlwind, we had only our faith in God's faithfulness to go on. Truthfully though, in any of life's challenging moments, do we ever have anything more valuable than a faith and hope in the character of God? All the resources and information and insight available cannot hold a candle to the power of a childlike trust in the midst of a storm.

Was Ecuador a mistake? At the time, it certainly felt to be so. But hindsight is always 20-20. We look back now and realize that our obedience to the instruction to "leave Long Island and go as a family to Quito" was as essential as any step that we have taken in the ministry. Our brief three month experience in Quito knitted us as supported missionaries to The Holy Spirit Christian Church in Hicksville, Long Island, where we would later serve for 11 years. We were in Quito when a team came in early December from the USA, including two Canadians, Pastor Ric & Deborah Borozny, who later became great examples for our faith, the closest of friends, and keys that God used to open up to us an entire world of international outreach.

Our willingness to move our family out of the country also caught the attention of Rev. Wallace Heflin, the man who would become our Pastor in Virginia for the next 15 months, teaching us principles that would greatly accelerate our effectiveness in the exercise of spiritual gifts. These gifts would in days to come open doors we never thought possible. When Patricio Robelly was removed as Bible College director and launched his own ministry, we were there to hear God's counsel to "stand by this man and be a friend and support to him". Over the past 25 years, we have done exactly that, watching as God's favor has built one of the largest churches in Ecuador, and fashioned one of the most powerful healing ministries in South America.

To this day Ecuador has remained one of the most cherished assignments in our life, returning there more than 25 times to serve and affirm the work of God. Perhaps we actually had caught a glimmer of reality when we declared it to be a life-long assignment and the core of our calling...for 27 years now into our Ecuadorean journey, we can look back and rejoice at how God has taken one small three month window of our pilgrimage and turned it into the platform from which He would launch His higher purposes through our ministry. Going to Quito was not a mistake. Planning to be there for 40 years was. Yet all things worked together wondrously for the good, for we deeply loved God, and were most definitely called according to His purpose. The promise of Romans 8:28 was unfailing. It has not failed since.

26 UNOPENED MAIL AND A CAMPGROUND COTTAGE

Rev. Heflin wasn't responding. It had been almost a week since we had express mailed a letter detailing our departure from Quito, our confidence that God was calling us to Ashland, and our desire for confirmation that they would indeed receive us. We were not going to drop in unannounced, and we knew that if we had heard correctly, then God would confirm the same to the man whom many worldwide referred to affectionately as "Brother Heflin". Wallace Heflin was known on every continent for his excellent preaching and healing ministry. He was a happy and loving man with a broad smile and a deep love for the nations. It would be a delight to spend some time with him, if only we could get him to answer.

Finally I could take the pressure no longer, and I picked up the phone to call. I should have done so to begin with, but simply lacked the courage. His secretary patched me through, and Brother Heflin greeted me cheerfully. "What can I do for you Brother Brake?" Everyone at Calvary was "Brother" or "Sister" so and so. I sheepishly asked if he had received an express envelope from me. "Well let me see...why yes, here it is...underneath the pile on my desk!". I learned later that Bro. Heflin was well known for the mountains of unanswered correspondence that accumulated on his desk while he traveled. Quickly I asked him if he would be so kind as to "open the letter, read it through, and then call me back after he considered my proposal". I still didn't have the courage to tell him exactly what the proposal was.

Within 15 minutes he was back on the phone: "I read your letter...can you be here in three days? We just had a cottage on our campground vacated, and it will take a bit of time to make it ready. We are thrilled to have you and your family join our ministry...welcome home!" I could have danced all over the room with relief after I hung up. We not only were being welcomed, but we were being provided for wonderfully with a new home, beds, kitchen and living room furniture...it was God's faithfulness unfolding all over again.

The next three days passed quickly in South Carolina as we enjoyed some great rest and relaxation with our oldest friends from seminary days, Ricardo & Margareth Lemos. They had commissioned a friend of theirs in Miami to meet us when we arrived with a car rental already paid, and then graciously shared with us their home and food for the week since our return. God used that time to renew and refresh us after a bruising time emotionally in Quito. They had imposed no judgments, but simply loved us when we needed to be loved. They remain today the longest standing friendship we have. Faithful friends are one of the greatest treasures in life, and especially so when in full time ministry.

We pulled into Calvary Campground in Ashland the fourth week of January, 1993. The staff of approximately 60, including several other families with young kids, rolled out the red carpet of welcome. Brother Heflin had been one of the men who advised me to confront and expose the subterfuge at the church in Quito, so he was more than sympathetic and supportive toward our situation. We were plugged in immediately and encouraged to get right back on the horse of world missions. But we soon learned that not everyone who knew us would celebrate our relocation.

27 YOU WILL TRAVEL THIS YEAR MORE THAN EVER BEFORE

The man who managed our bank account back in New York was disappointed. He had endorsed our missionary move to Quito and his church had invested in us significantly. He was understandably upset about the effect our decision might have upon his own credibility, and thus declared to me that out of remorse for our mistake, we should not embark upon any new mission outreaches, but sit in silence for the foreseeable future. It was the exact opposite of the counsel I heard as I took these painful words to prayer. Always so gentle and gracious, God spoke this promise to my soul: **"You will travel more for me in the next year than you ever have before. This is not the end, but it is merely the beginning; I am launching you out into the nations of the world"**.

We had no money, no contacts outside of Calvary Camp, and no plans to go anywhere; but God held true to His word. Rev. Heflin was planning five major outreaches that year, two to Israel, two to Russia, and one to China...and God impressed us to commit ourselves to every one of them. We had thought it took great faith just to get to Ecuador, but to travel to all of these places in an eight month span of time? It seemed completely out of reach...and it was. But it was time for us to discover just how far reaching was the arm of God. The trips would cost several thousand dollars each, much more than what it was costing us to live month to month in Quito. But the call of God was before us, and we would take a few dollars here or there and put them down in faith toward each trip as it came up. Repeatedly that year we experienced sudden and supernatural provisions. People we hardly knew would step forward feeling compelled to give money to sponsor tickets or travel expenses.

Israel was exhilarating. Lenora had been previously in 1992, prior to our departure from Glen Cove, but I had never been. It was sensory overload, as the Bible came alive at every turn. Being an administrative person, I thoroughly enjoyed assisting Brother Heflin in managing our large group as we traveled as well to Syria and Jordan. In Damascus, I tracked down the location of my Grandfather's agricultural materials store, and enjoyed conversing with his employees. My Grandfather, after whom I received my middle name, Khalil, had passed in 1980, but his business had continued to flourish under the management of my uncles.

We often spent our last dollar to participate in the opportunities before us, but we never lacked for food or clothing. When I left on the first trip to Russia, I had $5 in my wallet and left Lenora with $10. It was a new and radical kind of faith for us, but our hearts were in agreement and the provisions kept coming. In Russia I experienced the fulfillment of a seven year old boy's dream, the dream I had pondered when first hearing Brother Andrew in early 1970. The Iron Curtain had recently come down, and the Soviet Union was fast disintegrating politically. I had never seen such a desperate hunger for God and His word. We distributed Bibles everywhere we went, and at times the crowds surged so fervently that our team members would be pressed to the ground under a sea of outstretched arms and fingers. I'll never forget preaching in one village outside of Moscow to the entire population of 900 that filled the local Communist Town Hall. This entire village of 900 responded in unison to the offer of salvation that was extended at the end of the message. I was sure they had misunderstood, for I could not comprehend every single person in a town coming simultaneously to a personal relationship with Jesus. Yet even as the interpreter reiterated the call, the response was the same. I was beginning to see with my eyes the reality of

Paul's words to the Romans when he said, "For I am not ashamed of the Gospel of Christ, for it is the power of God unto salvation to all who believe...". Group conversion was to happen more than once in the years ahead.

In the Summer we took a break from international travel to devote ourselves to the 12 weeks of annual Camp Meeting held at Calvary. Folks would travel from all 50 states and multiple countries every year to enjoy the ministry of anointed preachers and teachers. We pitched in with occasional preaching, working in the office, and caring for the many guests. It was a crazy, hot, non-stop Summer. For 74 consecutive nights we were in church, along with our children. It is amazing how much church culture has changed in just a quarter century. It is quite an achievement now to have a midweek service, and some churches have abandoned even this in a surrender to the busyness of 21st century life. But those 74 nights did not kill us, and far from it. Our kids would dance around to the "campish" choruses, and then promptly fall asleep under the chairs...while we would fight sleep on top of the chairs!

God was teaching us much and teaching us fast, but still, camp life was far from idyllic. Several of the senior staff were dour and legalistic, and there was some deficiency in the finer points of doctrine and methodology. But as we have learned in every place we have served, God's grace and mercy flow not because people are perfect, but because He is faithful. He loves deeply His church, with all its spots and blemishes. He longs to touch the lives of hurting people, and will stretch Himself out through very flawed vessels to do so.

One of the greatest lessons God has taught us in ministry is to remember the words of Paul in Romans 14:4 - "Who are you to judge another man's servant? Before his own master he stands or falls". It is good to "work out our own salvation" before trying to sort out everyone else.

28 COMMANDING THE BREATH OF GOD

On Sundays that Summer we would always head into the main church facility in Richmond, Virginia, where the large congregation of Calvary Pentecostal Tabernacle gathered in an old but spacious sanctuary. People came primarily to enjoy the outstanding preaching of Wallace Heflin, as well as the freedom of worship, and always the opportunity for a miraculous touch from God. The ministry of Divine healing was common at C.P.T., but one Sunday in particular it rose to a new level entirely.

That morning I was participating in the order of service, and so was seated on the platform next to Rev. Heflin. We had observed a commotion going on toward the back of the sanctuary for several minutes as folks had clustered around someone to pray, but we couldn't see clearly from where we were sitting. After a short time, someone rushed up to the platform to inform us that "an ambulance needs to be called right away...brother Smith seems to have passed". Brother Smith was an elderly gentleman, and his wife was weeping and calling upon Jesus as two nurses in the church attempted to resuscitate him. He had suddenly fallen over and was totally unresponsive.

After administering C.P.R. but finding no pulse or breathing, they had hurried up to inform us of the emergency.

In the calmest voice possible, Rev. Heflin looked over at me and declared: "My parents planted this church 45 years ago, and no one has ever called an ambulance since, and we are not going to start now - - c'mon Brother Brake...let's go raise Brother Smith up!"

Honestly, I'm quite sure that if I were in charge that morning, I would have dialed 9-1-1 immediately. But Rev. Heflin was an unusual man of faith, and I jumped up to race behind him as he hurried to the back of the sanctuary. We arrived to find Bro. Smith laid flat out on the pew looking deader than a doornail. Rev. Heflin put his large hands on Brother Smith's forehead and began to declare with extraordinary confidence, "I command the breath of God to come back into this body!" Wow, I really did not know what to think about this, but there wasn't much time to think, only watch and wait to see what would transpire next. The rest of the crowd stood back and prayed loudly, while I stood beside Rev. Heflin hoping for a miracle.

This went on for about five minutes, when suddenly, as if it was the most normal thing in the world, Rev. Heflin looked down at his watch and said, "Oh...it's 12:00...I've got to get on the radio; Brother Brake, you take over and finish raising Brother Smith up!"

Rev. Heflin's Sunday preaching was always broadcast live at exactly 12:00 noon, and he wasn't about to fail his thousands of listeners. To him it was the simplest thing in the world, and Brother Smith's resurrection was already an established fact in his mind. What difference did it make who prayed for him?

I wish I could say that I was that calm and composed, but when Rev. Heflin told me to take over, I thought I would just as soon fall over dead on that pew right next to Brother Smith! I looked with alarm to Rev. Heflin with an obvious expression of my need for help, and his reaction was, again with great simplicity, "just command the breath of God to come!"

Rev. Heflin wheeled around and marched back up to preach, as all eyes now turned in my direction. I was **not** brimming with faith, but following the instruction, I began to repeat the prayer. I felt nothing, and it was obvious that Brother Smith, void now for multiple minutes of measurable pulse or breathing, also felt nothing. The poor man's death sentence was assured by being placed into the hands of a novice. I was certain that finishing the job should be a greater priority for Rev. Heflin than getting on the radio!

But this was a wonderful thing about our Pastor. He loved seeing others used by God. He was a big believer in encouraging everyone to step out in faith and exercise spiritual gifting. He wasn't looking for the glory for himself, but truly had a vision for God's people to discover that they too could be used mightily by God.

And so I stood there numbly repeating my prayer. In about two minutes however I felt the atmosphere change. A tremendous surge of boldness came into my spirit; I didn't really know from where. I certainly cannot attribute it to my own faith, and perhaps it was the collective prayer of those gathered around. At any rate, I found myself not simply saying the words, but actually feeling the authority to forcefully declare the life and power of God. Faith began to come alive in my heart, and in the hearts of everyone interceding. In a flash, as if struck by lightning, Brother Smith shot straight up in the pew, with a speed that was not natural, and simultaneously inhaled a massive breath of air.

We had been "commanding the breath of God", and it was as if the very breath of God had blown like a mighty gust into his lungs. It was identical to what I had witnessed when praying for the woman in Glen Cove with the cancer in her lungs three years earlier.

The breath of God, or the wind of the Holy Spirit, or the power of resurrection life...I cannot say exactly what the right terminology should be; but in both cases the result was the same. Something powerful and external had rushed down upon these souls in need, and that "same Spirit who raised Christ from the dead", was now on the scene raising up those for whom the world could hold out no hope.

Brother Smith looked around in shock, while his wife and those gathered began to whoop and shout praise to God. And true to the simplicity of his faith, Rev. Heflin interrupted his radio sermon to announce matter of factly to his listeners, "well, Glory to God, we just had a man brought back from the dead in our sanctuary...another typical Sunday at Calvary Tabernacle!". Brother Heflin loved any opportunity to brag on Jesus and be humorous at the same time.

Of course we cannot contend with certainty as to whether or not Brother Smith had truly been clinically dead. The medical members of our congregation certainly thought his absence of vital signs over prolonged minutes warranted calling an ambulance. But no one disputed the unusual manifestation of God's power that was visible when Brother Smith shot straight up, or that it could have been anything other than the gracious healing breath of God. For our lives, what was important was that we had witnessed and participated in an entirely new dimension of faith and healing. And we have ever since had a completely new understanding of the 37th chapter of Ezekiel, when the prophet was instructed by God to "prophesy to the breath" and to call for the "wind to come, and breathe on that which was dead", the dry bones representing the people of Israel. And indeed, just as Ezekiel prophesied and then witnessed the power of the Spirit of God to raise up dead things, so we too were beginning to see that resurrection life was not an occasional or rare bestowal of mercy, but rather the lifestyle of the church of Jesus Christ, commissioned to move out into a broken world with a living Savior who could fix and heal anything; if only we who represent Him would believe.

A humorous conclusion to this story took place the following Sunday, when Mrs. Smith stood up on the platform to testify. She was a very elderly and demonstrative Southern lady, and with a sing song preaching cadence, she held forth: "Last Sunday, my husband was dead...he died flat out on that pew back of the church; but I was praying and telling Jesus, it ain't his time...Lord, please bring him back! We set ourselves to prayer, and Brother Heflin, he quit prayin' and went on the radio...but **that** man...he didn't give up!" I suddenly realized Mrs. Smith was pointing straight in my direction. "**that** man... he BELIEVED! He kept on praying and commanding the breath of God into my husband, and he raised my husband back from the dead!!...Hallelujah!...Glory to God!". Mr. Smith sat beaming in his usual row, I sat basking in the sudden fame of being falsely credited with Mr. Smith's longevity, and Rev. Heflin sat delighted up on the platform, winking at me as he smiled from ear to ear, not interested in any glory for himself, but simply thankful that God was real, Mr. Smith was alive, and one of his staff had known the joy of participating in the higher realities of the Kingdom of God.

29 RISE UP AND WALK....
IT'S CHRISTMAS DAY!

Lenora and I enjoyed ministering as a team, praying for the sick and speaking God's word into the lives of people. Slowly we began to receive invitations to other churches, and almost always there would be testimonies of immediate physical healing. One of those visits was pivotal for our future, when we followed up on the invite we had received while in Ecuador to preach at Eagle's Nest International in Thorold, Ontario. Back in December of 1992, Pastor Ric Borozny had stopped by our small apartment in Quito and given me his business card, inviting us to come by whenever we might be back in North America. Otherwise we hardly spoke a word to each other during his team's visit, and I stuck the card in my briefcase, assuming I would probably never be in Thorold. We have preached nearly 100 messages in Thorold since then, more so than any other local church besides those that we have pastored or served in. The kingdom of God is an unusual place, where destiny can turn on a whisper, a seemingly tiny open door, or the smallest act of obedience. Our first visit to Thorold in May of '93 cemented this relationship, and we saw God's grace of healing as we preached and prayed for the people.

Rev. Heflin always taught that a preacher should not only preach, but he should minister by prayer to the needs of the people whenever possible. We could see this model in the ministry of Jesus and the Apostles, but it was not common in the circles we had grown up in. One of the other great lessons we learned from Rev. Heflin was to look directly into the eyes of people when praying. Each one was a precious person that God loved, not simply a project or a number on a prayer line. Each one deserved individual attention and care. Brother Heflin had a powerful ministry of healing, but he never separated it from a deep and compassionate love for people.

Another invite that year made me nervous. The banquet director for CBN, Christian Broadcasting Network in Virginia Beach, had been given permission to host monthly healing meetings at Pat Robertson's headquarters facility. We were asked to come and minister for one of these monthly meetings, to which folks from all around the region would travel in hopes that they might receive a touch from God. The invite was not from Pat Robertson himself, but just the fact that we would be ministering at the CBN facility was quite a bit beyond the exposure we were accustomed to. The meetings were promoted and they promised to house us in a lovely hotel room on the grounds, along with our children.

We were still learning how to flow in faith, trusting God for results rather than putting pressure on ourselves. But that particular evening I was feeling a massive amount of stress from what I knew would be the expectations of people coming to a healing meeting at CBN. One of our children was out of sorts that evening, talking back when I attempted to correct. I lost it. All my tension erupted into an outburst of yelling, excessive discipline, and ultimately harsh words with Lenora as well. This was 30 minutes prior to the scheduled meeting, but I stormed out of our hotel room, out to our vehicle, and sat fuming, ready to drive away, forsake the meeting, and probably quit the ministry altogether. I felt in that moment that I was utterly unqualified and in way over my head. I was mad at the world and especially at my kids for not making things easy.

Into my clouded mind of anger God's voice penetrated: "You need to go back into that hotel room and apologize to your family; you need to ask their forgiveness; and, you **will** get up and represent Me this evening. I am not giving you the option of driving away".

I knew God's voice, and I knew He wasn't negotiating. I calmed myself for a few minutes, went back into the room, and apologized for my actions, and everyone dried their eyes. We now had only a few moments before heading down the hall to the conference room for the meeting. As we left our room, the door to the adjoining room opened, and out came a very well dressed older woman, one who obviously had a lot of class. Being next to our room, she had clearly heard the screaming, yelling, and crying that had gone on only moments before. She cast a piercing look directly at me that said, "you are obviously the worst husband and father on earth!"

I was humiliated. But nothing like the humiliation I felt when we entered the conference room, only to see the same woman enter right before us, proceeding directly to the front row and planting herself as close as possible to "whomever the man of God might be that was going to preach that night". The look on her face when she realized that I was the guest speaker is one I wish I could forget. She looked at me with double the condemnation that she had stared at me with before, and it was no problem at all to read her mind: "I know what you are!...you might fool all these people, but you won't be fooling me tonight!" I was beyond mortified.

To add to my misery, they immediately wheeled a woman in a wheelchair to the front of the room, parking her chair close to the pulpit area. I looked at that woman and all I could think of was that she had picked the worst night ever to believe for a miracle. My faith had dropped lower than my shoes, and I knew I was absolutely incapable of helping anyone that evening - they would all simply have to go home disappointed. It was truly the lowest I had ever felt preceding the preaching of the Word of God.

Into my self-pity, the voice penetrated once again: **"Tonight I'm going to demonstrate to you that the healing ministry is not about you...it is always and only about Me...it is all about Jesus!"**. I heard God speaking, but wasn't sure what He intended to do. Things quickly became a whirlwind of activity, as guests filled the conference room and those who attended the woman in the wheelchair were eager to explain to me her predicament. She was the mother of young children and had been involved in a terrible car accident 6 months previously. Since that time she had not been able to walk. Her friend told me over and over, "She is very bitter...she is bitter against God; you have to get her to repent of being bitter or she won't be healed!"

"Well that's just wonderful" I thought: "She's mad at God, the well-dressed socialite in the front row is mad at me, and I don't have an ounce of faith to help anyone...we are **all** in trouble tonight!"

I preached as best I could, but things felt flat as a pancake. Finally it came the time to offer to the people what most of them had come for, an opportunity to receive the healing grace of God. And then it happened. The Holy Spirit spoke to me, "I want you to pray for her first!" I looked at the woman in the wheelchair, the one whose friends had told me several times already that she was extremely bitter, and indeed, she looked quite despondent. I'm certain they had worked mightily to get her to agree to come to that meeting. Now God was telling me to pray for her first. Surely the hardest case in the room should be saved for last...why kill everyone's faith right off the bat.

But God has His own ways, and there were two things particularly that He wanted to accomplish that evening, the first being to mercifully touch that woman, and the second being to demonstrate to me a lesson that I would need to remember for the remainder of our ministry: "healing would never be about me or credited to my spiritual condition, but it would always and only be about Jesus". Seems like a no brainer, yes? But in fact these are lessons that must be cemented into us by God, to keep our doctrine sound, and to spare us from the errors of pride or a self-congratulating faith.

The woman with her wheelchair was lifted up the step to the platform, while her friend, continued to whisper that I had to deal first with her bitterness. God apparently was not preoccupied with or prevented by this issue. He was present to heal. As I looked into her pain filled eyes, I felt the compassion of Jesus flood my spirit. I forgot all about the fight with my family, the condemning woman in the front row, and my own feelings of worthlessness. This is a wonderful byproduct of God's anointing. It transports us beyond ourselves and our human limitations and self-centered way of thinking. It consumes us with love for the person before us who God is desiring to minister to.

"What do you want God to do for you?" She looked back up at me and declared plainly, "I want to walk by Christmas". It was late November at the time. I did not plan my response, or even have time to think about it, but suddenly it rose forcefully from my spirit, and with great joy I announced to her, "**It's Christmas Day!**" She looked at me blankly, but when I extended my arm to her, she took it and rose slowly to her feet. "Are you willing to walk", I asked? She nodded her head slowly and we proceeded across the platform, arm and arm, her first steps since her accident six months prior.

I honestly don't remember any of that meeting following this moment. My euphoria at God's mercy to both of us, the embittered and the unbelieving, was through the roof. Even the angry socialite seemed to accept that perhaps I was not a devil in a suit after all. Such lessons regarding God's power have served us well in the years since. Whether we are feeling up or down is no longer a key factor. Faith is connected to neither our feelings or our performance. It rests solely on the accomplished work of Jesus who paid the price for the healing of all on Calvary more than 2,000 years ago. We would never again try to pay that price by being spiritual enough, praying enough or fasting enough. Nothing we could do would ever be enough. Jesus had paid the price in full. Our job was to rest in His righteousness, and then trust that this righteousness of His would be the sufficient legal ground upon which healing could be dispensed freely and with full confidence in days to come.

30 THAT CAR YOU ARE CONSIDERING....GOD SAYS TO GO AND BUY IT!

Over many years of international travel, we have come to realize how blessed we are in the West to have access to a personal vehicle. So many of our friends and colleagues are believing just for bicycles or even motorcycles, and in these developing nations the acquisition of a car for most would be a monumental provision. Even to this day we never take the privilege of owning a car for granted.

We had always had a vehicle since college days, but now with our return from Ecuador we found ourselves for the first time without a car. Rev. Heflin had graciously given us use of his personal vehicle for several preaching excursions around the East coast, but we recognized that with three small kids and an increasing ministry schedule, we would need to find our own set of wheels. During our final three years in Glen Cove we had greatly enjoyed a leased Chevy Astro van. With captain's chair seating and room for eight, we had great memories of family trips down to Myrtle Beach, the Smoky Mountains, and our frequent runs up to Maine. I had wandered around a couple of dealerships and was quite infatuated with the new GMC Safari vans, which were designed similar to the Astro but with some upgraded features, including 6 captain's chairs. With almost no steady income, this was akin to a fantasy vehicle, totally out of our range. For that matter, any car in 1993 was out of range.

One day I was standing in the back during a service in which Rev. Heflin was preaching. I became quite caught up in daydreaming about my hoped for GMC Safari van. In fact I became so distracted with thinking about that vehicle, mentally examining it's interior and pondering all the options, that I became totally disengaged from the sermon. It was not my nature at all to tune out during the preaching of a gifted preacher, quite the opposite in fact, for I almost always sat in the front and on the edge of my seat. But on this particular day, I was not even pretending to listen.

Suddenly, and quite firmly, I heard my name: "Brother Brake!" I snapped to attention, assuming that I most certainly had been more than obvious in my distraction. Rev. Heflin had stopped mid-sentence in his sermon, something I had only seen him do on a couple of occasions prior. But he was not stopping to correct me. Right in the middle of a thought, he had been arrested by the Spirit to deliver to me a message from God. It was a message that left me shocked: "Brother Brake! God says to tell you, that the vehicle you are thinking about, you have His blessing to go out and buy it!" And just like that, Rev. Heflin moved right back into his preaching. I honestly don't know if he even realized exactly what he had said, for he was not one to encourage excess spending.

We had never shared with Rev. Heflin about our desire to purchase a car, and we had certainly never shared our thoughts about a GMC Safari van! At that time such a vehicle was over $20,000, almost double what our taxable income would be during that year. Even if he had known of our hopes, he certainly could not have known what I was thinking at that exact moment in the middle of his message. Only the Spirit of God could have known then the thoughts of my mind, and through Rev. Heflin's obedience to speak out in response to a momentary whisper, God had graciously communicated to us that it was His good pleasure to provide the impossible for our family.

We were tentatively elated. At this time in the early 90's we had never used credit cards, and had no established credit rating. Even with God's permission, how could we ever buy a car? We asked God for further confirmation, and it came immediately.

Within just a few days of God speaking, we received a phone call from my mother. She had felt a burden to contact us regarding our need for a vehicle, and this was her message: "If you ever decide to buy a new vehicle, and you need help in regard to credit, I want to offer to co-sign for a loan." This was amazing to us, as no one had ever previously called us to offer to co-sign on a loan for anything. The timing could not be coincidental. Brimming now with excitement, but not knowing the first thing about purchasing a car, I called my older brother David who was the go to guy in our family for any questions regarding business or negotiation. He relayed that he would be more than happy to conduct the negotiation for us.

Both my mother and brother lived in the Dayton, Ohio area. Wanting to surprise Lenora upon her return from a mission to China, I traveled to Dayton in early November and with the help of my family, became the elated owner of our new GMC Safari. With zero money down and a 1.9% interest rate secured by my mother's co-signing, we would have 48 monthly payments until the debt was retired. The payments were over $400 per month, and they might as well have been twice that, as any payment at all was a step of faith for us, and without God's help we would not be able to meet the obligation. But He had promised, and He, as always, was faithful. We never missed a payment and paid the loan in full exactly 48 months later.

It is important to note that those who often deliver a "personal word" from God's heart to individuals might themselves at times wrestle with the graciousness of that word. We hear God saying generous things to those we pray for and preach to, while we ourselves might unlawfully judge the worthiness of the recipient to receive such a measure of grace or opportunity. Lenora and I certainly did not "deserve" such a beautiful vehicle. But our loving and generous Heavenly Father wanted to provide not only a ministry need, reliable transportation, but also to demonstrate His particular delight in giving His children "extras", that even though non-essential for living, become expressions of His intense paternal love. This we have seen more times since than we could ever recount in one book alone.

And so as the children and I pulled up to the Richmond Airport, beside ourselves with excitement at surprising mom with our miracle as she returned from China, it was not strange that Rev. Heflin walked up to my driver's window, and far from congratulating me, instead uttered two words: "what gall!" I burst out laughing, reminding him that he was God's instrument for confirming our shocking purchase, and reluctantly he had to agree. Our kids were proud as peacocks now to ride with mom and dad into Richmond for church each Sunday, no longer having to cram with the crowd into a 15 passenger ministry van. We now had wheels for family adventures, exploring the Virginia countryside on days off, running up to Pennsylvania or Ohio to visit family, and driving together to preach at churches on weekends.

For six wonderful years we drove that van all over America and Canada, mindful constantly of the goodness of God. We drove it until the day that God spoke to us to pass it on as a gift to a family in our Long Island church. That van was a precious symbol to us, and not something we parted with easily. But the life of faith must not cling tightly to material things. Everything must be held loosely, as things freely come and freely are let go again. There is a joy in receiving, yet there is a greater joy in giving. The years have proven that God will never run out of cars, homes, or any other thing that might be needed for navigating this journey. He is truly the One who owns the cattle on a thousand hills, and as we would continue to learn, He is quite proactive about distributing those cattle to His kids.

31 MISSION VS. MATERIALISM

As pleased as we were with our new van, we talked often about the priority of seeking Christ's kingdom over material things. From the time we first dated in Bible College, up through our distribution of furniture when moving to Ecuador, and now living in a cottage on a Christian campground in Virginia, our aim had been to live a life free from the quest for the American Dream of material security. Not that we didn't dream, as the previous story well illustrates. But our constant prayer was that the dreams of God's heart in reaching the world with the love of Jesus would always take precedence.

In the Fall of 1993, the same time frame when we purchased the van, we continued traveling to the nations at every opportunity. Over a nine week period we joined outreaches to Israel, Russia, and China. The trip to China was the one opportunity that Lenora had that year to be out in ministry while I stayed home with the children. She had an extraordinary time with a wonderful team that went into factories to pray for and minister to the factory workers. That trip alone was close to $4,000, and with the other outreaches combined, we invested an amount into mission that Fall that would have more than paid off half of our new vehicle. But we believed strongly in the mandate of Jesus to "seek first the kingdom of God and His righteousness, and all these things will be added to you". The "all these things" He spoke of referred to the necessities of life. We were confident that if we obeyed His call, not in a haphazard manner of running here and there, but in sincere response to His leading, He would always be there to add to our family anything that might be lacking. We have never deviated from that path, and God has never failed to keep up His end of the promise.

But life has had its moments when this belief system was tested - more moments than we would have chosen. One day a strong storm system moved over central Virginia. A river ran just behind the camp property and fairly close to our cottage. Lenora was preparing dinner, a happily anticipated feast of hamburgers with all the sides. A hasty knock on our door revealed one of the camp staff, there to warn us that the river was rising rapidly and there was a strong probability that our part of the campground was going to flood. They didn't know how much we loved hamburgers.

Sure enough, within a few minutes water began rushing under our door and into the living room. Dinner was about 10 minutes away from being served, and what would have been a common sense evacuation for most families turned for us into a discussion of whether or not we could bear the pain of leaving our hamburgers. We tried not to be materialistic when it came to possessions, but food was in another category altogether. With the water now rising quickly, we hit upon a brilliant solution to protect our sacred family dinner moment. I took out large plastic garbage bags, wrapped one each around everyone's legs, tied them off at the top, and there at the table we sat and enjoyed one of the most memorable family meals in our history. Laughing at our own craziness, and having nothing cherished to lose by staying (God having had the foresight to encourage the distribution of all our fine furnishings a year earlier), we feasted as the waters rose around our ankles and up to our calves.

One spiritually imbalanced woman stopped by to poke her head into our front door, which was now open as closing it kept none of the swirling waters out. "When thou pass through the waters, I will be with thee; and through the rivers, they shall not overflow thee," she melodramatically pronounced in perfect King James English as she attempted to reassure us from the 43rd chapter of Isaiah. I shouted back our confidence in decidedly contemporary Virginia English: "Thank you Sister...but you are too late...the waters have already overflowed!" She left appalled.

In spite of some imperfect circumstances, our first year at camp had been a time of tremendous advancement in our ministry and in discovering a completely new way of working in world missions. We had gone to Ecuador with only one paradigm in our thinking, that of the career missionary who is planted in a singular culture for life. But through Rev. Heflin and his team, we learned that God can and does send people to multiple places with a gospel message that can transform people, churches, and cities through the demonstration of resurrection power; through signs and miracles that would point people decisively to Jesus Christ. The revival we had tasted in Glen Cove became a template for international outreach. That wonderful year of 1993 was the year we discovered our larger calling to bring God's word into multiple places, as well as discovering that there are no limits of provision for those who accept such a calling. There was no ceiling. There were no constituted limitations on how far we could go or how many trips we could take. Limited only by the parameters of the sphere to which He assigned us, we were free within that sphere to believe for the impossible, and to genuinely discover that it "would be unto us, according to our faith."

We had run fast and fervently for a full year since Quito, living a life we had not known was possible. In the space of 12 months we had seen childhood dreams fulfilled as we stood on the slopes of Andean volcanoes, distributed Bibles across the former Soviet Union, moved discretely through Communist China, shared Christ's love in Muslim nations of the Middle East, and witnessed Scripture come alive as we walked through Israel in the footsteps of Jesus. Yet camp was not a long term place for bringing up a family. It's outreaches were geared toward an adult staff and community, and nothing much was available to help develop a structured and healthy spiritual life for children. Though our ministry overall was in full bloom, we realized as the year came to a close that God had sent us there for a season of training and faith development, but not as a permanent home. The idea of leaving Rev. Heflin who had been so gracious was tough, and we wrestled about it for some time. Where would we go anyway? We had no offers in front of us from any other mission organization. We didn't want to become part of a limiting structure when we had enjoyed such incredible freedom to hear from God and pursue His plan for our lives. We found ourselves once again praying for guidance from above. We were not under any external pressure to leave and had the luxury of time. But the conviction that we needed to find our next assignment still weighed continuously upon our minds. God, as always, was one step ahead, subtly now steering us toward the answer to our prayer. He was plotting a course that would provide a stable environment and community for our continued growth as a family and maturity in the exercise of our ministry.

32 THE VALUE OF ONE SOUL

While praying for clarity, a request came in from Ecuador. Our friend Patricio Robelly had planted a church shortly after our departure. Being an ethical man, he started only with his parents and children, though with his strong healing ministry he could have easily had many follow from his former place of employment. Watching him launch with such faith and humility gave us a strong desire to cheer him forward, and especially with the sense we had during our goodbyes that we should remain as faithful and supportive friends. Patricio's year old congregation was now flourishing, and he was inviting us to come in to hold a week of special revival meetings.

It seemed an impractical time to travel, as our long term plans were still up in the air. It was February of 1994 and the Winter Camp four week season was in full swing, but we resolved that I at least would go to Quito for the special meetings while Lenora and the kids remained in Ashland. Once again, God was sending us into an experience that would further enlarge our lives.

The opening night of the meetings was wonderful. An entirely new experience of Holy Spirit gifting began to occur, with words of knowledge that were much more specific than what had been experienced previously. A Biblical example of such would be when Jesus spoke to the woman at the well about her previous husbands. These things seem unsettling to some, but if we truly believe that God knows all things, then is it too much of a stretch to believe that He might sometimes want to communicate that information for the purpose of catching the heart of a listener? Jesus told His disciples that He would not leave them alone, but would send a Comforter, who would "teach them, and lead them into all truth". We must grant that God has the right to reveal as He pleases those hidden things that communicate His loving awareness of a person's need.

Sometimes we might see those who exercise the gifts do so in an irresponsible fashion, using unnecessary melodrama to capture a crowd, or operating with a mixed motive. Gifts are to be exercised only for the purpose of ministering God's grace into the lives of people. They are not given for self- promotion or the securing of personal position. The moment a gift becomes about us, and not about the Giver, we have become those who are abusing the gracious gifts of God.

In spite of such gifts operating that first night, not all was going smoothly. There was a terrible commotion and carrying on by a group of rowdy teenagers who all sat in the first three rows. I found myself repeatedly having to preach over their noise, and even as folks were being healed these teens seemed completely detached and unimpressed. I was irritated and somewhat offended by their lack of respect. God however was not.

As the meeting concluded and I looked at the chaos of those youth who had joined in from another church (they were not members of Patricio's congregation), I heard distinctly another one of those heavenly instructions that I did not immediately like: "I want to bring a great breakthrough to these meetings...but you will need to separate yourself from a normal schedule and mealtimes in the week ahead...I want you to fast and pray for the capturing of these young people's hearts.

"Fast & Pray." I was not particularly delighted. Quito is over 9,000 feet in elevation, and under normal circumstances it takes us two or three days of healthy eating just to get adjusted to the altitude change from sea level. I normally got a bit desperate and food preoccupied by day three of a normal fast (and sometimes even by lunchtime on Day one!). Why on earth did I have to fast at a time like this, and why for the entire seven days? We returned home from that first night's meeting and I informed Patricio and his wife of my resolve. Being those who passionately pursued

God, they didn't bat an eyelid. "We will gladly join you" they announced, and for the remainder of the week we consumed only water and a daily bowl of broth soup.

The meetings continued, though with less sensation than the opening night. Traveling there for the second evening I again heard a distinct instruction to my spirit: "You are not to pray prophetically over anyone individually tonight; My people need to value the message, not only the miracle". I knew that this would not go over well. These were advertised as miracle services. It was true we would still pray for healing, but many after that first night wanted personal words from the heart of God. One woman brought her friend to the front and demanded that I release to her some specific word of knowledge. I guess she thought this might solve all her friend's problems. But God had been very clear with me, and though she walked off in a huff, I knew that the program that night, just like the very different program of the previous night, was one of God's design. The Holy Spirit should always have the first and last say on order.

Through six consecutive nights I preached as the visiting teenagers wreaked repeated disruption on the service, laughing, flirting, and fooling around in a manner that might not have been too visible from the back, but for whatever reason they were purposed to sit directly under the pulpit, and I plowed passionately with the preaching to overcome their inattention. The culture in Quito is an exceedingly polite one, and no one wanted to be the bad guy who would humiliate these kids in public, several of whom were the sons and daughters of local pastors and elders. Being relatively young myself and not a seasoned Ecuadorean missionary, I too did not want to overstep the bounds of what was culturally acceptable by correcting them from the pulpit. I'm sure I would handle things a bit more intentionally today, but as it was then, God's focus was to teach us all a lesson about converting hearts through prayer and patience, and not extracting conformity solely through coercion.

On the seventh night, after a week of fasting, the service proceeded as usual. The same youth were all assembled. But something was different in the atmosphere that night. A strong presence of God to convict hearts was in the room. The Holy Spirit was moving powerfully. During the closing altar call, those same kids who had ignored me for an entire week, forced into attendance by their parents, were suddenly overwhelmed by the mercy and love of God. They flooded the altar, and tears of repentance flowed freely. I didn't know who any of them were, but one young man was among them whose destiny and mine would be intertwined from that moment forward.

I can still see the face of Jeremy Diaz as he cried out to God at the altar, a teenager with no idea of the plan God had, but only a heart's desire to give Jesus everything. No one knew that Jeremy would grow to become one of the most gifted and faithful men in that nation. Twenty three years later, Jeremy is in full time ministry, and has been for his entire adult life. He is the key leader under Patricio's ministry, a fledgling ministry in 1994 that has since grown to impact tens of thousands all over the nation of Ecuador. I had the privilege some years ago of officiating at Jeremy's wedding to his wife Gaby. He has led worship and organized services for dozens of meetings that we have held since that time, becoming one of our most cherished spiritual sons.

I often look at Jeremy and the great impact of his life, and then I imagine, "what might it have looked like if I had loved my belly more than those disinterested teens back in 1994?" I think of the value of one soul, and the economy of God, in which He will choose again and again to send you or I half way around the world for the sake of rescuing one seemingly innocuous life, or for the sake of answering one faith filled mother's prayer. It was not easy to fly away from Virginia that Winter, our money tight, our future undetermined, and my family preparing quietly for transition once again. But these are the lessons that have become the building blocks for a ministry passion that pushes us again and again to be outward rather than inward. We have to go; someone is waiting to hear. Someone who might change a nation one day, or simply someone who needs a cup of cold water that might lead to eternal life. Who, but God, can determine the true value and return of the resources that are invested into missions? It is not ours to quantify, but it will always be ours to willingly obey. In the midst of a year traveling five times around the world for the masses, it was wonderful to again be reminded of the value of a single soul.

33 THE LONG AND QUIET HALLWAY

Pastor Tony Stewart at Citylife Church in Tampa has a wonderful message he shares on navigating the hallways of life. If each major place of focus or assignment on the Christian journey can be thought of as a room in a house, then the time between leaving one room and arriving at another can often be compared to the time spent walking through the hallway. Familiar rooms are comforting and secure. But the moments in between that security can be our greatest times of testing.

We had never before been in a hallway. We moved directly from college to seminary, from seminary to Glen Cove, from Glen Cove to Ecuador, and from Ecuador to Calvary Camp in Virginia. Even those moments of wondering "where to" from Quito lasted only a few days...and those days seemed long and frightening.
Returning home from Ecuador, we set about to determine the next location from which we would continue to carry out our ministry of missionary evangelism. This time around there were no crystal clear words of instruction, no dreams, and definitely no audible voices. God does not like us to think that we have Him completely figured out. His ways are higher than our ways, and just when we begin to think that we have perfected our ability to

hear, He will speak in a new and unexpected way, or He will allow us to sit in a seeming silence as our faith seeks to stay rooted to the faithfulness of His character.

By the end of March we thought we had figured it out. A wonderful Pastor in North Carolina had really impacted our family during several services we attended. We felt drawn to his style of ministry and it seemed a perfect fit. I drove down one day to share our heart, and he showed delight at our willingness to move to his area, and even more, confirmed that he believed this to be God's plan. He assured us that they would be waiting with a red carpet welcome. We had also shared our ideas for relocating with an older preacher that we relied upon for counsel, and he as well thought the plan to be right. And even our friend who had originally been upset when we left Ecuador, telling us to sit still for a year, had gained an entirely new perspective on our calling. Praying over us one day that Spring, he shared this word: "you cannot make plans to satisfy others...you cannot live for the approval of men...God has made you into rolling stones, and you must continue to roll forward as He leads you." We knew that it had taken a real heart change for him to adjust his view and offer us that encouragement.

Rev. Heflin was disappointed to see us go, but he did not attempt to discourage us. He understood our need to find a place of stability for our children. We were so thankful to depart at a time of good relationship, as a short two years later he was called home to heaven at the young age of 63. We will always be grateful to God for giving us 15 precious months of training and partnership with one of the most loving, joyful, and gifted men we have ever known. Much of what we carry in our hearts today was imparted to us from the generosity of spirit carried by Rev. Wallace Heflin.

The plan was made to travel from early April to early June, visiting friends and family, preaching every weekend in churches, and sharing with all who might listen about the expansion of our mission. Support came easily when we were at the Camp, as thousands of folks passed through there annually, and many would feel a heart connection when hearing us or meeting us. But now we would be out of their sight...and as is often said in the ministry, "out of sight, out of mind." We are grateful that though this might be true of men, it is not true of our faithful God. None of us are ever out of His sight...and none of us are ever out of His mind.

Nevertheless funds dipped precipitously. We lived for eight weeks from one tank of gas to the next, driving our Safari van all over the USA, until finally we arrived in early June of '94 to what we believed was our next home city in North Carolina. What followed was the most painful and confusing experience we had yet known in ministry. The host pastor completely detached himself from our arrival. It was as if we had never had a conversation regarding our relocation. A thousand things raced through our minds as we struggled during four days in a hotel room to figure out where we had gone wrong. Did we miss God completely? Was it the devil trying to stop us? Was it God? We had heard God's gentle whispers with real clarity and confidence for several years leading up to this, and had no frame of reference for missing something so completely. It was true that we had mistakenly presumed the parameters when assigned to Quito, but at least we were supposed to be in Quito! But in North Carolina, we quickly found out we didn't belong at all.

Leaving Ecuador was deeply disappointing. Leaving North Carolina was devastating. We felt completely lost as we silently drove north toward Coudersport, Pennsylvania, Lenora's home town and the place where her parents still resided. It was bad enough that we had told our many friends that we were heading triumphantly to North Carolina. But to make the pain worse, Lenora's parents still were uncertain over the fact that we had left our denomination three years earlier. This would provide incontrovertible proof that we had erred in leaving the traditions of our upbringing.

It is easier now, in retrospect, to process this hallway period of our lives. We have learned that no matter how well we hear, think we hear, or may have heard, the words of the Apostle Paul will always ring true: "for now we know in part." No one but Jesus has ever heard the Father's voice perfectly 100% of the time. Because of the potential for hearing imperfectly, many have been scared away from listening for the sweet sound of His voice. But we cannot allow the unexplained moments along the way to intimidate us from pursuing the extraordinary privilege we all have to fellowship and communicate with our Savior. We never did discover why the door was so completely closed to us in North Carolina, and perhaps it was God saving us from a major directional error. I would rather be temporarily wounded by the detachment of a church leader, than to plunge headlong into an assignment that might detour or derail us from a greater purpose that God had planned for our lives. He indeed had a greater purpose, but it would require us to endure the hallway for several months longer.

God's grace is so amazing, for in the midst of our regret and confusion, an invitation came to participate in an evangelistic crusade in the capitol city of the Dominican Republic. This seemed hardly the time, but again, we lived by the principle of "seeking first His kingdom." In ourselves we had no courage, and would have said no. But as Lenora and I prayed, God confirmed that I should go at the end of Summer in the month of August. We now had absolutely nothing, our bank account being down to exactly $25, and no idea where our car payment would come from, let alone the costs of an outreach in another nation. I put my head down in prayer asking God what to do, and in a moment He provided the answer: "give your last $25 for another team member's expenses, and I will provide for yours." To be honest, I was almost embarrassed to write out a check for $25 and send it as a contribution to the man who was to be our team leader. His costs would be in the thousands. But God does not look at amounts. He looks at faith, and at the intentions of our hearts.

With Lenora's agreement, I wrote out a check to my colleague for our last $25, and placed it in the mail. Literally one hour after I mailed it, the phone rang at my in-laws. It was an old friend from Glen Cove who himself would be a member of the Dominican team. "Do you need funds for this mission?", he asked, "because God just spoke to me to pay your entire fare if you are planning to go!" I put down the phone, once again in shock. So many times along the way God's amazing grace has left me in momentary shock. Why do we get so surprised when God so supernaturally and instantaneously responds to our giving, our dilemma, our opportunity, or our need for direction? I preached once that His grace should always be "amazing"; I don't want to ever get to the point where His uniqueness as God becomes commonplace and unimpressive. He will forever be Almighty God!

This provision infused fresh life into our family, and though we still had no clear direction, we were certain that God was still with us and would in due time point us to our next place of residence. My mother and stepfather in Ohio had a home situation that was much more conducive to receiving a slightly disoriented family of five, so after just three weeks in Pennsylvania we loaded up our van and headed over to Tiffin, Ohio. It was here in Tiffin that we would again experience the extremely specific intervention of God, an event so unusual that we still speak of it regularly all these years later. If Lenora and I had not experienced it together, I would think that perhaps it had only been a dream.

34 A DIVINE ENDORSEMENT FOR BUGLE BOY CLOTHING

My mother and stepfather were gracious hosts, but I had not lived at home since I was 17 years old. It felt humiliating at 31 to return with a family and no ability to satisfy the normal parental questions regarding our future. "God will provide" may sustain our own faith, but it does not usually appease the anxiety of extended family. This becomes for many who are called the real place of testing, for the last thing any of us want is the derision or doubt of our loved ones. Yet it seems that throughout history God has put many into this same crucible, where the calling and vision are irrevocable, yet the crowd along the way has no insight into the inner workings of God and your own heart. We cannot take offense at their skepticism. Joseph's brothers did not have the dream that Joseph had. Why should they believe? The humility which bears the cross of misunderstanding must be allowed to work its way into the deepest parts of our soul.

Even though the Dominican Republic trip was approaching, I struggled to stay afloat emotionally. For our kids it was the best Summer ever. Their Granny was and still is an amazing grandmother. Every day was a new adventure, with outings to the city swimming pool, exploring the woods behind Granny's house, and eating Granny's amazing Middle Eastern cooking. No more 74 nights in a row of camp meeting for them! No, the kids weren't complaining at all. It was a peaceful time for Lenora as well, who always had a special bond with my mother. But I was weighed down by the need to find direction. I was the leader of our home, and we had always had adequate or abundant provision. But now we were living in part off of the hospitality of my parents.

One day we went to a department store to look at kid's clothing. We had a very limited amount of money, and as my eyes fell on a certain section of clothing for boys, I felt the pain of remembering a time not too distant when we had substantive income in Glen Cove, and I could buy our children whatever they needed. There was a clothing brand at the time for young boys called Bugle Boy. These clothes were especially sharp and trendy, more expensive than other brands, but we loved to buy Bugle Boy for our sons and to have them as well dressed as we could afford.

Sadly for me, the price of Bugle Boy clothes was totally out of our present range and circumstance. We went home with a few bare necessities, and for whatever reason, this became a tipping point for me emotionally. I sank that night into the deepest slough of despondency. I felt utterly defeated. It wasn't so much the clothing, but it was the total loss of our independence. There we were with a beautiful van parked in my parent's driveway, yet without an extra dollar for any of the necessities of our family. I went to bed and woke up the next morning in an even deeper state of discouragement. I just could not get out of my head the mockery of those unaffordable Bugle Boy shirts and jeans.

Like it was frozen in time, I can still see myself sitting in the family room chair quietly that next day. The phone next to me rang, and as I unenthusiastically answered, the voice on the other line asked for Rev. Kelly Brake. "Wow...are you ever hard to get ahold of...I've had to call three different people before I finally found someone who knew your phone number!" The caller was a Christian Psychologist who had been a team member on our outreach to Russia a year earlier. We had seen Dr. Kay perhaps once after Russia when she came through Ashland, but we certainly were not well acquainted, and had never to my recollection had any conversation together. She proceeded to tell me the purpose of her phone call: "I was in prayer early this morning, and God spoke something to me. He told me that I was deliver this message to you. Now Kelly, I don't have any idea what this means, and I don't know if you will either...I hope you don't think that I'm crazy for calling you...but if I didn't call I would be disobedient.. so here it is - - God told me to tell you that '**He**

knows how to provide Bugle Boy clothing for your children'...does that make any sense to you?

She did not have to wait for my answer. I started to cry right on the spot. I knew that God was a speaking God, but this was a whole new level of demonstration of the profound love and care of God for the smallest details of our family life. My brain was stunned trying to fathom not only His grace, but the ability of a prayer intercessor to hear from God so specifically. And not only to hear, but the obedience level she must have had to pick up that phone and call me with such an obscure message, one that had to be 100% accurate, or indeed, she would be deemed crazy. I was immediately catapulted into a deeper hunger for knowing the ways and voice of God.

Within a few hours of that phone call, I received another call, this time from my father who lived at the time in another state. "Son, I don't know what you need, but while praying this morning God spoke to me to send you a $200.00 department store gift card so that you can buy new clothes for the children!" My tears just kept flowing. Naturally, the card was for a department store that carried the Bugle Boy line of clothing. And naturally, the minute that card came in the mail Lenora and I raced out with the kids and gleefully bought all three of them what they needed...including our boys' heaven sanctioned and not so cheap Bugle Boy outfits! Does a person need such to be happy? Of course not. But God wanted to make a point. "I am Almighty God, who knows your every thought. I love you with an everlasting love. I care about the deepest desires of your hearts and the smallest details of your journey. I am with you...and I will never leave you or forsake you!". Our faith has been resuscitated many a time as we've reflected back on God's penchant for the Bugle Boy brand. Truly we serve an amazing God!

35 BE HERE AT 2:20 PM

After God's grace in showing such care for our kids, it was easier to fly off to the Dominican Republic and trust that God was charting out our next steps; easier, but not easy. I knew that upon returning we would need to find our new home by Summer's end. In spite of that preoccupation, God moved wonderfully in the D.R.. Words of knowledge regarding physical needs and healing continued to occur, and God did not fail to meet the hunger and need of those we ministered to. One moment in particular sticks out, when a word of knowledge was given regarding someone with a painful hernia, followed by a tap on the back of my shoulder. It was the Pastor of the church standing on the platform behind us. God was faithful, as always, and the Pastor was immediately healed of his pain.

Our conditions on the ground were difficult, with rats overrunning us in the night as we stayed in the home of a very poor pastor in the poorest part of the capitol, scorching Summer heat and high humidity, and local church leaders who fought tenaciously about the details and protocols of the large open air crusade we were conducting in the final three days. When we finally flew out, even with the good results, I was so appalled by the divisions of the churches that I vowed to never return. It is foolish to vow anything about where we will or will not go in the work of God. That vow was overturned in dramatic fashion by what turned out to be one of our largest projects ever 21 years later, a story that will be told toward the end of this book.

True to expectation, we packed up our van in early September, said our goodbyes to the grandparents, and drove off into the sunrise with a month's itinerary of preaching, but not the slightest idea of where we would land. It was truly an Abrahamic moment for us of going forward into promise, but not knowing where that promise would lead. We knew only that it was a "land He would show us."

Our first stop was at our now familiar field of Thorold, Canada, where our friend Pastor Ric proposed that "perhaps God will send you back to Long Island". I announced to him emphatically and dramatically: "that is the **one** place that God will definitely not sent us back to!" "We have already lived there twice, in Baldwin and in Glen Cove; we don't want to live there again, and it could raise ethical questions if we return as former pastors to our old stomping grounds." I may not have known what the will of God specifically was, but I certainly was sure of what it wasn't!

From Canada we drove to Long Island, preaching in several churches, including our previous Glen Cove church. We were staying with a friend in Glen Cove as well. With the preaching concluded and eager to move on to visit friends in New Jersey, where we would preach for an Arabic fellowship that coming weekend, we continued praying about our permanent location. No insight came, but the day before departure I received the clearest instruction in prayer: **"stay in town for two more days."**

The last thing we wanted to do was stay two more days on Long Island. We were loved there and could spend a month visiting friends, but we really wanted nothing more than to move on and figure out our future...which was most definitely not on Long Island. I could see no practical purpose to sitting around for two more days, but the directive in prayer was clear. The first extra day we sat twiddling our thumbs, trying not to feel crazy, and asking God for clarity.

On the morning of the second day, I received a strange phone call from Pastor Burns of our former church. "I need a big favor from you" he requested: I need you to come to my home...at 2:20 in the afternoon. His home of course was our former parsonage in which we had lived for 4 1/2 years during our ministry there. He went on to explain: "I have an appointment with another pastor who wants to talk through a few issues. He is coming at 2:00, and I prefer to have someone else present, but it might be awkward if he arrives and you are sitting there...would you mind coming by around 2:20?"

"John, I really would rather not do that", I responded; "can't you sort it out without me." As John continued to ask for my cooperation and "this one small favor," I finally agreed to help my friend out and promised I would come by. "Okay", I responded, "but I'm only coming by for a short visit, and then we have to get ready to head out." All I could think in my head was that there were a thousand things more important I should be doing with my time rather than sitting in on a meeting between two local pastors.

Wishing that I was anywhere but in Glen Cove, I dutifully showed up at 2:20 PM, knocked on the door, and joined Pastor Burns and his colleague around the dining room table, where after brief greetings they attempted to continue their discussion, which was now somewhat difficult with my being present. I was agitated at myself for agreeing to be there, as my visit seemed to add nothing more than a buffer for their exchange.

And then it happened. Within five minutes of taking my seat, just after 2:25 PM, I looked out the window to see a man hurrying up the parsonage sidewalk, heading directly for the parsonage door. I knew this man well, Dr. Louis Hamada, an evangelist in Lebanon who had spoken twice before at our church. I had not seen him in at least two years, but was so amazed at the sight of his approach that I jumped up as if I was still the resident in charge. "That's Dr. Hamada" I announced, heading to the door to let him in, forgetting for a moment that it was no longer my home. I swung open the door just as he rang the bell. "Dr. Hamada, what are you doing here?" His answer was just as surprised: "what are **you** doing here? I came to speak to the new pastor...but you aren't the pastor anymore...why are you answering the door?" Which in fact was a very good question, and one I didn't answer, as I hastily invited him to come in and join us at the table.

As Pastor Burns and his friend listened quietly, Dr. Hamada and I launched into a happy and animated conversation, catching up on our mutual ministries. When we had known one another previously, it was to connect on the few days of each year that he passed through Long Island to visit his sister in her Glen Cove home. But now, he informed us sadly, his sister had passed away. He was tasked with settling her estate. Dr. Hamada's next words made me wish the conversation had never started:

"We were supposed to leave by this weekend, but we haven't been able to find the right family to rent her home. We feel we should rent it out rather than selling it, but we also believe it ought to be a Christian family whom we can help, and this will give us the security of knowing it is in good hands while we travel. Perhaps you pastors know of someone? And tell me Pastor Kelly, where exactly is your home base at this time?"

I hemmed and hawed and did all I could to avoid the question. I knew that if Dr. Hamada knew we were looking for a place to live he would immediately conclude, incorrectly, that his house was the Promised Land...and we were **not** moving back to Long Island! But I could not evade his question forever, and finally I had to admit that we were in the process of relocating from my mother's home and finding a more permanent location.

In a moment he was on his feet, passionately exclaiming the wonders of God: "This is God! Oh, this is clearly of God! I didn't even know why I was coming to this home; I knew you did not live here, and I was not even in town long enough to preach...but I felt compelled this morning to get out and walk, and then compelled again to walk through this neighborhood...I was not going even to stop, but somehow I felt compelled to come up the sidewalk and ring the bell...Oh can't you see it!...it is so clear...God brought you and I here together at this moment to answer both of our prayers!!"

Pastor John Burns and the other pastor sat as witnesses to an unfolding drama of no man's making. And I...well I was not up rejoicing with Dr. Hamada. I was in the process of calmly explaining to him why this could not possibly be God's plan and purpose for our present season of ministry. But he was unrelenting. "At least come over for coffee and cookies...come over this evening...just to talk; bring the kids. It will be wonderful for my wife to see your family again. Promise me you will come."

What else did I have to do? There were no excuses, and fully prepared to burst his bubble, we joined them that evening for some fellowship in his sister's expansive home.

The Hamadas got right to the point, pointing out that they were looking for $1,200 per month, but for our family, they would reduce it to $1,000. They needed no down payment and no security deposit...for after all, they knew us. We steadfastly insisted that we were certain it was not God's plan, but inside our hearts were wrestling mightily with the thought that indeed this could be, totally unexpected, and totally out of left field, maybe...just maybe...the hand of God.

"Stay on the Island two more days." "Come to my home at exactly 2:20 PM." Dr. Hamada, fervently praying for a renter of God's choosing, came up the sidewalk at 2:25 PM. These crazy coincidences kept replaying in my mind, even when I tried pushing them out. We loved Long Island, but we did not want to settle in the same region where we had pastored. We did not want to be guilty of reestablishing ourselves in another man's vineyard. And we most certainly did not want to rent a house six blocks from our former parsonage! It is amazing how often we put God into a box of how we think He can or should move.

"Would you at least agree to pray about it?" When they asked this question, we knew we had no grounds for refusal. We would go to New Jersey as planned, preach that weekend, and return to Long Island on Sunday night to give our answer on Monday morning. The Hamadas would postpone their departure as well to await our return.

It was one of the longest weekends of our lives. Our brains could not compute the plan and purpose of God. True, the set up seemed impossible to deny. The timing of the events were an impossible coincidence. But why on earth should we return to the land we had left so decisively when we moved to Ecuador just two years prior?

Sunday night I lay awake until 4:00 AM, wrestling with not only the issue of returning, but the larger faith issue of a $1,000 per month rent. We did not have sufficient monthly support to sustain that kind of a commitment. Was God seriously asking us to sign our names and reputation to a figure that large? It had been a monumental step of faith for us to purchase the van, and indeed God had been faithful. But this was entirely new territory. Since marrying we had resided only in student apartments at minimal cost, or church provided living quarters. We had never paid substantive rent.

As I wrestled into the early hours, God's voice broke through firmly, yet still gently: **"If you cannot believe Me to provide for your family, you will never be able to believe Me to be a blessing to the nations of the earth."** That was it, and it was crystal clear. We knew we were called to serve and bless nations with the gospel and to lift up the poor with His Kingdom resources. But it would not just happen because of our good hearts and intentions. We had to be a people of faith, not just for travel, and not just for clothing, and not just for vehicles...but for every area of our family's life and future. God knew that we had to get this right if our ministry was going to successfully move forward. The provision of a free home would have put a roof over our heads, but God wanted more than a roof over our heads. He wanted a couple who would trust unwaveringly in His ability and determination to care for their lives.

Still hesitant and in the tradition of Gideon, we laid out one final fleece: "Okay Lord, we are willing...but we have to be sure that we are obeying and not just presuming." We determined to put some fairly unappealing conditions before the Hamadas, which in retrospect were somewhat ludicrous, but such was the weight of deciding to settle for a third time on Long Island. We will tell them that "we are, like them, a faith based ministry, and if they want us to rent their home, then they will have to join their faith to ours that we can pay them in a timely fashion each month!" Surely no one would agree to such an audacious proposal.

We had set ourselves up, for the Hamadas didn't blink. "Wonderful!", they exclaimed; "no problem at all! We will pray together and God will provide for us all!" That was it. Our destiny was sealed. With a half-hearted smile Lenora and I both signed the lease for $1,000 per month. We had enough accumulated from preaching to pay the first month, and a few days before October 1st we were moving into a wonderful home that was God's means of getting us to the right place at the right time for the next 11 year assignment of our journey. We had no beds, no furniture, and a less than heroic faith...but He who had called us was about to be faithful yet one more time.

36 THE CLOCK IS TICKING, AND WHERE IS OUR $1,000 FOR RENT?

Those first weeks of October were a cascade of blessing. Friends brought furniture that filled every room. In the eleven years we had been married, we had purchased one item of furniture, a $300 couch for our first apartment. Since then, in each of our major moves to Long Island, Quito, and Camp, God had abundantly filled our homes. We never sent out pitiful pleas or announced our empty rooms. God's faithfulness always went ahead and made the provision. We had left Ohio with our van and personal sentimental possessions such as photo albums and souvenirs from our travels. We had known what we were assigned to do as evangelists to nations, but we had not known where we would land. Three weeks later we were settled into a fully furnished home.

Pastor John Burns in Glen Cove was especially gracious to us, encouraging church members to grant us a warm welcome back into the Long Island community. Our fears of conflict had been unfounded.

As kind as everyone was, we knew it was not appropriate to make our former church the base for our traveling ministry. That would be unfair to Pastor Burns, and unethical by any measure of ministry. Where would we go to church? This was the paramount question, and the first order of business. It would not suffice to attend just anywhere, or to pick and choose a church like a consumer Christian. We needed to know God's assigned place for our family.

Within 48 hours of moving in, our family was eating out at Mykonos, our favorite Greek restaurant in Glen Cove. Lenora and I had prayed, asking God to lead us, and in the middle of our dinner conversation it dropped into our hearts, not as a good idea, but as a statement of fact: **"Your new church will be the Holy Spirit Christian Church in Hicksville"**. It wasn't vague, and the whisper was in fact unmistakable...but this church was not at the forefront of our consideration. We had other ministry friends on Long Island whose churches we knew far better. We had attended the church in Hicksville only once previously, to preach before going to Ecuador. They had taken up monthly support during our time in Quito, as well as helping us during the transition to initially get there. But other supportive congregations were located closer, and we barely knew the folks in Hicksville.

I spoke with Pastor Dan Beaulieu who led the Hicksville Congregation, and he was more than welcoming. The very next Sunday we attended and he introduced our family.

We were familiar with no one, yet we felt at home. God, for whatever reason, had decided to plant us in what we later realized was a very different type of church community than any we had known previously. A church of over 200 with 90% being ethnic Italian, these dear folks were full of passion and humor, loud and very much alive. Many of our members on the North Shore of Long Island in Glen Cove had been from a more reserved Scandinavian background. But we were soon to be fast indoctrinated into the wonders of Long Island Italian culture.

Church home being resolved, we turned our attention back to our calling, looking ahead at the calendar for those places God would send. A first trip to India was already slated for February. But I could not concentrate too well on ministry planning. Though flooded with furnishings, our cash flow had become a trickle. We bought our food, and paid for our vehicle, but November 1st was fast approaching and nothing was in hand for rent.

Lenora has always handled financial pressure better than myself. I often used the excuse that I was the one paying the bills...the same excuse used by many a church treasurer for being anxious regarding the flow of funds. But it is not an acceptable excuse to God. All of us our called to live by faith, whether pauper or millionaire, whether treasurer or visionary - - each one must learn to walk in perfect peace that the One who promised will be true to His word.

With the deadline fast approaching, I began to feel overwhelmed by the thought of failing on the very first month. We had taken the bold faith step of signing the lease, but now I needed to remain in a bold place of faith and trust God to supply miraculously, even if it was manna day by day. I did not stay in a bold place of faith however. By the 31st of October I was practically sick to my stomach. Lenora was a sea of calm while I bemoaned the end of the universe. Our promise was to stop by Dr. Hamada's lawyer's office by the 1st of each month to drop off payment. On November 1st, I realized that we were not going to keep our promise. It was devastating to my morale, and one moment I would pace like a crazy man frantically trying to come up with a plan, and the next I would sink into our couch and stare blankly out the window. Why had God not come through? Why had He allowed such a humiliation? He was supposed to take care of our family...had I utterly failed in my faith as the leader of my home?

On Nov. 3rd, my 32nd birthday, God spoke to me and set me free. He showed me during my prayer time that morning that the problem was not the money. The problem was my pride. I had not been concerned about the ministry. I had not been concerned primarily about housing for my family. I had been concerned about my reputation.

Seeing this with such clarity as the Holy Spirit probed my heart, I repented of being more concerned for what people thought of my faith, my reputation, and my leadership. I had allowed this test to become more about what Dr. Hamada would think of me as a fellow evangelist, rather than about what I really thought of God.

It was a liberating and profound moment. I felt suddenly so free from the burden and pressure. The money would come, whether late or on time; but I would no longer allow these moments to dictate my emotions, or my view of God.

I had a breakfast appointment with Pastor Dan that day. We shot the breeze for an hour or so, during which time he asked if I would be willing to teach now and then for the midweek service. He asked if I could meet with our mission board and give them some advice on the structure of the mission program. I assured him that we were glad to do whatever we could to assist the congregation.

As I got up to leave the church office, Pastor Dan suddenly remembered something and stopped me. "Oh, I almost forgot to give you this." He opened the desk drawer and pulled out an envelope. "I'm sorry I didn't call you about this earlier...it just completely slipped my mind. Our board met four days ago and decided we would like to help with your housing costs...as a donation to your mission ministry; this check has been sitting in the desk." He handed me a check for $1,000...a check that had been issued October 31st. I stared at it, my emotions alternating between overwhelming gratitude to God and a slight desire to throttle Pastor Dan for somehow forgetting to call me. And then he dropped the real surprise: "And we would like to commit to this for the next 12 months. Our secretary will have a check for $1,000 for you at the end of every month over the coming year".

I was quite emotional that wonderful birthday morning. The money had been there all along. The money, we have since learned, is always there, all along. God knew the check was sitting in that desk drawer, but He allowed my faith to be matured and developed. Faith refined is of greater value than all of this world's gold. He owns all of the world's gold and silver, but our loving Heavenly Father knows that our life is far more effective and fulfilling when we learn to walk in the full confidence of His love.

Delay is not denial, and in God's economy and timetable, He is never late. He is not the God of 11:59, the last minute God so often found in our limited theology. He is the God of 12:01, after the last hope has expired, after the Midnight deadline has come and gone...the God of resurrection who comes in the midst of our mourning and reminds us that He still has the mastery over death and the grave.

I paid the rent that November morning, three days late. In the 23 years since, we have never again been a single day late with a housing payment. I would not have chosen that painful lesson for myself, but it has paid dividends for life. All these years later, the foremost aim of our faith is still to live in the peace of His promises, one day at a time. It was not incidental when Jesus told His disciples "Therefore, do not worry about tomorrow...don't worry about what you will eat, or drink, or wear...for your Heavenly Father knows that you need all these things. But seek first the kingdom of God, and His righteousness, and all these things **will** be added to you."

37 THE SOUND OF AN ABUNDANCE OF RAIN

As we continued settling into our new home church, we also continued preparing for upcoming mission assignments. I received an invitation from Pastor Ric in Canada to join a team to India. This trip to India changed all of our lives. It launched one of the most important assignments of our calling, and it set the stage for events that would impact individually every member of our family.

Much of that impact had to do with Dr. K.R. Singh, our host and dear friend ever since that first visit. We call Dr. Singh the Apostle to the Jungle. Challenged by God to pioneer outreach to unreached tribes and people groups in the remote forests of the

Indian states of Orissa, Madhya Pradesh and Andhra Pradesh, Dr. Singh spent six years going from village to village before winning his first convert.

It was an elderly man, seated on a tree stump on the fringes of a dusty village near the Orissa border. K.R. Singh shared with him about Jesus, to which the man responded: "Why have you come so late with such good news?" Why do you come so late with news of a God who sacrificed his son? I have already sacrificed my only son according to the instructions of our village witch doctor. There was sickness and we were told that only the blood of my son would make the spirits go away. But it did not work. We are still sick. We are still poor. And I have lost my only son."

Child sacrifice was still practiced at that time 35 years ago, and even today still occurs in remote places. K.R. was broken hearted by the old man's words, "why have you come so late with this good news of a God who gave His only Son?" He prayed to God, "let me never again hear those words that I have come too late!" The old man received God's comfort and salvation through Jesus that day, becoming the first to profess Christ in his village. Today, among hundreds of villages and dozens of remote tribes, more than 100,000 have been baptized. It is one of the great revivals of modern history.

Into such a setting we landed, crossing rivers by dugout canoe and trekking through the hot sun to become the first Westerners to enter several villages. We were allowed in more as an oddity, our very light skin attracting the curiosity of the chiefs. In addition, the promise was made by K.R.'s team to provide schooling for the children, none of whom had opportunity otherwise. These places were completely off the grid of modern society.

In the first place I preached a maniacal looking witch doctor, complete with literal bones in his nose, performed his incantations and gesticulated wildly during the message. It was a bit unnerving, yet he became the first to respond to the offer of security and permanent forgiveness through Jesus. As soon as the villagers saw their leader's response, the entire group followed him in embracing the Son of God. It was a 100% turning from pagan idolatry and witchcraft to the light of the gospel of Jesus Christ. A pastor, church, and school in that village are all dynamically functioning to this day.

The main event of this three week outreach was to be a gathering for over 10,000 tribal believers and inquirers. They would travel down out of the jungle to one of K.R.'s ministry centers, by foot, by bus, and any other way they could get there. Some would walk for over a week. They would come to hear God's word and celebrate Jesus. A small army of volunteers would cook and provide for their needs.

We were in the final days of the conference, and it had been a wild affair. Thousands of the attendees had never been to such a gathering, and managing the food distribution was a monumental task of steaming piles of rice and vegetables served 3 times daily on banana leaves. The bathrooms were across the road - over 10,000 people attending to their daily needs on one small piece of land with only the cover of trees. No running water, no flush toilets, no paper or privacy. Not one person was complaining though, for this was how they lived in the forests. They were simply excited to be there and enjoying the atmosphere of communal celebration.

On the second day, disaster struck. There was one well that served the needs of the ministry center. It was the sole source of water, and it had never run dry. This well was the supply for cooking and for drinking water for all 10,000 people, but there had never been so many gathered there before. Dr. Singh approached us very solemnly that morning, informing us that we had an emergency that required a miracle: "we have no more water, and we cannot send these people away. We do not have even water for them to drink. It is the dry season, and there will not be rain for at least 3 months. I've called all our friends in Europe and asked them to pray. Please my friends, pray with me...we need a miracle from God."

The people gathered that evening for the service, and we decided to inform every one of the situation. We were going to ask God to demonstrate that Jesus was indeed alive. All of those gathered knew that rain in early March was not going to come. But we had told them about the God of miracles. We were going to ask for rain. We were going to worship and sing. No more preaching, no more speeches. Just 10,000 desperate people who needed the God of the Bible to come upon that mass of humanity and meet their need.

Fifteen minutes into the worship, with our team sitting on the platform, I suddenly felt a strong breeze blowing. In that same moment, the 200 orphan children seated on the ground just in front of the platform suddenly began to leap up and point over our heads. All of the children were pointing, but we could not see whatever it was they were pointing at. Then just as suddenly, all of the children raised their hands, many of them weeping and worshiping deeply with their eyes now closed. The atmosphere was electric. We didn't know what was happening to the children, but we knew that something we had never seen before was unfolding, as the orphan kids one by one began to worship in spiritual languages they had not previously known. The Holy Spirit began to fall mightily upon the kids. At that very moment, there was a thunderous clap and a waterfall of rain began to pour from the heavens. The crowd went ballistic with joy, dancing wildly in celebration. The children began to dance wildly. There were many dignified pastors visiting from other denominations who came for the meeting that night, standing prim and proper in their suits and ties, and they looked stricken with confusion. They had never seen such a manifestation of the power of God, and many of them were almost in a state of fear.

But for our team, it was not a time for fear. We too had on our suits and ties, as was the cultural custom for preachers in those days, but we did not stand by analyzing. God had heard and answered the cry of His people. We began to dance with the crowd, as the rain fell harder and harder upon the ministry center. It did not simply rain. It poured down as I've never seen anywhere else other than during the rainy season in the Amazon River basin. The water began rising everywhere, and was soon several inches deep on the ground. The people danced and celebrated on. Still the rains came, and being a practical North American, I began to worry about the electrical lines that had been strung up and attached to generators.

Light poles began falling, and lines were landing everywhere. "God, these people are all going to be electrocuted!" My mind was racing even while celebrating. I watched poles and lines one by one fall over and equipment blow out, even as the water rose five to six inches in depth, yet no one seemed affected. The entire grounds became a splash pool for kids. I have never to this day seen such an outpouring of joy and ecstatic dancing as we all witnessed that night. And suddenly, just as it had started, the rain stopped. The waters receded, and the well was completely full. Ten thousand tribal people had just seen that Jesus is alive!

The follow up was almost as spectacular. We asked the children the next morning, "What were you pointing at?" They responded through the interpreters as if we were theologically behind the curve: "Oh, when we were praising, Jesus came down. He came down and stood on your heads!" Every child we interviewed had seen the same vision. As we led the crowd in worship, Jesus Himself appeared, standing over the platform mid-air, just over the heads of all the preachers. For reasons we don't know, only the children were granted the ability to see this, but each of their testimonies aligned. At the moment they saw him, they were all descended upon by the Spirit of God. And the very next moment, the rain began to fall.

We learned as well that rainfall had been confined to the immediate area around the conference center. In fact, the paper of the nearest city was brought to us that next evening. On the weather page was a map of India, with symbols of bright sunshine dotting the entire nation...and one symbol of a very dark thundercloud directly on the map over our area of India, with the following weather observation: "a meteorological phenomena was picked up by radar over one localized spot in Andhra Pradesh, which resulted in an unseasonable and very heavy rain". This was the gist of the weather center's attempt to explain why rain had fallen when it wasn't supposed to rain. What God had done was brief, but so intense that it had been noted and recorded. It was also noted and recorded in the hearts of every man, woman, and child who were present that evening, for they had in fact been visited by the Creator of heaven and earth.

38 EVERY PEOPLE, TRIBE, AND TONGUE

We learned so much over many trips to India about the variety of methods the Holy Spirit will use to reach the hearts of people. People have the same concerns around the world, but their cultural perspectives can be vastly different than our own. No matter how much education we have, education alone is not sufficient to master the art of communicating the gospel in such a way that it penetrates deep into the heart of another human being, especially one with the limited world view held by many remote tribespeople. Without the aid and anointing of God's Spirit, we are often guessing at best. But with wisdom from above, the impossible can be attained. It seemed to me that the task of preaching to unreached tribespeople was an impossible one. I still believe that effective preaching is impossible for man on his own. The commission Jesus gave us, to make disciples, to convert the hearts of people, to deliver the captive soul...all of these require God's supernatural grace. Churches and ministry have never found success by virtue of Bachelors, Masters, or Doctoral degrees. These are excellent tools and can be much commended...but all of our learning and training must then be saturated with power from on high.

We were told on one foray into Madhya Pradesh that we would walk some length to a village that had not had previous guests from the West. I knew nothing of the tribe or what to speak, only that we bumped along for too many hours on a rutted road in our effort to get there. My nerves were on edge as they always were at the prospect of preaching with simultaneous translation through two different languages, first from English to Telegu, and then from Telegu to the local tribal tongue. Like so many times before, I quietly prayed for God's help.

"Noah's Ark"....the two words that resounded in my mind were crystal clear.

Immediately I began the all too common and unhealthy practice of trying to logically figure out God. "Noah's Ark? Seriously? How in the world do I tell the story of Noah's Ark to people that have never seen a boat bigger than a dugout canoe...to people who have never even heard the creation story? I wrestled with my questions, but in the end I would do what I had always done, which was to plunge ahead in faith that what I had heard was the familiar voice of God, and not a manifestation of jungle madness.

We arrived to find close to 300 people gathered under a large thatched structure. They were eager to see the white people, and more eager to hear what was spoken. After greetings and formalities, I took a deep breath and plunged ahead with the story of Noah's Ark; a story of a world filled with sin, where men turned away from God, and suffered the judgment of a great water that filled the earth. All had died and it was terrible...only a man named Noah and his family survived. I felt a bit awkward relating this tale of judgement to such a primitive people even though I knew it was leading to a happy ending: Jesus, God's only Son who was sent to be the sacrifice for our sins, so that we could trust in Him and never again live in fear of such a flood or such a judgment. God was Love, and he did not want to hurt anyone, but to save all who would trust in Him.

I didn't make it to the invitation before the wailing began. Once the part about the flood unfolded, the tribespeople present began shaking and weeping. As soon as I finished the story of Jesus, and offered His salvation from judgment, there was a rush to the front of the crowd. Every single person came forward in a state of great emotional distress, crying out in their language for a Savior who would save them from the flood.

Suddenly I was beset upon by the tribal evangelists who worked in that region: "Who told you? Who told you what happened here? How did you know what to preach?" They were themselves in a heightened state of excitement, and naturally I asked what they were talking about, as no one had told me anything. "The flood", they responded emphatically; "the terrible flood...it came last year during the worst rainy season this area has ever seen. The Chabari river rose higher than it ever had before. The village of these people was swamped. Many, many families lost members and many children were drowned...how did you know to preach about being saved from a flood?"

It was another of those priceless moments that adjusts our view of God and ministry. How great a communicator is the Holy Spirit! How tragic it is when He has no role in our 21st century preaching. Whether a sophisticated North American audience, or a group of illiterate tribespeople in a remote jungle, God alone knows the deep secrets of a man or woman's heart. Why do we consult Him only in emergencies? Should He not be the Master of Ceremonies and the choreographer of our messages in every venue in which we gather? We left that place rejoicing, redoubling our determination to have a hearing ear for the ever ready voice of God.

39 THE TRANSFORMATION OF TERRORISTS

India has waged a battle for several decades with Communist guerrillas known as the Naxalites, and the years when we first began working in the tribal region were particularly difficult times of persecution against believers. The Naxalites used force and intimidation to persuade the villagers to join their ranks. They were particularly hostile to the Christian message, which offered freedom to the people without the use of violence and anarchy. Christian evangelists and pastors therefore became the greatest threat to their movement.

On more than one occasion we narrowly escaped an ambush. Heading down the highway one afternoon, we were flagged down by our advance team returning from the other direction. The church where we were to meet in just a few hours had been attacked. Eighteen of the villagers were speared, and several even shot with flaming arrows. We turned around thankful that we had been spared, but grieving for those who were paying a high price for their faith.

On another occasion we had a large meeting planned outside of the ministry headquarters in Sileru, a remote community near to where three states came together. Heading up the mountain we had a flat tire, which seemed to take forever to repair. It was frustrating to be so late for the outreach. Just as we got started again, one of the evangelists came racing down by motorcycle. The Naxalites had again prepared an ambush for our team, and just moments earlier the police had been tipped off and swooped in to pursue them. Without the flat tire we would have driven directly into their trap.

Yet Jesus loves even the Naxalites. We trekked one night far into the bush, escorted by dozens of tribespeople carrying torches. Once again the Holy Spirit dropped His chosen word into my spirit, the message of the Prodigal Son. Moments before the preaching began, after which we would show the Jesus film, Dr. Singh approached me soberly. "There are several 'brothers' here in the crowd; let the Holy Spirit give you wisdom in the words you speak." 'Brothers' was the code word we used when talking about the terrorists in mixed company.

As I preached it was evident who they were. They stood on the fringes, their dark and angry eyes illumined by the firelight. All of them were armed, but we were armed with weapons far greater, the love and power of the gospel of Christ. As the story of the remorseful Prodigal unfolded, their hearts began to soften. When the surprise ending of the Father's passionate forgiveness and joyful welcome was told, three of these Naxalites were among the first to raise their hands to receive Jesus. Such stories have been repeated scores of times over the years. Growing up in hopeless poverty and indoctrinated into a message of violence against the perceived oppressor, most of these young people have no idea that there is another way. When they hear of God's love and mercy, many renounce their violence and embrace the way of the cross. What a joy we have had to lay our hands in prayer upon dozens of these men and women as they have stepped forward to receive their diplomas from Bible College. Most of them, when they are converted, want to go as full bore for God as they formerly did for the devil. Some of the most effective preachers in the jungles are former terrorists.

On another occasion we crossed the Sileru River and walked a ways into a no man's land in Orissa. This was an area controlled completely by another group, the Tamil Tigers, a violent movement fighting for ethnic independence in the nation of Sri Lanka.

They had established drug running corridors through this part of India and would use the proceeds to purchase weapons for the battle back home. (The Tamil Tigers movement has since been defeated, but at this time in the mid 90's, they were at the peak of their influence).

For some reason or another the Tigers gave permission for us to access a particular village under their control. They did not have the level of antagonism toward the preachers as did the Naxalites - as long as they got their drug money, they were happy.

The fields all around us were full of opium poppies, and drug trafficking was the primary means by which the people made a living. We entered the village through a group of heavily armed guards, all of them carrying automatic weapons. The military and police never entered this area. It was completely controlled by the drug trade.

After preaching, we were asked to pray for a local man who had only a few weeks earlier accepted Christ. One of the tribal evangelists had made some inroads into the community, and several locals were going to be baptized in a small creek by our team. This man was one of the candidates for baptism, and he had requested that we first bless his "business". We assumed that they were referring to his crops or goats, but when we approached his small thatched hut, we were surprised to see a well-fortified heavy wooden door with a giant padlock. He pulled out an old key, opened the door, and we all crammed inside into a space that might have had room for six people to sleep on the floor.

The smell hit me like a freight train, immediately resurrecting images from some less than stellar high school moments. Stacked floor to ceiling against every wall were bale after bale of freshly harvested drugs. I couldn't resist the temptation to turn to our church Mission Director, Ruth Vopelak, and whisper that I had just had an incredible idea for financing international missions for the next 50 years. Ruth was not amused.

"Please pray for God's blessing on this man's family and economic situation." I looked a bit helplessly at Dr. Singh as if to say "seriously?...you want me to pray for God's blessing on this?" Well no one of course wanted us to bless the business of running drugs, but this man was sincerely asking Jesus to help his family and home, so with that I began one of the most circuitous prayers I have ever prayed. For all I know I may have prayed for his home, the salvation of all India, and the N.Y. Yankees to win the pennant...I just wanted to get to the end of that prayer! All present seemed satisfied enough when I finally said 'Amen,' and off we trotted for the baptismal moment.

Baptism in India is a holy and sobering experience. For the tribal believers, they are laying everything on the line when they step into the waters of Baptism. Their identity card will be changed, and they will no longer have access to government subsidized prices on rice and other staples. Their children will be prohibited from attending schools. And very often they will be run out of their homes, physically beaten, and in some cases even killed.

As we stood in the waters and baptized those gathered, a small group of the Tamil Tigers stood guard up on the embankment. One young man was eyeing us intently, when suddenly he laid his automatic weapon on the ground and climbed down to where we stood in the water. There was a brief exchange as the local evangelist translated for Dr. Singh what appeared to be a very intense and sober conversation. After a few moments K.R. (our affectionate nickname for Dr. Singh) turned to me and said, "he is asking if he can be baptized." "What will happen to him if we do?", I asked, for he was a sworn devotee of the Tamil Tiger cause, not just an unknown local. "They will likely kill him; but he knows that, and wants to be baptized anyway. He felt Jesus calling to him and offering him forgiveness during the preaching. He is serious about this decision."

We took the young man by the arms and gently led him into the center of the flowing water. K.R. asked the three questions he always asks of those being baptized in the tribal region: "Do you believe that Jesus Christ is the Son of God?" "Do you believe that He died as a sacrifice for your sins, rose from the dead, and now offers you eternal life?" And finally, "Will you now turn from your sins, and be faithful to Jesus, even unto your death". The young man quietly assented to all three questions, and we joyfully immersed him in the river in the name of the Father, Son, and Holy Spirit.

On our next visit to India I was eager to ask K.R. the outcome of this young man's life. "Did he come to the Bible school? Has he been faithful to grow as a believer?" "Yes, he was faithful", replied K.R.. "They executed him after we left the village because he renounced their revolution. He is enjoying now his reward in heaven."

These are the scenarios we have seen and heard again and again. Why does one become a martyr and another a powerful and unstoppable evangelist pioneering into the remotest of people groups? Such answers are only known by God. But it is fellowship with such men and women that began to powerfully shape our missions burden and call. It became impossible to insulate ourselves from the hidden world of these heroes of the faith. We could not simply return home and live a typical North American life. Having walked with such giants, we were imprinted with a passion to return again and again.

On one of our earliest trips to India we drove to the highest point in the Eastern Ghat mountains. From there one can sit at a viewpoint and look dozens of miles to the West, across a horizon of mountain ranges where hidden peoples have still never heard the good news. As I sat reflecting on the heroism of our colleagues, the voice of the Spirit again came so clearly: "I have other sheep that are not of this fold; I must go and bring them also". These were the words Jesus used in the Gospels to explain why He had to keep moving from one town to another. These words have never left me. They are the reason why 22 years after our first visit, we continue to return as often as we can. We ourselves cannot effectively go into those furthest of villages. But we can support and encourage the men and women who can. We can cheer on those Indian believers who risk everything because their hearts burn with a God given passion to reach every nation, tribe, and tongue.

40 PLEASE SIR...CAN I HAVE SOME MORE?

The Spring and Summer months that followed that first trip to India in 1995 were filled to capacity with ministry in various churches, a return visit to Ecuador, and a full schedule at our new home church on Long Island. I began to teach the weekly mid-week Bible study when not on the road, as well as continuing to work with the church missions committee. Lenora was home schooling all three of the kids, and this gave us the liberty to travel together frequently as a family.

In September our friends in Ontario launched a 30 day revival called "30 Days Ablaze." It wasn't quite the 74 days of Summer Camp, but it was unusual for a North American congregation to attempt this many consecutive days of church services. God moved powerfully in those meetings, with wonderful expressions of His presence and healing nightly. K.R. Singh from India also flew in for a week, and we had a great time together experiencing the grace of God. In the middle of it all, I experienced a vision that once again dramatically shaped the course of our ministry.

An opportunity to return to Israel had come up, and Lenora and I both felt it would be good if Melissa could travel there with me. She was only 10 years old at the time, and to a few folks this seemed like a needless expense. We didn't have a word from the Lord about it, and we wrestled with whether or not it was okay to commit such an amount of funds on something that was not essential. Was it proper for us to believe God to include our children on trips like this one? Melissa had a strong desire to visit the Holy Land, but was it legitimate to spend $2,000 to include her?

Half way through the 30 days I was spending time in prayer, specifically asking God for direction regarding the trip to Israel. Though we had often experienced God's direction through dreams, we rarely had experienced what some would call a vision, and in the case of what happened next, an open vision. Our understanding of most "visions" would be defined by brief pictures that we might see in prayer, particularly as we would pray for an individual. But an "open vision" is defined by many as more akin to a movie. God allows a person to see an uninterrupted sequence of events. It is not merely a "word" about what will happen, but it is a visual and life like display of something that is on the heart of God. It can be literal or illustrative, but an open vision is unmistakable. It is not fleeting. It is not a glimmer or a shadow. It is as vivid as a distinctive dream, only the one seeing the vision is conscious and fully awake. I was not in a trance or in a stupor...I was simply in prayer. And in that moment I experienced my first open vision.

I saw a scene from the movie Oliver, as clearly as if I were watching it in a theatre. The story of Oliver is the story of a young orphan boy in London in the 19th century, a boy who was much mistreated by the headmaster of an orphanage. There is a famous scene in the movie in which Oliver gets up from the breakfast table, and to the shock of all those present, has the audacity to approach the man dispensing porridge where he utters his now famous line: "Please Sir, can I have some more?" For this he was resoundingly disciplined.

But that was not what happened in my vision. I watched Oliver rise from the table, and I watched the disdain of children and adults both as he approached to make his request. True to the movie, he then spoke his famous line requesting more porridge. But then the vision deviated from the movie. Suddenly the ladle became huge, and reached deep down into the pot. When it came back up, porridge was pouring out over every side, and a massive portion was dumped into Oliver's bowl, filling it to overflowing. The other boys and orphanage workers simply stared at Oliver in shock and disapproval. And then I heard the voice of the Lord:

"I want my people to dare to believe Me for more. I am a good and gracious Father. There is so much more that I am willing to do, if only My children will have the confidence to ask; but this you also must know, that just as Oliver was disapproved by those watching, so also you must endure at times the disapproval of those who are offended by the audacity of genuine faith."

With that the vision came to an abrupt end. I was somewhat shaken, as I had never before seen a full screen moving vision in such a manner. I was also shaken by the implications of what God had spoken. Was this Biblical? We firmly believed then as we still do now that no vision can be legitimate if it in any way contradicts the written word of God as found in the Old and New Testaments. But this was a window into the Father's heart that went beyond my current understanding. Yes, we had experienced the wonder of Divine affirmation for our vehicle, but reliable transportation was a need for traveling ministry. Surely the perks of comfy seating and automatic everything were one time exemptions to the "pray only for what you need" religious dogma we had grown up with. Was God now telling us that He actually took pleasure in going beyond the minimum? This wasn't a couple hundred dollars' worth of clothing to remind us that He knew our every need and desire. We were talking here about thousands of dollars for a child to travel half way around the world, a child with a childlike faith to inform her parents that she wanted one day to go to Israel. We might not have known to recognize immediately the validity of such a desire, but someone much higher up had no problem with the validity at all.

If our view of God had not been matured, and if we had never discovered the lavish nature of our Heavenly Father, we would not be writing this book today. We did not know then as we know now that our calling would require us to ask largely and impossibly of God over and over again. At this point in 1995 we had experienced a handful of nations outside of North America: Thailand, India, Russia, China, Ecuador and the Middle East. We could not have dreamed that two decades later that number of nations would be nearing 100. Without the freedom granted by that window into the heart of God, our children would not have accompanied us into the dozens of nations to which they have each traveled. We would not have thought to ask for the hundreds of thousands of dollars that have since been poured into meeting the needs of pastors, churches, widows, and orphans across five continents. But He did allow us to see something of His heart that we had not fully seen before...and the ladle has been serving up overflowing portions of porridge ever since.

"I want My people to dare to believe Me for more." Those words have never left us, and along with their promise, their caution regarding human behavior has also come true. The spirit of dead religion is forever condemning the concept of an extravagant God. But will we live for the Father's good pleasure, to give us the Kingdom, or will we live in a desperate bid for the approval of men? It was a happy 10 year old girl who accompanied her Daddy on that long flight to Israel, soaking in the wonders of Jerusalem and the Galilee, walking where Jesus walked, traveling on horseback down the narrow canyons of Petra, Jordan, and hiking the hills of Masada. It was an equally happy woman 18 years later when Melissa accompanied us again to Israel, this time with her husband Derek, newlyweds with a lifetime of expenses ahead of them...yet free to enjoy the "more" that continuously flows out from the open hand of their loving God.

So often we do not have...simply because we have not dared to ask.

41 HIS DELIGHT AND OUR DESIRE

Psalm 37:4 is an oft quoted verse, "delight yourself also in the Lord, and He will give you the desires of your heart." Delight in Him must precede fulfillment in us. "Seek **first** the kingdom of God;" this had always been our mantra. Some teach that when we delight in God, our desires will automatically conform to His purpose. That is certainly true, but what is also true is that He has made each one of us with unique personalities and interests. Your uniqueness matters to God, and He is not looking for an army of robots with no individual hopes or preferences. We once heard a terrible sermon entitled "God does not care about you," with the preacher declaring that God only cares about preserving your eternal spirit, but your human personality and life situations mean nothing to Him. Nothing could be further from the truth.

Having dreamed since childhood of a long term assignment to one particular foreign field, Lenora and I were still adjusting to the concept of traveling from nation to nation. We had a God birthed love for the nations and for the calling of cross cultural ministry, and felt wonderfully at home with whatever people group we found ourselves in.

Perhaps that was partially the source of a unique desire we had. Or perhaps this particular desire was implanted in our hearts as we pursued the delight of walking with Jesus. But wherever it came from, it was certain that at some point early in our children's lives, we had a strong desire for them to all be baptized on the foreign mission field. Emboldened by a fresh revelation of the Father's heart, we were now daring to ask for it.

Melissa was the first. It was exhilarating to step with her into the Jordan River in Israel as she professed her commitment to follow in the footsteps of Jesus. It was our first adventure together as father and daughter, and the trip was the stuff of dreams. We bobbed together in the salt heavy waters of the Dead Sea, walked the rampart walls around the Old City of Jerusalem, and enjoyed scampering around the amazing archaeological ruins that are everywhere in that part of the world. In the first week of November the Prime Minister Yitzhak Rabin was assassinated by an ultra-right wing Israeli. Under heavy security we crossed over the Jordan River into Jordan on the date of my 33rd birthday. Eating cake that night in Petra, I thanked God for giving Melissa and her mom and I the desires of our hearts.

In early 1997 Omar traveled with me for the first of several trips he would make to India. He was 10 going on 11 years old, the same age as Melissa at her baptism, and the same age as myself in March of 1973 when baptized at Lincoln Avenue Baptist Church in Southern California. Omar too was ready to be baptized, and his was a unique setting in a small reservoir that had been made to supply water for villagers north of the city of Vishakapatnam. Along with 150 Indian believers, Omar stood as the only Westerner that day, surrounded by myself, Dr. K.R. Singh, Pastor Ric Borozny, and Pastor Homer McKeithan, a dear friend whom we had met while on one of our outreaches in Russia. These three preachers all knew Omar well, and the joy of standing in Gambiram Lake under the hot Indian sun while my son was prayed for by each man in turn was an experience I could never have designed on my own.

We became bolder in our prayers, and though traveling with one child at a time was a delight, we longed for the whole family to be together on the field, and particularly to be together in India where we were on constant sensory overload from the sights and sounds of primitive cultures, amazing kingdom miracles, and masses of people coming continuously to faith in Christ. Was God willing even for the five of us to travel at once all the way to India? This was something we secretly brought to the Lord in prayer, not telling a soul of our radical dream. But God, who sees in secret, has a habit of rewarding His children openly.

We received a phone call one day from a church member. One of their household had been awakened that night, with an urgent conviction that "Pastor Kelly's family needs to travel together to India." Along with the conviction came a commission to cover the costs of the tickets for the children. "Are your children traveling anytime in the future with you to India?" We had not made a specific plan for it, but had held it close to our hearts as a dream. That dream now became reality, as a check was handed to us for the full sum of what it would cost to bring our children.

In November of that same year that Omar was baptized, off we all flew once again with a great team from the Holy Spirit Christian Church. This time it was Jonathan's turn, he also having just turned 10 in June of that previous Summer. The setting for Jonathan's baptism was perhaps the most dramatic of all, high up into the tribal area, again with the hot India sun shining down as we stepped into the Sileru River. There had been plenty of crocodiles pulled out of that river in the past, and one in particular had been a record breaker, with the authorities in Delhi traveling in to record its girth and confirming in fact that it was one of the largest ever measured. We made sure to point out this reptilian reality just prior to our son stepping into the water. The added blessing of Jonathan's baptism was that his mom was able to stand with us as a witness. Missing both Melissa's and Omar's baptisms was not easy for Lenora, but the joy at God's faithfulness to grant our desire compensated for the sacrifice of sending us out while remaining at home. It was a great day of celebration on that memorable November 28th up in the mountains, as the five of us now stood together, each as professing and baptized members of the wonderful body of Christ.

42 FROM CELEBRATION TO EVACUATION

Dr. Luke in the Acts of the Apostles records many stories of the Apostle Paul's courageous faith, and Paul himself makes reference in the Epistles to the stands he took more than once in the face of great opposition. There is also however that less than heroic story of Paul escaping his would be persecutors by being lowered over a wall in a basket in the dead of night. I've often wondered why sometimes God has us face down the devil and other times has us flee. It is good to know the voice of God, for that is often the only way in which we can know the difference between fight or flight.

Heading back down the mountain after one of our trips to Sileru we came to the village of Gumma, a village in Orissa where members of the Bonda tribe would come down from their remote mountain communities and barter for simple goods. The Bonda were the most primitive people we had seen anywhere in the world, even still to this day. Aside from simple loincloths and beads they were entirely naked. The women were required to keep their hair cut close to the scalp by sharpened rocks. This was their punishment imposed by the creation myth of their tribe, in which the first woman shamed herself by appearing naked before the gods. The men were constantly hostile, fighting with bows and arrows and killing regularly. No prohibition against murder was enforced by the civil authorities, for the Bonda were off limits and considered a culturally protected people group, completely free from external intervention.

Pastor Amos is one of the most spiritual men I've ever known. His face radiates the glory of God. Many years ago he approached Dr. Singh after his Bible School graduation, sharing that God had called him to pioneer the gospel to the Bonda tribe. The Bonda were extraordinarily difficult to communicate with, their concept of good being "dark" or "black", and their concept of bad being "white" or "light". That requires some linguistic gymnastics when translating the word of God into a message they can understand. Amos was sent out, and has labored fervently for close to 25 years. In the first decade they saw barely a dozen converts, the first a woman whom they renamed Lydia. We were arriving into Gumma to see Pastor Amos' school for Bonda children and his beginnings of a small church.

Almost immediately our group was surrounded by an angry group of non-tribal Indians who had somehow received word of our intended meeting and gathered a group in opposition. These were not just vocal protestors, but radical Hindu members of the BJP, a virulently anti-Western and anti-Christian religious political party. Dr. Singh was in a sober discussion with them, nothing of which we could understand. What we could understand were the angry expressions on the faces of around 15 young men who sat poised in the back of a pickup truck.

Calmly and quietly, K.R. turned and with a look that invited no retort, commanded me to get everyone back on our bus immediately. With the same look I instructed my family and our team and we all complied, though disappointed to be pulling out of Gumma so quickly after arriving there from a 5 hour drive over torturous roads. As we pulled away I asked K.R. what had transpired. "They told me that if you even opened your mouth to preach one word, they were going to kill everyone. I decided it was best that we leave." I was happy to concur with K.R.'s sound judgment.

The men were not making an empty threat. Only a few years prior in that same area, an Australian missionary and his two young sons were burned to death in their vehicle by a mob of radical Hindus. I was more than happy in that moment to be slipping out in a basket and lowered over a wall.

Being Spirit directed can mean the difference between life and death in many parts of the world. Yet even then, the Spirit led life does not always guarantee the outcome of our choosing. The Apostles were Spirit led men, and heard God's voice clearly...but most of them died a martyr's death as they followed their Savior's lead even to the point of the grave. Thousands today continue to lose their lives to persecution. These are not careless or unspiritual people. Quite often they are powerful men and women of faith and prayer. They hear God's voice and follow, but it has not always led them into a basket and over a wall. We are humbled and grateful for God's assistance during more than one of these close calls, whether by means of a flat tire, an angelic intervention, or the wise word of a team leader like Dr. Singh who does not put others at risk for the sake of his own glory, or for the acquisition of a sensational story.

43 NOT OUR OWN WILL, BUT HIS BE DONE

Even as we enjoyed becoming increasingly involved in the dynamic of tribal missions, things were changing at our new home church. The Holy Spirit Christian Church turned out to be an amazing base for a world mission ministry. They were extremely generous with both our family and with international mission projects, paying our housing regularly now for well over two years and supporting all of my ticket expenses as we led short term teams out of the congregation. In the Spring of '97 Pastor Dan took a trip with me to Quito. We had a great adventure together, though at the end I became seriously ill and he ended up doing most of the preaching.

Just a few week later Dan dropped the bomb on me that he was planning to accept a full time teaching position at a Bible school in Upstate New York, Pinecrest. The school had been founded as a place where young people could learn to hear the voice of God and develop a Spirit directed method of ministry. They had some great teachers and many a fine pastor had graduated from their program, Pastor Dan being one of them.

Dan sat now with me in his office, not only to tell me of his coming departure, but to share as well his conviction that I was the replacement Senior Pastor of God's choosing. Lenora and I had felt that our time of serving in a leadership capacity with the missions committee might actually be coming to a close, but we had not interpreted that as a change of this magnitude. We wanted to spend even more time on the mission field, not less, and for that reason had concluded I would give up the Tuesday teaching meetings, which by now I was responsible for on every Tuesday we were home.

The very moment in early Summer when I was certain my role would henceforth be different and I would no longer teach, was the same moment when Pastor Dan told me of his plans. We did not want this. HSCC was a wonderful and growing congregation, but we loved the freedom of hearing from God and traveling freely as He would send. We had ample support through the mission program by now, and had no need of a fixed paycheck or an income that would certainly be more stable by virtue of a senior position. But it was not about what we needed or wanted. It was about what God wanted and was requiring of our lives. For purposes of His own, which would later become more clear, His plan and design all along had been for us to return to pastoral ministry on Long Island. This was why Dr. Hamada had ventured down that sidewalk at the moment that he did. This was why we had heard the word while sitting over shish ke babs at Mykonos, "Go to the Holy Spirit Christian Church". And this was exactly what we were going to do for the next eight years of our journey. It did not matter that **we** were done with pastoring Long Islanders. God was not done with loving Long Islanders, and God was not done with shaping and developing our call.

It likely was not right, but I determined to make it difficult. It was truly for us a deep wrestling of the soul to even allow our names to be considered. I asked God for two very unlikely signs: a unanimous vote of the membership, and their agreement to our one condition: that we would always have the liberty to go out on mission if the Holy Spirit so directed. We had lived in this manner for the past ten years, and we certainly did not want to sacrifice now the most precious aspect of our calling, which was to hear and follow the specific leading of the Lord. We would not abuse the privilege...but we needed to be certain we could still preserve the integrity of our walk with God.

Both conditions came to pass on the day of the congregational meeting. We were bound by our own words...but also at peace in the assurance that this truly was the will and purpose of God. HSCC was not a place of unfamiliarity. In the three years we had developed some wonderful friendships. Many of the members and youth had traveled already with us to the foreign field. We had developed great relationships as well with the two church overseers, Rev. Bill Pepper, a pioneer missionary in the Peruvian Amazon, and Dr. Jack Buskey, a highly respected minister in both the United Methodist and Church of God movements.

Dr. Jack was used much by God to train leaders in Russia after the Iron Curtain fell. In 1996 I accompanied him for 3 weeks of teaching in Ishevsk. We developed a great friendship during those days of teaching in 25 degree unheated classrooms, bundled up in our coats and hats as the students diligently tried to take notes with their gloves on.

Being in Russia on tourist visas we were not supposed to be teaching, especially as Ishevsk was in a sensitive military area. On the night before we were to leave, a church member brought us a warning from the Lord that we must leave earlier than we had planned. They did not know why, but there was an urgency to the message. We decided to leave at 5:30 AM to return to Moscow, rather than 7:30 AM as we had planned. Thirty minutes after our departure, the security services showed up to the apartment where we had been staying to detain us. Thankfully we were already bundled into our van and safely on our way out.

In truth it was a great privilege God was granting us. To be the shepherd of God's people is not a punishment. It is an honor and a high calling. Whether pastoring 10 or 10,000, God's people are the most extraordinary people on the planet. To be among them at any time for any reason is a blessing. To be called to lead them is one of the greatest gifts that God can bestow. We accepted His gift, and began to feel an excitement grow in our hearts for our third Long Island pastoral assignment. All three churches were in Nassau County, Baldwin on the South Shore, Glen Cove on the North Shore, and Hicksville in dead center. A line could be drawn on the map South to North and it would run through all three communities. By God's design, we were inextricably connected to the spiritual landscape of Long Island, New York.

We needed a new home, closer than the Hamada's home in Glen Cove. Quality rentals were few and far between, and we prayed once again that God would provide our housing. One of our board members had a friend in real estate who called her with a head's up on a home that would be listing the next day. It was less than one mile from the church. It was a perfect home that met every item on our wish list. It had a fantastic back yard with 12 foot high hedges all around. This home wouldn't last an hour on the market, but we were the first to look at it and we grabbed it. The rent was $2,500 per month, but the leadership didn't blink. They wanted us to have a wonderful home for our family. We had left Ohio seeking a stable place for our children, and God had arranged for it all, well in advance, and well beyond our own expectations. In a matter of weeks we were moving in, being ordained into the new position by Dr. Jack Buskey, and taking up the baton from Pastor Dan Beaulieu. The whole Summer had been a miraculous whirlwind of Divine assignment, change, provision, and vision for the days to come. It had not been our will at first, but we soon became glad that His will was done.

44 A HORDE OF PLAGUES FROM INDIA

Just three months after being installed as the new pastor in Hicksville we embarked with our large team to India, the trip where Jonathan was baptized in the Sileru River. We came home triumphant, having completed four outstanding outreaches to India in less than three years. But our celebration did not last long.

I was standing in the teller line at our local bank on Long Island, when a sudden chill coursed over my body. By the time I was up to the counter my hands had begun to shake uncontrollably. I knew before I even left the bank that the severe chills and tremors that came seemingly out of nowhere could only be one thing: Malaria! I knew what malaria was, and I knew what the symptoms were, but what I did not know was that you can contract malaria at any time of the year in India. I had been told by a colleague that malaria wasn't an issue during the latter part of the year, India's Winter. Someone failed to pass on this information to the parasite carrying mosquito that bit me.

I went home, crawled into bed, and informed Lenora that I would be just fine...I would ride this out and conquer it with my faith like so many other physical maladies before.

Forty eight hours later, dehydrating and with a sky high fever, I lay on our bed repeatedly soaking the sheets with sweat and moaning under the torment of a headache that I could only describe as feeling like someone had parked a semi-trailer on my skull. I randomly recited Scriptures like Psalm 91 and Psalm 23, desperately looking for relief. It was about that time that God decided to intervene and save my life, because left to my own stubbornness I was on a fast track to the cemetery.

"Go to the hospital right now!" Through my misery I heard God speaking. It was an urgent command. Could He have just as decisively healed me on the spot? Of course He could have, but God has His reasons for doing things the way He does. He has no problems with the medical profession, and modern science and medicine have never been and should never be seen as contradictory to the ministry of healing through faith filled prayer. All medical knowledge comes from God anyway. The problem was that my faith was nowhere near the level I thought it was, and in my desire to be a super faith filled believer, I was pushing myself into a corner that was not of God's design.

The command was so unmistakable that I instantly picked up the telephone, called one of the members of our church who was a physician's assistant, and asked him to come over right away and drive me to the hospital. If I had known how bad my condition was, I would have called an ambulance.

Long story short, there are four primary types of malarial parasites, and I had the worst of the four. Malaria is even to this day the #1 cause of death worldwide over any other sickness or disease annually. The greatest medical breakthrough of our current era will likely be the malaria vaccine that is very close to being approved. Bill and Melinda Gates have invested hundreds of millions of dollars into developing an effective vaccine, and may God bless them for it; but no such vaccine existed in 1997. The milder forms of malaria afflict tens of millions every year without causing permanent damage or death. But the most dangerous of the parasites kill ruthlessly by attacking the major organs of the body. With the eggs being laid in the liver of the host, the parasite lives on and reproduces repeatedly.

I didn't know any of these details back then. I only knew that when they rushed me into the emergency room at a hospital on the South Shore, it was quickly apparent that not every doctor had expertise in managing this type of tropical parasite. My kidneys were failing, my fever spiked to 107, and in desperation they immersed me in some type of ice bath to lower my temperature before more serious damage occurred. I was told that if I had arrived 6 hours later, I would have likely not survived. I was glad to have heard God's voice issuing a prescription for a hasty trip to the hospital. Sometimes we put faith in our own faith, rather than putting our faith in the specific words and directives of God. Faith is not producing what we want with our effort. It is producing what He wants and what He has spoken through the power of His grace which flows freely through the conduit of our belief. The Old Testament King who was chastised during his illness after he went to the physicians was not chastised for going to the physicians. His failure was in not bothering to consult with God.

This was fast becoming my December of despondency. As I lay shaking in my isolation room at the hospital, I was certain at one point that my number was up. I called Lenora emotionally to say goodbye. My great friend from Calvary Camp days, Mike Lynch, called me in the hospital and I broke down on the phone with him as well, letting him know what a great friend he had been and dramatically announcing my soon departure from this planet. Thankfully he saw through my fever induced delirium and told me

I would be just fine. I came out of the hospital after several days, pushed myself right back into routine, and within a few weeks relapsed and was re-hospitalized.

While my mosquito induced nightmare unfolded for a second time in the hospital, another nightmare of plagues was unfolding at home. As Melissa brushed her hair one morning, she called to Lenora to point out that bugs were spilling out onto the table. It was a dreaded infestation of lice, picked up while combing the hair of some kids from the Indian slums. While malarial parasite eggs were riding home in my liver, lice eggs were riding home on the scalps of our family. Lenora and Melissa both had lice, and the boys' heads were treated for it just as a precaution. The lice had taken one look at my bald head, scorned the barren landscape, and searched out greener pastures.

Next came a severe burning on Lenora's scalp, and an urgent trip to the dermatologist revealed another hitchhiking pest - scabies! Our house was a house of microscopic horrors from the Sub-Continent. And then came the final blow: Lenora was hit with the worst back spasms she had ever had, ones which immobilized her for 10 days on the couch, with crawling to the bathroom being her only means of getting around.

Church members turned out in droves to help our pitiful family, cleansing the house from top to bottom to rid the rooms and beddings of lice, making meals for the kids, doing laundry, and every other kind of errand and chore that needed to be done. We were not having a fun start to our first full calendar year as the new lead pastoral family of the Holy Spirit Christian Church!

But this too would pass. We have adopted this wonderful phrase, whenever an unexpected trial or test may come: "This too will pass." The Scripture tells us that with every temptation there is a way of escape. Afflictions will come, but God delivers us from them all. Weeping endures for a night...but for the believing Christian, there is always a joy filled morning on the way!

Unfortunately there were lots of self-appointed scholars who had researched malaria and offered me this tragic forecast: "sorry Pastor Kelly, but you will have this for life. Malaria never leaves your system. You will have relapses when you get over tired. It is a medical reality...no way around it." Well I may not have had the maturity of faith to knock out the malaria in round #1, but there was no way I was going to wave the white flag of surrender and let it beat me in repeated rounds for the rest of my life. I informed all who pronounced my fate that "my case will be different." "I am not going to live with malaria the rest of my life. Those parasites and their nasty eggs will just wither and die within me. They have picked the wrong host organism. I am a faith filled follower of Jesus Christ, and He is the Healer of ALL diseases!" We were not going to accept the negative forecast of those whose expectation was limited by the natural boundaries of the physical realm.

The lice finally were conquered, the scabies died, the back spasms dissipated, and I suffered one more serious bout of malaria a few months later in May of 1998. My dear friend John Burns came over to pray for me as I lay shivering and feverish in my home. A day or two later, my dear partner in Indian ministry, Dr. K.R. Singh, flew in from Germany and he too laid his hands upon me in faith that I would be fully healed. A final mild flare up occurred several months later, more than 18 years ago, and I have never had the slightest evidence of malaria again. By His stripes I had been, I was, and I knew that I would continue to be fully and completely healed. I'm thankful for the Blood of Jesus Christ, a sure prescription for the plagues and parasites that inhabit this imperfect world.

45 THE RESURRECTION OF RONALD GULMI

We opted to stay close to home for most of 1998 to recover strength and settle in more fully into our new role at the church. God wasn't just moving in foreign lands. Just as in Glen Cove, God moved wonderfully in the lives of many families in Hicksville. People often ask "why does God do miracles overseas, but not in North America?" They are mistaken. It is true that we see a greater frequency of the supernatural overseas because in many cases the people are more desperate for God's intervention, not having the support systems of a prosperous economy and first world medical care that we enjoy here at home. But God is the same in every land. Wherever He finds faith and a people who will believe in the power of His Name and His Word, it is there that He will without reservation pour out His Spirit. That has always been His promise.

One Sunday morning I was up early preparing to preach, when a very strange instruction came to my heart and mind: **"I want you to preach in a quiet and steady voice this morning."** There was no explanation, but God's instruction as I prayed was clear. My normal preaching style, 99% of the time, is a louder volume and a more demonstrative presentation. I had never to my recollection preached in a quiet or monotone style.

People worldwide enjoy preaching that is "alive" and dynamic. That is the style of most evangelists. A monotone and subdued presentation can put people to sleep quickly, though at times I have heard soft spoken men and women who have had such an intensity of God's presence on their lives that every whispered word hit home like a hammer. But that was not the way I had been created or called, and I knew as we drove to church that our congregation was not going to appreciate my passivity, most likely suspecting that I was having a physical relapse of some sort.

Lillian Gulmi was one of our faithful prayer warriors, an older woman nearing 70 years old who had prayed fervently for her husband Ron for over 20 years. Ron was a good man in the community, but he did not appreciate Lillian's penchant for churches with a Pentecostal style, especially those with loud preachers. Ron preferred the quiet reserve of his Roman Catholic upbringing, and these were the services where he felt at home. Lillian though was certain that her husband needed a personal encounter with Jesus. She believed that if she could just get him to go to church with her, he might have that encounter she had prayed for. But for twenty years Ron steadfastly refused, telling her over and over again that he was not going to sit and be yelled at by some loud mouthed pastor who was all about hype and drama.

Then lo and behold, unknown to me that Sunday morning, the day had finally come when Ron decided to silence Lillian's pleadings and come at last with her to service...at the Holy Spirit Christian Church in Hicksville! Ron sat up front with his wife that morning as I preached my message in the softest and steadiest tone I had ever employed. I didn't know at that moment it was for the sake of Ron. All I knew was that afterward everyone wanted to know what was wrong with Pastor Kelly. They had come expecting the style of presentation they were accustomed to and that they very much enjoyed. The truth was still there, but some did not like the packaging.

I learned a great lesson that morning about God's love for the one lost lamb. Jesus tells a story of the shepherd leaving the 99 to find the one. I have seen this happen over and over, where the direction of a service or outreach will shift completely for the sake of one person in the room that God is endeavoring to reach. It might come through the spontaneous selection of an unplanned song. One day in Glen Cove I began to sing from the platform an old hymn that we had never sung in the church. It simply dropped into my mind during the worship. A woman came to us weeping at the end of that service, sharing that she had not been in church in years and was now overwhelmed at the love of God because we had sung the hymn that was her favorite. This told her that God had not forgotten her and was still desiring to work in her life. Jesus surely loves the 99 that have everything on track in their lives - but He will always take a detour when needed to secure the wandering "1" who has yet to turn back to the Shepherd.

Ron did not have a dramatic conversion that Sunday morning, but what God was doing was creating a receptivity in his heart toward a man for whom he would have otherwise had no time. We chatted briefly after service, and he expressed his appreciation for the message. He had been disarmed by the Holy Spirit, and set up for the greater moment that was soon to come.

A short time later Ron was afflicted with a severe gall bladder attack, and the gall stone was so large that there were secondary complications and he was hospitalized in Brooklyn. Lillian had asked that I visit her husband to pray, but I was not certain he would want a Protestant pastor barging into his hospital room. At 5:00 AM on a Sunday morning I awakened with an urgency in my spirit, **"go to the hospital and pray for Ron Gulmi."** It was so strong that I knew it could not wait until after church, and I would have to leave immediately in order to drive to the hospital, see Ron, and get back in time for our morning worship service. I got dressed for church and hopped in the car, praying as I often did before a hospital visit that God would give me a specific selection from the Bible that I could read to the person I was visiting.

I was not expecting the answer I received, for immediately I heard the word **"Naaman."** Naaman was the Syrian General with leprosy who was instructed by Elisha to bathe seven times in the Jordan River in order to be healed. Naaman was offended and angry, declaring that surely "the rivers of Damascus were better than all the waters of Israel." He stormed off from Elisha in a rage before later relenting and agreeing to the instruction. I was truly mortified at the thought of reading the story of Naaman, an obscure Old Testament passage about an arrogant leader, to a man who was sick in the hospital and in need of pastoral care. Yet I had asked, and God had answered. It was my responsibility now to trust His voice and obey what He had spoken.

I walked gently into Ron's room that early Sunday morning. He welcomed me weakly and thanked me for coming. I asked his permission to pray, and if he would allow me to first read from God's Word, to which he readily agreed. Barely believing myself that I was doing so, I began to read from the beginning of Naaman's story, of his leprosy, of the Jewish slave girl who recommended he go to the prophet Elisha, the counsel regarding the waters of the Jordan River, Naaman's rage and offense, and finally his healing when he retreated from pride and obeyed the prophet's instruction. As I neared the final verses of the story, Ron began to weep intensely.

Suddenly he was crying out, "that's me...that's me! Oh Pastor, pray for me...I am the man in that story! I need to know Jesus!" I was astonished by the power of God's word, that the most seemingly random passage of Scripture from an Old Testament story could be the right key for unlocking a man's heart. Neither Lillian or I could have ever figured out what it would take to reach Ron. But the Spirit of God knows the key for the heart of every human being. How limited we all would be without the Spirit of God!

Ron and I prayed together for Jesus to become real in his life. And his transformation was dramatic, far more so than any of us could have imagined. Ron Gulmi became a man on fire for Jesus. From that day forward he never missed a Sunday at the Holy Spirit Christian Church, sitting front row and center, now one of the loudest people in our praise and worship services. He would throw his hands high in the air and over and over declare the name of Jesus. "Jesus...I love you....Jesus....You are so wonderful!"

The man who had refused for twenty years any suggestion of attending "one of those loud Charismatic churches" became the most charismatic of us all. He had bathed in the river and come out fully clean. His joy was childlike all the way until his end. A couple of years later Ron had open heart surgery on a Tuesday. He was discharged on a Friday, and walked into service on Sunday morning. "Pastor, I don't ever want to miss a chance to come and worship Jesus!" We were all amazed by the fiery passion of Ron Gulmi. He is with the Lord now, and I love the thought of seeing him one day in heaven.

46 I WANT TO BLESS THE LEPERS - ASK THEM TO GIVE AN OFFERING

Fully recuperated and with the church flourishing, we ran at full speed in 1999 all over the world. The year began with a team of our men spending the New Year on a mission trip to Quito, where we were now returning annually. Patricio Robelly's ministry was exploding, with hundreds receiving miracles of healing and many more coming to faith in Christ. Ecuador and India were great places for our church members to see how God was working in the nations, yet God was opening new doors and sending us to places like the Peruvian Amazon for our first trip with Bill Pepper, or to the mountains of Lebanon to minister in Druse villages with Dr. Hamada. There was plenty of excitement and fruitful ministry as we enjoyed God's favor everywhere that we went.

The greatest miracle though was reserved for our final trip of the Millennium, right at the end of 1999. Many in the New York area were panicked and preparing for the mayhem and digital meltdown that was expected for Y2K, the changing of the clocks into the year 2000. At HSCC however, we had no time to become preoccupied with cataclysmic end of days scenarios. The fields were white unto harvest, and cataclysm or not, Jesus had instructed that we must "occupy until He comes." Keeping hands to the plow and eyes on the field ahead has always been our aim, for when one gets excessively caught up in eschatological predictions of impending peril, it is easy to become self-focused rather than outward in our mission. Even in times of trouble, and even as the end may draw near, we must continue reaching souls and advancing the Kingdom of God.

In December we took another team to India, and on that trip we had one of the most memorable experiences of our ministry. There was a community of families in one part of the city that suffered from leprosy. Leprosy was curable, but once the ravages of the disease became evident to others, there was ostracism and banishment across many parts of India. The lepers who were missing parts of fingers, faces, or hands would be consigned to begging, as no one would employ them normally. Their children might be disease free, but because they were the children of lepers, they would be kept out of school. Dr. Singh would take many of these children into his orphan homes to provide for them a place of dignity and education. And we would conduct outreaches with God's word of comfort and hope to these isolated pockets of families that lived in slums or on the fringes of society.

The community we visited that particular day occupied crude homes built on land owned by the city. They also had a small church building that Dr. Singh's partners had put up. We were holding an outreach service in this church, worshipping with around 40 men, women and children. Many of them were raising their disfigured hands in passionate gratitude to Jesus. They loved to hear of the promise of heaven, where they would be made completely whole again, and never would be outcast or despised.

The privilege of worshipping with these saints was a highlight for any of our visiting teams.

Over the years we have become accustomed to God's Spirit speaking some very unique and unanticipated things. He is not confined by our traditions or protocols in the least. But what He spoke suddenly during that worship service put me into a sweat:

"I want to bless the Lepers...I want you to receive from them an offering." Non-traditional was one thing, but this sounded downright scandalous! Receive an offering from the Lepers? Could there be possibly anything done that would be more awful for a rich by comparison North American preacher than to walk into a gathering of the poorest people on earth and ask them to give an offering?

Yet the Spirit's voice was insistent, "I want to bless the Lepers." I wrestled for a solid 5-10 minutes of worship over the potential impropriety of such an action, arguing with God about what I would even do with such an offering. Where would it go, and who was it for? Certainly I could not pack it up and haul it back to the USA? This seemed almost criminal. We were there to give, to serve, to bless...we were not there to take.

Yet God was also there to bless, and He was about to do something that would reverberate for years to come. In the middle of my wrestling, a family in our church dropped clearly into my mind. They had been abandoned earlier that year by the father who had become a drug abuser. The wife and three children were left alone with nothing. Our church benevolence ministry had been paying their rent and providing a living allowance until they could become self-supporting. Their need was legitimate, and God was now indicating that they were to be the recipients of this offering.

I finally worked up the courage to share my impressions with K.R. Singh. There was no way I was going to take this offering of my own initiative or without his permission. All of us, no matter how clearly we believe we may have heard from God, must have others in our lives who can confirm and recognize what God is saying. K.R. looked at me like I was crazy, but then bowed his head in prayer. After a few moments he looked up at me and declared: "this is of the Lord; but you must know that nothing like this has ever been done in India." Tell me about it! I was well aware that we were fearfully about to tread where no sane person had tread before. We were going to take up a missionary offering from lepers in India and carry it home to a family in America! "Dear God", I prayed, "help us to get this right...and help me not to be out of my mind!"

We quieted the worship team, and I began to address the families seated before me. I explained about a very poor family in our church, abandoned by their father. I explained that we helped them weekly with food. And then I asked the lepers if they would be willing to give to help this poor family. I made no promises of what would happen for them. I did not tell them that God had spoken that He wanted to bless them. I simply shared the need, and waited to see what would happen.

The Spirit of God fell upon those people. I have never seen such a weeping come over a community as they were granted for the first time in their lives the dignity of being told that they could make a difference in someone else's life. Frantically they began unfolding their meager rags where the coins they had gathered by begging were carefully tucked away. They became fervent with the joy of giving, crawling over one another in an unstoppable determination to give away all they had. Not one of these lepers were gainfully employed. Their only living was what they could acquire by begging in the streets, or by the charity of local churches. But suddenly they were empowered as the givers and not the beggars. All of K.R.'s staff were weeping. There was not a dry eye among our team. K.R. himself turned to me and with tears explained, "no one has ever believed in these people to such an extent before." "They have never imagined that God would use them to help someone in a place like America."

The pile of coins was solemnly counted that afternoon, amounting to the equivalent of $40 in U.S. currency. K.R. explained that it would take one family 6 months of begging to gather such an amount. We converted the funds and I carried it home as if I were carrying gold. That envelope has always been to us the most precious gift we have ever been entrusted with, and with equal solemnity we presented it the very next Sunday in Hicksville to the family for whom it was designated. It was a powerful teaching moment for every member of our church.

God however, was far from finished with the lepers. He had declared that He wanted to bless them, but none of us realized to what extent. We had seen the spiritual blessing of their liberation into service and usefulness for God's kingdom. But an even more shocking miracle was on the way. Within weeks of our visit, the city notified the lepers that a development plan was under way for the community where they had established their small houses and church. Not wanting the scandal of evicting them outright, the city officials thought to save face by offering them the chance to buy the land...knowing full well that it would be impossible for the lepers to do so. If they could produce an amount equivalent then to over $100,000, the city would provide them title to the land and they could stay permanently. Otherwise they would have to leave and their small dwellings would be razed.

A man in Germany was awakened in the night on that very same week. He heard the voice of God's Spirit speaking, "My people are in trouble and I want you to help them. I have a work for you to do for the lepers in India." This man was a friend of Dr. Singh's and called him the next morning, telling him of God's message to him in the night. "What is it that the lepers need?" Dr. Singh shared the crisis, the demands of the city, and the impossible dilemma that these precious people were facing.

"I will go to my bank this morning and instruct them to transfer the full amount required for purchase. I know that I have heard from God, and I know that I am to put the funds into your hands so that you can represent them". K.R. quietly put down the phone, his next call being to a Christian lawyer that assisted them with property purchases. Some days later Dr. Singh marched with the lepers down to the city offices with the full funding that had been demanded, and because the sale price had been given to them in writing, there was no way for anyone to renege on the agreement. Reluctantly the property was sold, and joyfully the newly wealthy leper community took their deed to the land and became the talk of all the town. Their community exists to this day, only with much finer buildings, a much larger and beautiful church, and a dignity as sons and daughters of God they had never known was possible on this side of heaven. Their property has also skyrocketed in value since then, far beyond the initial purchase price. God had said to "take up an offering, for I want to bless the Lepers." They joyfully gave all that they had, and God joyfully did what He loves to do, lavishing them with the love of a generous and good Heavenly Father. May God help us not to place limitations on the extravagance of His perfect care and love. He truly is a good, good, Father!

47 FAITHFUL FRIENDS IN GOOD TIMES AND BAD

God calls no man or family to a ministry of isolation. We all need friends and people on our team, and God's anointing and gifts are not meant to become substitutes for healthy relationships within the body of Christ. Without a love for the church family, we can never be successful in ministry. Some have been wounded and set out on their own, but their journey eventually falls short. As the new millennium began, our own loyalty to God's family was about to be greatly tested. Without faithful friends, we would not have made it.

Some of the most wonderful friendships we have began forming during those first years at the church. Joe and Rosemary DeVito had begun attending HSCC only a few months after our family arrived, and we fast became friends. Married the same weekend as Lenora and I in 1983 and with kids the same age as our own, we found much in common, but it was their zeal for the kingdom of God that really caught our attention. Joe quickly became a wonderful prayer partner and also a partner in mission, traveling with me to Quito where we had a wonderful reunion with Pastor Zenon Rivera of the original host church where the apartment had been built for my family. It had been eight years now and the disappointment of our separation was long since passed.

Joe also went with me to India, where he was unfortunately sliced by the poison tipped point of a Bonda arrow which we had failed to clean before packing it up to carry home. I returned from the bathroom at the Bombay airport to find Joe lying on the terminal floor, dizzy, and with all our team alarmed. This became somewhat of a crazy and in retrospect humorous incident, as we found ourselves calling Dr. Singh before flying to ask him what antidote there was for the poison in the arrow. Somewhat incredulous but always polite, K.R. let me know that the Bonda people had not been known to publish antidotes for their arrows of warfare. I sort of expected that response. Joe was seriously ill for a full three weeks back home on Long Island, and the doctors never were able to determine what had happened to him. It is truly a devoted friend who overcomes the offense of being cut by his team leader's careless handling of a poisoned Bonda arrow!

Another very key couple came into our lives during the Spring of 2000, David and LaRae Pepper. I had met LaRae when traveling with her father in law Bill Pepper to Peru, but did not yet know David. The Peppers had been commissioned by God to plant a new church in the city of Wasilla in Alaska, and Bill thought it would be beneficial for them to visit our congregation to see the multi-cultural model we had developed. By this time there were a number of ethnic groups and nationalities represented, though the church make up was still at least 80% Italian.

Right around the time we were making plans for an ordination service for the DeVito's, David and LaRae arrived for our Easter weekend. Church on the Rock in Alaska had only started a few weeks prior, but David had a family gathering in Maryland, so it provided an excellent opportunity for them to shoot up to Long Island. It was a wonderful Easter Sunday with standing room only, and I derived great amusement in watching our warm and affectionate Italian members greet David in the same way we all greeted each other on a Sunday morning: with a big hug and a kiss on the cheek. My new Alaskan friend was getting a serious invasion into his personal bubble. Alaskans are warm and friendly, but they do not kiss on Sunday mornings! After church and a follow-up massive feast at an Italian home with about 75 kissing and hugging people present, David & LaRae were on Long Island overload. But our hearts were knit by God that weekend for greater things to come. Our church mission committee voted that following week to begin sending a monthly offering to assist in the fledgling church plant known as Church on the Rock.

The amount was minimal, but it was one more outgoing gift on top of a great deal of money that by now was moving monthly through our church. More than $50,000 per year was going into the work in India through monthly support and special projects, and there were many other missionaries and projects we were supporting in addition worldwide. Our own facility had been undergoing a major renovation, and there was plenty more to be done. The strong focus on outgoing giving began to weigh upon some of our leadership, though I was unaware of their concerns. However, that soon changed.

We had quite a large board of elders and trustees at HSCC, and most all of our meetings were pleasant and hilarious times of great fellowship and laughter. But one night our meeting ended differently. One of our leaders asked to introduce a final item before concluding in prayer, and then he dropped the bomb: "several of us feel that going forward, we would like you to ask the board's permission before committing to being away for mission trips."

I was certain that everyone at that table had been present three years earlier when the congregation had voted me in as the senior pastor under the sole condition that I would have liberty to obey the Spirit's leading when He called us to lead a team out to the nations. The nations were our childhood calling and front and center in the DNA of our church. Without the liberty to hear from God and obey His command, I could never fulfill the Great Commission in the unique manner in which He had called us to obey it.

This was part of the reason why God had called us out of our denomination, not because of any flaw in that organization, but because our calling was broader than what we could have fulfilled within the structure. There are a diversity of church leadership structures, some having a stronger role for the lead pastor than others. We believed strongly in working with a team model, and arriving at consensus before anything major was initiated, especially consensus in regard to the distribution of funds. But in this one area of mission travel, our liberty to hear and obey without restraint was essential. I took this same approach regarding the subjects and content of my preaching.

I responded poorly, and with little humility, laughing in a high minded manner, and firmly informing my brothers that under no circumstances was that ever going to happen. A deal was a deal, and whether they paid my salary or not, I was not about to be told when and where I could travel!

When someone has a genuine concern, whether or not that concern is unfounded, it is unwise to meet their issue with ridicule. The worst thing I could have done that day was to laugh at their request, but our church was riding high with God's favor on every side; why should I listen to such an upstart proposal? I was naive, and had no idea how passionate people in church government can become about issues of money and authority. The issue was not just about my being absent five to six weeks per year. A lot of resources were going outside of the church, and some were wondering if there was a limit to how much the radically generous missions committee was willing to give away.

I failed to recognize the rift that was developing and turned a cold shoulder to their concerns. I wish today I had handled some things differently, but hindsight never fixes the past. Our leadership team polarized fairly quickly between those who wanted me to yield the point and those who supported my view. Suddenly everything was an issue and what began originally as a proposal was fast becoming a referendum on my suitability to lead. The issue of missions soon became minor compared to the hard feelings and rumors that ran rampant. Some of the elders believed I should step down in such an atmosphere of conflict, a type of conflict the congregation had not previously experienced. I knew that God would not allow me to do so, though at times I wished I was anywhere but home in Hicksville. We had not wanted to pastor again anyway. Why should we have to endure this headache? Resignation would have been easy.

Our church became a case study in why every local church, especially the independent ones, should have an external leadership structure of overseers or apostles who can be called in for exactly such situations. Dr. Jack Buskey very graciously flew up from Florida and gave three days of his time to sit for endless hours with all of our leadership team, staff, and elders, and to hear every side of every person's story. At the end of this marathon he rendered the judgment that there was no legitimate ground for my resignation, at which his authority was promptly renounced by those who were unhappy.

Dr. Buskey gave me some painful counsel, but it was the wisdom of the Lord: "You need to let this come to a congregational vote. Otherwise it will be conflict and discord for months to come. Let God judge this through the constituted process. If He means for you to stay, you have nothing to fear."

We survived that congregational vote, but it was the most painful and humiliating experience of our lives. I voiced my complaint to the Lord prior: "Lord, this is unfair...I'm innocent!" It was one of the times in my life when the Spirit spoke to me sternly and with force: **"No one is innocent! Jesus is the only One who was completely innocent. You may not be guilty of what they charge...but never reduce a conflict among my people to the issue of whether or not you are innocent. My Church is about Jesus...it can never be about you!"** That was a serious rebuke, and I took it to heart. I had been full of self-pity for the unfairness of it all. Adding to my sense of humiliation, God further instructed me as we prepared to drive to the church for the congregational meeting: **"As a lamb before it's shearers is silent, so you are to answer not a word to any accusation made against you today."** I was troubled, as I knew that to fail to make my own defense would immediately discourage those who might be sitting on the fence, and there were many of our members who were waiting to hear what their Pastor had to say.

Yes, we remained in our position at the church that day, but we lost many precious people whom we had loved and had wonderful fellowship with. One of the most painful parts of the process was in facing people who loved us dearly but explained as they chose to depart: "Pastor, if only you had defended yourself we would have stayed; but your silence left some of us in doubt." Didn't God know this was going to happen? Why did we have to be like the "lamb before it's shearers? I was angry at first with the ones who had been most antagonistic, but in time my heart softened and I realized that they also were precious members of the family of God. No one emerges a winner in times of division. The best we can all do is forgive, heal, and move forward into His calling.

Those two men I mentioned in the beginning of this story became two of the most important men in my life in the season of painful reconstruction that lay ahead.

Joe DeVito was passionately loyal as a friend but more importantly, as a brother with integrity. I remember so clearly the day he sat with me in my office some time later.

After the split I was edgy about any negative responses to my ideas, and very lovingly he shared that "some people are afraid to tell you when they disagree." "Well if they are afraid to talk to me, that's their problem...it's not my problem!" "Actually," said Joe, "it **is** your problem." "And you are going to have to figure out how to resolve it." Joe's honesty that day was one of the greatest services anyone has ever provided to me, and it transformed my style and manner of leadership. After all, if we are not like Jesus in our leadership style, then what does it matter what we are building or leading? We all need friends who are more loyal to Jesus than they are to our personal position and any strategic advantage that they might derive from association with that influence. To this day Joe is one of the most trusted men in my life, not a counselor who says what we always want to hear, but one who like Nathan the prophet will declare the Word of the Lord that is needed.

David Pepper became one of my closest friends and a favorite companion on the mission field for the next 17 years and counting. Church on the Rock continued to flourish even as we built a friendship and partnership that would go far further than either of us imagined. There was great loss we would have to process in that Summer of the year 2000, but God, as always, was laying the foundation for the greater things to come. If we will keep our hands to the plow, even through our tears, He will bring us out into the joy of a new morning. There was still an abundance of grace ready to rain down on the families who remained with us at the Holy Spirit Christian Church.

48 THE COMMANDING OF SKEPTICS AND MEN

The next 12 months were the most difficult yet most important in my personal life.

Dealing daily with the disappointment of having the church divide under my watch, I frequently wished to pack up and leave Long Island for good. We were so happy on the foreign field, and neither Lenora or I could understand the necessity of remaining in pastoral ministry. But God had a deep work to do in our hearts. He wanted us to learn forgiveness on its deepest levels. He also wanted us to learn much more about faith. We thought we knew much about faith, but truthfully our knowledge and experience were elementary at best. In our time of crisis we were forced to press deeply into Him, and the words of Psalm 119:71-72 became my sincere confession: "It is good for me that I have been afflicted, that I may learn your statutes. The law of Your mouth is better to me than thousands of coins of gold and silver."

We entered into a season of great need, but also a season of great insight into the Word of God. Principles of faith flew off of the pages in ways we had never seen before. Prior to the conflict we had been well paid and everything was coming up roses. Our church had a reputation as one of the few independent churches in the area that had never suffered a split. Finances were abundant and we were able to operate in great generosity toward the work of world missions. Now all of that was gone. We took a drastic cut in our salary in order to keep some funds flowing to our supported missionaries, albeit at a significantly reduced level. It had been a while since we had needed to pray for our basic living expenses, but now we were living very much on credit cards and prayer. We began once again to experience the miraculous provision of God.

One day things were terribly tight, and we spent that Monday's day off with our kids at the beach, a cost free outing, but not one free of worry. As we lounged in the sunshine I tried to get my mind off the mounting bills, particularly the pressing obligation of $1,000 for something that was coming due. But the worry kept pushing in. In His way of speaking to me, I heard suddenly the voice of the Lord: **"I am able anytime I want to command a man to give you $1,000."** I wasn't really praying about my problem, so God's voice seemed more like an interruption to my line of thinking. I thought to myself "I already know that, but your ability is not the issue...the issue is my problem believing that You are going to do it!"

The next night we had our regular Tuesday Bible Study and a man approached me at the end of the service, a man who had only attended two or three times previously. "Pastor, I don't know why I'm doing this...in fact I've never done anything like this. But God has been compelling me all day long that I need to do something." With that he peeled off 10 crisp $100 bills and placed them into my hand. "I suppose you need this for something" he shrugged, and that was the end of our conversation. God's words from the day prior were ringing loudly in my ears.

On another occasion we had a $1,200 tax bill, and three weeks before tax day I began to worry myself silly over it. We didn't always worry about finances, but sometimes the weight of an obligation could seem overwhelming during that season of far less than what we had been accustomed to. I fretted about it all the way up until the week the taxes were due. Early that morning in prayer, I heard the voice of the Lord again: **"Why don't you just ask Me?"** I realized in an instant that I had never once prayed and asked God for the funds; I had just spent my time worrying. I immediately asked God's forgiveness for not honoring His character by asking for His help, and I prayed for the provision of the $1,200. Within 10 minutes my telephone rang, and on the line was a woman from our church who had a particularly keen ear for the voice of the Holy Spirit: "Pastor Kelly - what is it that you need?" "Oh, we are fine" I answered, somewhat less than honest. "Well, I know that you need something specific, because I was driving down the road to work and the Holy Spirit told me that you have a particular financial need, and I am to provide it." I was embarrassed, but at her insistence I finally admitted the specific need that we were facing. Twenty minutes later she was in front of our house with $1,200 in cash.

On another occasion we were in a board meeting discussing some renovations in the church. We would often pray as a leadership team and ask the Spirit to give us direction or insight if there was something important to Him that we were overlooking.

In that moment of prayer I heard the distinctive sound of running water, and saw a quick vision of a cascading fountain. I submitted this impression to my fellow team leaders, sharing my belief that this indicated we ought to install a decorative fountain into our church lobby to go along with the theme of living water that flows from Jesus. This was going to be a non-essential and added expense, but everyone was in agreement that this was an idea originating from the heart of God. How to pay for it was the problem. As we continued to discuss the challenge of financing items that in the past might have been non-issues but were now very demanding, I again heard the voice of the Lord, with a similar but more peculiar wording than what I had heard on the beach:

"I can command even an Atheist to provide money." Well I didn't think that I knew any atheists, at least not any who were lining up to donate money to our church. But a pattern was beginning to emerge, not of God stating what He was able to do, but of Him announcing in advance what He was intending to do. He was simply asking us to believe it.

One of the finest members of our church had passed away from cancer some months earlier. This woman had been with us all the way back to our beginnings in Glen Cove, and later commuted to some of our services in Hicksville. Her husband was an educated man in the field of natural science, but decidedly unpersuaded about the Biblical accounts of creation and salvation. He accepted with some academic amusement his wife's zeal for religion but he loved her dearly. Shortly after I heard this word about the commanding of an atheist, my phone rang and I answered to find him on the other end of the line. He was urgent and insistent, explaining to me the reason for his call:

"Pastor Kelly, I have to do something to honor my wife; I can't explain it to you. You know that I have never given money to the church. But I feel compelled and I don't know why. I am not going to rest until I do this. Please, is there any project you can think of that would make a fitting tribute to my wife?" Instantly my mind saw the fountain that we had purposed to purchase for the lobby. He did not waver when I shared the cost, and within 48 hours a check was in my hands. That beautiful fountain bubbled in our lobby for many years, with a lovely plaque in tribute to the wife of a scholarly scientist who had been visited by the presence of God. One important note from this story: we did not simply take the money and forget about this gentleman. People are always of far greater value than their resources, and we made it a point to reach out to him in the years that followed.

God wanted us to know that our need was about more than His ability. Of course He was able! But He was retraining us to ask, to have large faith in a time of trial, and to recognize His power to move resources through people in order to accomplish provision for His people and for the forward movement of His church. He was also teaching us to listen carefully to His voice, for He continued to be God over the tiniest of details.

49 I KNOW WHERE YOU CAN GET A PIANO FOR LENORA

We were hosting a marriage conference in our church one weekend in 2001, and the service concluded with an invitation for all of us to pray at the altar, committing ourselves to being more faithful covenant partners to our spouses. Like everyone else there I was on my knees, asking God to make me the husband that He wanted me to be. Once again He surprised me with one of the stranger words I've heard along our journey: **"I know where you can get a piano for your wife."**

I wasn't praying about a piano. I wasn't even remotely thinking about a piano. We had enjoyed having a piano in our home back in the 80's while ministering in Glen Cove, but this was like a forgotten dream now with funds being so tight. Once in a great while Lenora would mention her hope to have a piano again, but we never discussed it at length. We were more focused on buying groceries and not going deeper into debt. I listened quietly for the second part of the message, for if God had announced that He knew where to get a piano, He certainly was about to tell me . **"Call Matt Junge."** That was it, short and sweet, and I immediately felt uncomfortable. Matt was a great friend and had been so for years. We had stayed in his Glen Cove home prior to our move to

Ecuador, and he owned the roofing business that I had worked for that Summer. Matt had been very loyal to us over the years, but the thought of calling him and asking about a piano made me nervous. We did not solicit people individually and were even shy about doing so through newsletters when we traveled prior to pastoring again in Hicksville. Raised in the George Mueller philosophy of "asking no one but God" so that the provision is pure, we endeavored to be as delicate as possible when it came to our immediate needs, let alone something as unnecessary as a piano. But in the mind of a good Heavenly Father, a piano was anything but non-essential. It was the desire of His precious daughter Lenora's heart, and His mind was set to grant her that desire.

I knew God was speaking, so I worked up the courage to call my friend. "Hey Brother Matt...it's Brother Kelly." (Matt always called me Bro. Kelly so I always called him Bro. Matt - it was our affectionate way of greeting one another). "Do you by any chance know of how I could get a piano." "Wow! Are you kidding me Brother Kelly? This is unreal! I just got off of a job today for a lady that is a millionaire up in Bayville. She has a beautiful piano in her home that she wants to get rid of, but needs someone to move it. She just told me that if I came by to pick it up, I could have it for free...and it is worth a lot of money!"

Twenty four hours later Matt and I were pulling up to a beautiful home on the North Shore in Bayville and loading up the lovely piano that God had hand-picked for Lenora. I had been praying to be a blessing to my wife, and He had showed me a path to blessing her better than any I could have ever created on my own. It is so comforting to know that He knows the location of every single thing we could ever need or desire in this life, and even more, that He delights to bring much of it into our hands. Empty religious dogma declares that God provides what you need, but not the things you might want. Empty religious dogma has never met the God of the Bible. As we've said already before, He is a good and gracious Father.

50 DRIVE TO THE BORDER RIGHT NOW!

As evident from the above, God continued to speak clearly and provide supernaturally, despite a season of recurring pressure and depression over the people we had lost. Circumstances may change, but God remains God. The clouds began to lift as we moved into the second half of 2001 and key events for our future continued to unfold.

We made our first visit to Alaska that January of '01, speaking to the nine month old Church on the Rock congregation which already topped 100 people, as well as speaking for the annual Men's Winter Conference that Bill Pepper had hosted for over 20 years. It was -35º on the first day of conference, and along with nearly freezing, I was quite unsure of my qualification to speak at a conference. Our church had been through a shaking only six months prior. I hadn't even worked up the courage yet to return to the mission field, let alone speak in a conference. But Bill was gracious and encouraging regarding the future. He came through Hicksville that Spring with a word from the Lord for Lenora and I: "God told me to tell you to incorporate a 501c3 non-profit for your missionary outreach. You may not need it now, but the time will come when you will have assignments that you won't be running through the local church."

This seemed premature and irrelevant to our current situation, but in both our hearts we knew it was a true word from God. When discussing with Bill what name we should choose for the ministry, he was matter of fact: "Call it Brake Ministries International." That's your name...why call it anything else?" Bill Pepper's renowned practicality made perfect sense to us at that moment, so we set about incorporating an organization which at that moment seemed to have no reason for existing. We have often been asked how we chose the name of our ministry. I would like to tell of a profound visitation from God in the night, but it was by no such means. A fatherly visit from an Amazon missionary fit the need quite nicely. God quickly provided an experienced lawyer who assisted us in all the legalities free of charge. We were soon fully established as an IRS recognized New York State incorporated tax exempt charity.

Around this same time we had invited another local congregation to share our facility, the same congregation that had served as our sending agency when we first moved down to Ecuador. These dear friends had now come full circle into our lives, losing their own place of worship and now praying for a new location. We entered into a great partnership with them that lasted close to five years, sharing many special services and events with their Spanish speaking congregation of over 200 from multiple Central and South American nations. We weren't yet running back to the mission field, but God had brought the mission field through our front door. It was a much needed boost from a people that excelled in joyful celebration.

In one of those joint meetings we planned for a special focus on world missions. I preached and extended an invitation at the end for the young people to respond to the call of God if they were sensing such that evening. One of the first to the altar was the drummer from the Spanish speaking congregation, a young man who had come as a teenager from Colombia. Juan Pablo Martinez, or "Juampa" as we all called him, made a decision that night which would affect all of us in a profound way. He sensed God's calling and purposed to study for ministry at the Nyack College extension campus in Manhattan. Four years later Juampa would be installed as the Senior Pastor of the Holy Spirit Christian Church, a remarkable turn of events that could have only happened by the hand of God.

In the Summer Lenora and Melissa traveled back to Quito, where Lenora ended up ministering the word in 16 different meetings. Preaching the word was nothing new and she had done so off and on since our time in Glen Cove, but this was something of a turning point as more and more often there were requests overseas for special services and ministry to the women. As a mother of three teenagers, a pastor's wife, and one who had walked on the front lines of the life of faith, she had a vast resource of experience and gifting which would eventually be poured out all over the world. Melissa as well was beginning to connect more with the nations, beginning with her trip to Israel, several trips with our youth teams to India, a class trip with her Christian school for outreach in St. Maarten, and now remaining for a month longer in Quito after Lenora returned home. At every opportunity we made the effort to keep our kids connected to God's heartbeat for world evangelism.

The biggest event in everyone's life that year, for our family, church, and much of the world, was the terrorist attack on the World Trade Center and Pentagon on September 11th. I was in Canada at the time with our son Omar and Dr. Singh, who had flown to preach for Pastor Ric Borozny and a few other churches in the USA. We sat that morning at breakfast watching in disbelief like everyone else as the video of the first collision in Manhattan played repeatedly. Soon the second plane crashed into the second tower, and I heard the Spirit's firm command: **"Leave immediately and cross back over the border!"**

We had planned activity for that day, but I raced upstairs to our hotel room and told Omar to be ready to leave in 5 minutes: "throw everything into the suitcases and get ready to go. We have to leave right now!" I had told the same to K.R. who raced up behind me to his room to assemble his belongings. We called in a quick goodbye to Pastor Ric and within minutes our thrown together clothing was in the back of the car and we were driving quickly to the border crossing, 35 minutes away. The questions at the border were lengthy and the immigration officer understandably nervous. No one knew yet at that time what had happened, but everyone knew it was some kind of attack. We made it through as an extremely long line was forming behind us. Twenty minutes later every border in the United States was sealed, and would remain so for several days thereafter. But we were across, and with New York City sealed off, we had no option other than to continue on our pre-planned course of driving to my brother's church in Swanton, Ohio. It was there we would learn of the full extent of the horror that had happened that morning.

We were unable to communicate by cell phone as all service was disrupted, but the facts at home were shared with us many days later. Lenora had hurried over to Hicksville High School to secure Melissa where she had just enrolled for her Senior year. She then drove to the town of Jericho to pick up Jonathan at Lutheran High School where he was a Freshman. Everything was shut down, and everyone was in a panic. Many of those who lost their lives in the World Trade Center buildings had lived on Long Island. Several members of our church worked in lower Manhattan, including one who worked in the WTC tower itself, but all managed to escape. But the family members of many we knew were not so fortunate. It was a time of great mourning and loss in New York and all across America, and for several weeks the churches were once again full in every community.

51 THE MAN WHO WOULD NOT TAKE "NO" FOR AN ANSWER

We were glad to finally turn the page on 2001. With the shock of 9/11, the slow recovery of our church family from a bruising year prior, and some painful personal losses in the final two months of the year, we were glad when the New Year finally came. In a short span we attended the funerals of Lenora's mom Betty Groat, my beloved Uncle Omar after whom we had named our oldest son, and my stepfather Richard Kaiser. We had also said goodbye to Bob Vopelak, the senior elder and a founding member of our church. He had been a passionate supporter of our family and of the vision for world missions. I was broken hearted by his passing. But we can never camp within our grief or loss. The Holy Spirit is a Comforter for a reason, as temptation is ever before us to live with a mindset of loss; but as followers of a resurrected King, He empowers us to live with a mindset of life, progress, and a hope of things to come.

Good things began to come in rapid succession. The church returned full steam to the tasks of evangelism and international outreach. We renewed our outreaches to India and Ecuador, with many new fields opening as well. God began to send Lenora out more often, and she had powerful experiences traveling in Kenya, Tanzania, and Bulgaria. The Peruvian Amazon became an annual pilgrimage. We seemed to always find ourselves in jungles, off the grid or way into the bush, sent by God into places that others might have deemed a punishment. We were ecstatic, and the more remote a location, the happier we were to be there. Our hearts burned to reach those who were seldom if ever visited, and to comfort those who wondered if anyone cared.

A fresh excitement washed over our church family. We experienced God's presence continuously in both of our weekly services. Some indication of His favor always manifested, without fail, every single time we gathered. We believed that this was God's will and intent for the body of Christ. If God was Who we professed Him to be, then the concept of a boring service should be non-existent. The idea that we could gather and leave disappointed was completely banished from the culture of our community. Jesus was alive! The precious Holy Spirit resided in our hearts, and we never asked Him to "come" into our services, for we knew that we carried Him in with us. The key was to yield to His plan and purpose for each gathering, and in so doing, we never once experienced a service without a measurable evidence of grace, whether by virtue of someone converted, someone healed, or someone impacted by the power of His Word, whether taught, preached, or prophesied. He was not just Emmanuel for a Christmas long ago. He was Emmanuel, "God with us," in the 21st Century, and we delighted ourselves in the comfort of His continual and faithful presence.

As responsibility began to increase and invitations to other churches became more frequent, God knew that we needed someone to instruct us more fully in the principles of living by faith and leading with maturity. We had learned some painful lessons the hard way, through trial and error. But it is so much better to learn by the example of one who has a lifetime of successful ministry and experience under their belt. One day that person came quite forcefully through our door.

My friend Ric Borozny was on the phone, conveying a message from Pastor Keith Johnson of the Saskatoon Christian Centre in Saskatoon, Saskatchewan. We had met Pastor Johnson in July of 2002 while attending a meeting where he was speaking. His messages on the life of faith electrified our own, and we began to listen to his sermons in the car as we traveled. We had found a man who could understand our way of life, and his messages confirmed so many of the things we had been learning.

We had loved his teaching, but I was not prepared for his no nonsense approach to ministry. "Pastor Johnson asked me to call you and tell you that God has instructed him to come to your church in November." These were the words my friend Ric was hesitantly passing along by phone, but I wasn't having any of it. "What do you mean God told him to come to my church? God didn't tell me any such thing. Who does this guy think he is, calling someone up and telling them that he is coming to their church? Besides, I'm going to be in Ecuador. It's not possible."

All Long Island pastors were beset continuously with petitions from traveling preachers for a booking to preach. I did not appreciate being pressed for pulpit time, and I did not even consider that perhaps Pastor Johnson was being sent by God. He was after all the extremely busy senior pastor of a large congregation. He had oversight of dozens of other leaders and churches. He didn't need a place to preach. Maybe I had a problem with someone external supposedly hearing clearly for matters of our own ministry. Whatever the reason, I was disrespectfully unresponsive to Ric's message, and he let me know he would inform Pastor Johnson of my answer.

Ten minutes later the phone rang again. It was Ric calling a second time. "Umm, well, I gave him your message; and he told me to tell you that he has heard a clear instruction from God, and that God is sending him, and that these are the exact dates he is supposed to come...and will you please prayerfully reconsider?" I could tell that Ric was miserable with his middle man assignment, especially when I blew a gasket and began to rant about my non-negotiable commitment to conduct a healing campaign in Quito on those exact dates, etc., etc.. In the middle of my mini rant I heard the voice of God: "You haven't even consulted Me." I stopped my rant and told Ric I would pray and get back to him. I went out driving around the neighborhood, highly agitated but asking God for clarity. He quickly made His will plain: "I am sending Pastor Johnson. You are to cancel your outreach in Quito. This is important for your life and ministry."

I drove straight home, called Ric back, and told him to inform Pastor Johnson that we would receive him on the weekend he had specified. I had not the slightest clue of the caliber of the man I had initially rebuffed, but I am grateful for God's second chances, and I am grateful that Pastor Johnson had the humility and tenacity to persist without being offended at my first refusal. For this was a man whose influence would be essential, not only for that season, but for the 15 ensuing years of our ministry since that time. By the end of that weekend Lenora and I both knew that God had brought Keith Johnson into our lives forcefully. We needed him for more than just sermons on a teaching CD. We needed a pastor and an example in particular areas of ministry that were critical for our future success. We needed the accountability, counsel, and encouragement he would provide, for God knew that our greatest steps of faith were still ahead...and we were not going to fulfill our calling and destiny on our own.

52 SLOTH SLAYERS, TARANTULAS, AND RIVERS IN REVERSE

The Mayoruna Tribe in the Peruvian Amazon are one of the most remote people groups on earth. They live in small communities of usually 50-100, passing back and forth between the border that separates Brazil and Peru along the Javari River. Omar and I had joined David Pepper and two men from Church on the Rock in Alaska, Gary Oathout and Tim Sandstrom. The five of us headed down the Javari, along with two Peruvian leaders, for an unprecedented visit to one of these Mayoruna villages. Bill Pepper had dreamed for years of reaching this tribe, but was unable to go himself. Two ladies from Wycliffe Bible Translators had made it in years earlier, but due to the inaccessibility of the region, follow up visitors had been few.

We chugged along slowly, eyeing the warnings on the Brazilian side against any trespassing into the Javari Indigenous Reserve. "Is that seriously Brazilian territory?" I had to know, for I was incredulous that in the midst of nothing but jungle, monkeys, and fantastically colored butterflies, the sandbar only 20 feet to our left was actually Brazil.

"Yes, that is Brazil," replied our guide; "but it is not legal to land there - it is a protected area." That was all the justification I needed. "Pull over immediately! We have to plant our feet on Brazilian soil...especially the soil on which resides the last uncontacted tribes on the planet!...besides, who is there to protest anyway?" We had motored for hours down the river and were far from any outpost of civilization, so over to the left we went, somewhat illegitimately adding another nation to our growing list of places where our feet had wandered. "I'll go back someday to Rio or Sao Paulo to make it official" I promised my buddy David, after we had all taken our pictures on the sandbar as evidence of our conquest.

The Mayoruna were too deep in the jungle for us to make it in a day or even two. We would have to head further into the interior on secondary tributaries, lodging in small villages along the way. As we headed onto a tributary off of the Javari, our pathway now became a narrow and choked waterway barely 20 feet wide at some points. Towering trees loomed over us as all sorts of creatures scampered through the canopy. We passed and saw no one, as the only people present on this small river would be either local fishermen from the villages or once per decade missionaries like ourselves. It became evident that our way was becoming impassable, and as we pulled into a small cluster of huts for the night, we knew we would need a miracle to reach our destination. The river was simply too low for us to continue, and we could not drag the boat across dozens of miles of jungle.

As we lay in our jungle hammocks that evening, the ceiling itself seemed to be moving. Making closer inspection, we discovered we were sleeping in a house of tarantulas as we later named it. Spiders the size of small birds were crawling all over the ceiling and walls. Omar attempted a closer inspection only to have one spider spring forward directly toward his face. This curbed our interest immediately and we all zipped up our hammocks into impenetrable but sweltering cocoons. It was a long night of unsettling noises, but we awoke to a miracle, for the river had risen a significant amount for our journey to continue. The locals could not account for this reversal, as it was the dry season and there had been no rain in the area. We thanked God for the ability to press on toward the Mayoruna community.

Arriving at last when our backsides could endure the planks in the boat no longer, our Peruvian leader disembarked. A stern looking group of tribal leaders gathered next to the river, as Pastor Ramon turned back to us and said in a firm tone: "Please do not get out of the boat." Hmm...that was not the word we wanted to hear after traveling three days to get there. Lively discussions ensued with the aid of a young man who spoke both Spanish and the dialect of the Mayorunas, with the primary issue being that these leaders were demanding to know who had given permission for our visit. Someone was supposed to have given advance notice, but in the Amazon there are no guarantees.

The one guarantee we did have was that God had sent us and one way or another, we hoped He would persuade their hearts to allow us to stay for 3 days of outreach. A church somewhere back in the USA had provided funding to build a simple church structure, and the materials had arrived; it just seemed that the chiefs did not know the gift of building material included the package deal of listening to a wide eyed group of gringos.

Waved ashore in the end, we set about finding the hut where we would string up our hammocks. The location was around 10 feet from their internal cooking fire, which meant that we would be "smoked missionaries" by morning. Omar and I wandered about the village and stumbled upon a horrible sight, a young girl of no more than seven or eight years old slowly turning a sloth in a fire, and scraping the burning fur off of its skin with a crude machete. It was odd enough to see someone burning a sloth, but the real trauma was the fact that the sloth was alive and screaming as she repeatedly flipped him, bound at the front and rear paws, in the fire. We took pictures and got away fast, as the girl and her grandmother glared at us menacingly, likely in fear we were going to steal their supper.

We had three amazing days of ministry among the Mayoruna. We talked to them of Jesus, of salvation, and even of the ministry of the Holy Spirit, Who in the same manner in which the river had risen unexplainably to bring us there, could spring up through them with a river of life, filling their community with the righteousness, peace, and joy of God's kingdom.

One final note of humor which illustrates the unexpected cross cultural challenges of communicating in a tribal setting: I was fervently in the middle of a message, sweating in the humidity and heat but plowing forward to a climactic point. Suddenly an older man stood up, walked over to a huge brass plate hanging from a pole, and thunderously hammered it with a large mallet. There was a loud "gong" that reverberated, and all of the assembled villagers stood up from where I was teaching and walked away. "What just happened?", I asked Pastor Ramon. His answer was hilarious: "It is their lunch time; You are finished now." And with that, my sermon was indeed finished. Pastor David and all our team had great fun with that moment, never letting me forget the day I was "gonged" into silence in the jungles of the Amazon.

53 TELL THEM TO SHINE MY SHOES

During this same Summer of 2004 when we visited the Mayoruna, we also were busy at home looking for a permanent residence. Though our numbers had not returned to previous levels, we nevertheless enjoyed great peace at HSCC, and it was a season of real unity and excitement regarding the future. With the anticipation of being able to go out on mission outreach three or four times per year, we were at rest about making Long Island our permanent home. If this was how God wanted us to fulfill our mission mandate, we would not protest. We had wonderful friends, a very loving group of leaders in the church, the familiarity of Long Island culture, and the proximity of New York airports for international travel. It seemed the perfect set up, and we set our minds to leave renting behind and become committed New Yorkers for life.

My buddies in the Amazon knew we were house hunting, and Gary Oathout jokingly said "maybe God will send you to Alaska." I was not amused, and let him know that this was the least likely thing on earth that was going to transpire. We knew we would find a home soon. In fact it was quite the opposite. Financial obstacles were real - the house we had rented for close to seven years eventually sold for $650,000, Nassau County having one of the highest costs of living in the nation. An equal obstacle though was the lack of peace about any home we looked at. Nothing seemed to bear witness with our desire. Without financing, and without peace of mind, we seemed to be in a holding pattern which we could not understand.

Understanding came one day late in the year, and it was not what we had been looking for. Searching for the will of God in prayer, He surprised us with the unexpected: **"I am sending you back out into full time traveling ministry to the nations."** This was not a jolt from men. This was a jolt from heaven. The thing we had aimed for our whole lives was no longer the thing we were aiming for. Yes, we wanted to devote ourselves to the nations; but our minds had become accustomed to the model that had worked beautifully now for the past several years. We had once again a solid salary, we had a supportive community, and we had an abundance of open doors for evangelism. Why should we pick up and walk away from that security, only to start over from scratch once again?

We made no hasty decisions, determining to pray until we were certain we were hearing clearly from God. We could not imagine this going over well with our faithful friends at HSCC who had stuck beside us through thick and thin. After eleven years back on Long Island, we did not want to leave a third time without absolute certainty. And when, where, how, and what? These details were all unrevealed, with our only affirmation being the shared witness of God's voice that Lenora and I both carried in our hearts.

We made a fast decision to celebrate the New Year of 2005 in Manhattan with all three of our children, realizing that this might be our last time together as a family in New York. More than sixteen years of our children's lives had been lived on Long Island, and we were New Yorkers more than anything else. Melissa was home for Christmas from Oral Roberts University, and Omar was home from Faith College in Saskatoon. Jonathan was in his Senior year of High School. We took the plunge and braved the crowd of over one million in Times Square, standing for 8 solid hours in the freezing cold to secure our view, triumphant at Midnight, but also vowing to never do that again!

God was gracious to grant us that time together, for in the next two weeks the kids returned to their schools, and I flew off to India to spend some time alone with K.R. Singh, who by now was one of my most trusted friends and advisors. K.R. was not a sentimentalist. He was a man who would shoot straight with what he believed was the word of the Lord.

"I have a word for you from the Lord" he announced, within a day of my arrival. "God gave me this scripture for you," and he proceeded to read to me the 15th verse of Genesis 28: "**Behold, I am with you and will keep you wherever you go, and will bring you back to this land; for I will not leave you until I have done what I have spoken to you.**" He went on to share that he believed it was indeed God's plan for us to move out into full time traveling ministry. This took great integrity for K.R. to share such, as our church was a heavy investor into his ministry. If we left, there were no guarantees of the extent to which any future pastor might feel to partner with him.

I abruptly became ill, and in fact extremely ill. I had a high fever and felt like I was once again about to depart the planet. It was not malaria, but it felt to me very much like some type of spiritual warfare by an enemy that was determined to keep us from moving forward by faith into this next stage of our calling. We had planned several days of meetings with the leadership of K.R.'s organization, and some had traveled great distances to get there. I was distraught over my inability to get up and minister the Word of God. K.R. stood now in the doorway of my bedroom, asking me for instructions and whether or not I could make an appearance. I can't account for it exactly, but somehow a spirit of faith gripped my soul and I raised my head with this declaration: "Have one of the boys shine my shoes." This was an odd thing for me to say, even though K.R.'s staff were always keen to launder our clothing and keep the dust off of our dress shoes. I have always found it humbling to have someone shine my shoes, and would never dream of ordering it to be done. But faith raises its head in unexpected ways.

The moment the words flew out of my mouth I was hit by the power of God. I have only two or three times in my life experienced something similar. A heavy blanket of God's glory settled upon me - I could feel it physically. In an instant, my raging fever and burning throat and aching joints disappeared. I sprang up and into the shower, put on my suit, then went out and preached to hundreds of my fellow preachers under an anointing I had not imagined my body could have endured. Several of my dear Indian friends sought me out afterwards: "Pastor Kelly, do you know that you were glowing with the glory of God?" I laughed politely and told them it was simply the reflection of the ceiling lights off of my bald head. I had heard people make the same miscalculation more than once. They were not amused. "We know what we saw...many of us saw it. There was a visible glory of God when you were preaching. It followed you across the platform wherever you went."

I honestly don't know if it was the lights or if they had actually seen a manifestation of God's presence. I do know that the anointing of God's Spirit is an extraordinary and wonderful thing. It transforms with regularity men and women that are otherwise unsensational into those who can operate as if they are from another realm. It can make words come from the mouth of a jackass as witnessed by Balaam in the Old Testament. It can turn a carnal King like Saul into an overnight Prophet of God. No man can credit his own faith or spirituality for these extraordinary things God does. We are all weak and feeble on our own, but thanks be to God who raises up the nothings of this world and enables them to do something that counts for eternity. My experience in India sent me homeward with a renewed confidence that maybe, just maybe, full time travel would work out after all, even if it meant starting over from scratch once again.

54 CARRIED ON THE WINGS OF EAGLES

Lenora and I left for Ecuador, the place of our shared international beginning, determined to hear from God together and receive one more confirmation of His mandate. Prior to our departure Lenora shared with me a verse she believed the Lord had given her specifically for me. I had been wrestling of course with the concern about provision if we were to pull up our stakes and launch out once again into traveling ministry. She wrote out the words and they gave me real comfort, words that I have cherished repeatedly from Exodus 19:4-5: **"You have seen what I did to the Egyptians, and how I bore you on eagle's wings, and brought you**

to Myself. Now therefore, if you will indeed obey My voice and keep My covenant, then you shall be a special treasure to Me above all people, for all the earth in Mine."

It was an amazing week of ministry, rejoicing in God's faithfulness with the Robelly family who were now in the 12th year of leading their nation impacting church and ministry. God had granted extreme favor to Patricio, and we were delighted as access was given for us to enter the vacant office of the President to spend time in prayer for Ecuador. Each time we visited we shared in the wonderful miracle services that were conducted monthly. On this visit we again saw many being healed and many more being born again.

After a full week of ministry we took a day off to attempt the summit of Pichincha. The Pichincha volcano was active off and on, and for those willing to drive off the grid about two hours outside of Quito, there was access to climb up to the rim of its 13,000+ foot crater. This was not something that could be done upon arrival to Ecuador, as the altitude adjustment was too severe. After a week however at Quito's 9,000 foot altitude, we were adjusted enough to attempt something we had been able to accomplish only one time previously.

We drove until the 4X4 vehicle could go no further, and then the four of us got out and started the slow and torturous climb upwards: Lenora, Pastor Patricio, Jeremy Diaz, and myself. It was a long and painful climb, and more than once we thought of turning back. Towards the top we were managing only 10 - 20 steps at a time, with long intervals of heavy breathing in between. Lenora and I were 42 and 43 at the time, not old by any stretch, but also not physically fit. We sounded like two dying respiratory patients, but still we pressed upward to the crater. All the while I prayed and meditated on the Scriptures, asking God to confirm to me that He indeed would be faithful and take care of my family. I should not have needed such confirmation, but the fact was that I did; I was not a superhero of the faith, and found myself right back in that same state that I had been in the night before we signed the lease with Dr. Hamada to begin eleven years of residence on Long Island. "Lord," I prayed, "I believe…but help my unbelief." "Give me the courage to launch out one more time, and the faith that you will care for my family…else how can I believe you to use us to be a blessing to the nations of the earth?"

Finally we reached the crest of the crater, and all of us scattered to various points to walk and pray. A heavy mist of clouds floated in and out, but after some moments, every cloud in the sky parted and we were standing under an exceedingly hot and very intense Equatorial sun. The sky was brilliant blue, and the sun was somewhere behind me as I pondered my perfectly cast shadow, contemplative in the warmth of the sun.

Suddenly I froze. I stared down at the shadow of my body, blinking my eyes in disbelief. As if painted there by a Master painter, my head was framed, perfectly, by two extremely distinctive and large wings. It was as if my head were some creature, and in perfect proportion, one wing came out from the center and right side of my head, and the other wing came out of the center and left side of my head. The image was absolutely still, like a photograph, not shimmering, not fading in and out. Slowly it dawned on me that this was no vision.

Very slowly I lifted my eyes upward and tilted my head back. Less than six feet over my head, in perfect position, an eagle sat riding on the current of the wind. He hovered perfectly still, staring straight down into my eyes. I looked back down at the shadow that had not changed, then slowly back up again at the eagle. Still he stared down, directly into my eyes, and for a brief moment I felt a fearful fascination that perhaps he was ready to sink his talons into my face, but the word of the Lord suddenly resounded in my spirit: **"I have borne you on eagle's wings, and brought you to Myself. If you will obey My voice, and keep My covenant, you**

will be a special treasure to Me...for all the earth is mine." I don't think it meant a thing to that eagle, but it was one of the most holy moments God has ever given me, on the rim of a 13,000 foot volcanic crater, alone with my Maker and a messenger of His design.

Mission accomplished, the eagle turned and slowly drifted away into the wind. "Did you see that awesome eagle? It was hovering over your head!" Lenora approached me and began to exclaim about what she had witnessed from afar. She had no idea though of the shadow of eagle's wings that had been cast about my reflected head. I shared with her the power of that encounter with God's word of promise. Again and again over the past decade we have reflected on the wings that carry us faithfully through every season of life. The earth is truly His, and armed with this blessed assurance we returned home with all doubts removed regarding our plunge back into our life of missionary evangelism. The task before us now was to settle on the where and the when...and it was easier said than done.

55 NORTH TO ALASKA...PLEASE
SAY IT ISN'T SO!

Gary Oathout had been right! Every time we prayed regarding our next home base, the word "Alaska" kept wafting through our minds. Staying in the New York area seemed like the logical choice. Almost all the friends and family we had were in the Eastern half of the USA. I was past the struggle about the "what." We knew we were to launch out into full time traveling ministry, and the wise word Bill Pepper delivered in 2001 regarding forming our own 501c3 non-profit was suddenly not so irrelevant after all. But the struggle over the "where" was just beginning. Alaska is among the most beautiful states in America...but it was 5,000 miles away! Alaska's people are warm and wonderful, but our people all lived in places like Pennsylvania, Florida, Ohio, and New York. Alaska's Summers are amazing...but Alaska's Winters are dark and can be depressing. I did not want to move to Alaska.

My problem was that everyone I consulted who had influence in my life believed that it was in fact God's will for us to move to Alaska. K.R. Singh believed it was Alaska. Keith Johnson believed it was Alaska. And most imposing of all, my trusted counselor Lenora was delighted to discover that it was Alaska! God had spoken to her clearly, "you're going home." Alaska's culture is almost identical to the culture Lenora grew up in in rural Western Pennsylvania, with a small town atmosphere, cold winters, a population that loved to hunt, and the beauty of mountains and quiet country living. Long Island's breakneck speed of life had never invaded the stillness of her soul. For Lenora, Alaska was a reward. To my mind it was a trial intended to refine and break my spirit.

We received back to back confirmations after returning from Ecuador, first from Pastor Johnson who flew in to Long Island during an ice storm, which forced the cancelation of our services. It didn't matter, for he had only one overriding mission, which was to deliver us counsel from the Lord: "Missions is who you are; launch out into your calling." That very same evening I received a phone call from Bill Pepper, who knew nothing of our decision to leave the church. "I have a word from the Lord for you" he began; "I've written it down to make sure I get it right." And then he read to me the following statement: "Missions is who you are. God is calling you to launch back out into full time traveling ministry." I nearly dropped the phone. The words were identical to what Pastor Keith Johnson had spoken less than 24 hours prior. Bill added one follow up piece of personal advice: "In these kinds of decisions, the most important factor is that of the local church where you will be based. More than anything else, you need to be led by God to the right local church." He had no idea that the local church God had in mind was the one being pastored by his son David!

David Pepper was flying through to Europe a few days later, and I finally decided to broach the subject with him directly. I told him what I believed we were hearing, and asked that he solicit the prayerful agreement of his elders. If they were confident together that God was sending us, then we would take the next step and inform our leadership at HSCC. I got a thumbs up later from David. Church on the Rock was booming, with a recent attendance of 900 at their first Easter service in their new facility, just 5 years after they had begun with a few families in a living room. They would be glad to have us base our mission ministry out of Alaska, and would welcome us with open arms. Several other voices were added when I attended a conference in Canada, with one Pastor who did not know me giving me a word to "get ready for your transition, and, your labor has not been in vain." This was especially important to me as we wanted to leave Long Island with the confidence that we had fulfilled all God desired of us and left nothing undone.

By this time I counted seven distinctive confirmations of our transition and move to Alaska. At this point I heard a solemn caution from the Lord: "I have spoken to you clearly enough; don't ask me again." There was nothing left to do but obey.

I assumed from the start that my associate pastor Joe DeVito would obviously be the man of God's choosing to take the senior position, but I had assumed incorrectly. While preparing to speak with him about our transition, God spoke to me from the text in I Samuel where the prophet is looking for God's chosen among Jesse's sons. When he saw the one most naturally qualified, he was certain he had found the man. But God told Samuel that he was not the one. "The Lord does not see as man sees, for man looks on the outward appearance." Pastor Joe was more than qualified, inside and out.

As I prayed however, another name kept coming into my spirit. "Lord, that's impossible" I protested. "This could never happen. The people will never accept it. There are insurmountable obstacles from every direction!" God had spoken to me the name of "Juampa," the young man our church had assisted beginning four years earlier with his Bible College education after he responded to God's call to ministry.

Juampa was in his twenties and about to be married to Rachel Galloway in the month of May. He had no plans to rush into full time ministry. He was technically a member of another congregation, even though he helped us frequently with our Sunday worship and also with the young people in our church. Juampa spoke excellent English but would our people accept someone from another nation? I just could not figure out the logic of God's plan.

Thank God for the humility and sensitivity of Pastor Joe DeVito. He recognized in prayer that this was the wisdom and purpose of God, and threw himself fully behind it. He was more than willing to take the senior role if that was what God intended, but he knew in his heart that God was not asking him to do so. If God wanted Juampa, then Joe was going to fully support Juampa.

But first I had to tell Rachel and Juampa, and see if they even were open to such a crazy idea. I was asking them to assume a full time senior pastoral role only 6 weeks after they would return from their honeymoon. This was not the first year of marital bliss and romance they had imagined, but wanting God's will above all else, they agreed to pray. Their destiny was inescapable, and a few short months later the newly married lovebirds stood before a congregation that had voted their overwhelming consent. We joyfully ordained them and set them into the ministry of leading and caring for God's precious people at the Holy Spirit Christian Church. Lenora and I were now able to leave in absolute peace, knowing why we were leaving, where we were going, and who would carry the torch forward after our departure.

God does all things well, all the time. He is not a haphazard or disordered God. He plans ahead for times and seasons, days and dates and moments, with great specificity. When He sent us out of Glen Cove to Quito He faithfully established John and Robin Burns in our place. When we left Hicksville, the man and woman of His choosing were again in position to shepherd His flock, a ministry they carried out with excellence for the next 6 years. And as we prepared to shift into a higher gear of travel, He was going before us as well, putting things in order well before our arrival. Our faith however would still have demands placed upon it, for this life will always be a walk of faith. The Bible declares that "the just shall live by faith." There is no other option for the believer. Mountains that were large and imposing would always loom ahead, but grace would always be greater.

56 THE NEVER-ENDING TANK OF GAS

The first phase of our journey to Alaska started out all wrong. After 25 years together and all of those years in either school or ministry, we figured that God would smile upon our desire to drive up slowly. We had no arrival deadline, other than the goal of beating the Winter weather. We had planned to drive from New York to Florida in August, spend some time with family, and then embark upon a five week drive with an October 1st arrival. We took no furnishings, but did mail 91 boxes ahead of us by the U.S. Post Office, half of those being books. The church staff who retrieved and stored this massive weight of goods had to exercise a lot of grace and forgiveness toward this crazy missionary couple with their unconventional method of relocating. If we had to do it over we would have packed everything in a U-Haul and driven it up ahead of time. But media mail postage rates saved us a small fortune, plus we wanted to drive up slowly and unencumbered, soaking in the Pacific coastline, National Parks, and the spectacular drive up through British Columbia and the Yukon on the Alaska Highway.

On day one of our planned departure, Hurricane Katrina roared ashore and devastated New Orleans. The Big Easy had been our first planned stop, but now we would need to wait and skirt around north of the city. We did not wait long enough, and we had no idea of the mayhem we were driving into with the complete lack of gasoline across hundreds of miles of flooding and devastation. We filled up several hours after leaving the central Gulf coast of Florida, wrongly believing that we could fill up again in Alabama or Mississippi . No one had gasoline, and those stations which did had lines that seemed to stretch forever. People with empty gas cans were waiting in the heat. We moved up into Georgia then across into Alabama to avoid the worst of the problem, but it was the same there. There was a lot of panic and contention radiating out concentrically from New Orleans, with everyone desperate to get out. Gasoline and drinking water were the two items most in demand.

Driving past one empty gas station after another, I began to get nervous, realizing that we did not have enough fuel to reach our intended destination, the far Western side of Louisiana. We wound through Alabama and Mississippi with our gas tank now well past the point of when it should have been empty. With so many scenes of chaos in every community (we had left the primary highways), we prayed now for the same miracle we had experienced in 1983 on our honeymoon in Spain.

My Uncle Omar had given us the choice for our wedding: either he and my Aunt would fly in from Europe for the ceremony, or they would give us tickets to fly to them for our Honeymoon. They lived in a village of 30 people high up in the mountains in the Rioja region of Spain. It was a decision that required no contemplation, and off we flew 48 hours after our wedding for 3 wondrous weeks in Spain. Uncle Omar loaned us his behemoth of a car, a Mercury Monarch that he had shipped over from the USA. One of our adventures was an outing of several days up across the northern coast, where our route was to take us through Gijon then down through Leon and back over to the tiny village of Castroviejo, another several hours away.

I became hopelessly confused trying to navigate the highways and bypasses of the large city of Leon, heading off in a direction where it was soon obvious that we were lost. I had calculated that we had enough fuel to get home, but that was assuming we went directly home. We drove helplessly for a couple of hours, looking for fuel, but only finding ourselves in decreasingly smaller towns and villages. Our Michelin road atlas was not helping, we could not figure out the road signs, and we eventually ended up at the literal end of a dirt road with only a cow path in front of us. Our tank had no more than a gallon or two remaining, the sun was setting, and we were in a huge sedan that would quickly burn through whatever fuel remained. When I saw that cow path and the setting sun, I had a bit of a panic. I had brought my bride out into the wilderness to die. There wasn't even a shepherd around to give us pity, just some wandering cattle stopping to stare at the tragic foreigners who obviously had not the slightest idea what they were doing.

While I ranted about our predicament, Lenora began to sing a song of worship, and just as the restless spirit of Saul was stilled by the anointed music of David, our car was likewise flooded by the presence of God, and a great peace came upon my soul. Lenora's singing has often released God's peace into a troubled moment. Hope was stirred, and instead of panicking, we asked God to have mercy on my cartographic incompetence and help us get home...on an empty tank of gas. It was now nearly dark as we backed out of that cow path, turned around on the dirt road, and by a means we still do not comprehend, found our way by continuously turning right or left in the right direction, until three hours later we pulled into Castroviejo. Those three hours must have been at least 130-140 miles...on an empty tank of gas.

Here we were 22 years later in need of another miracle of multiplication. We stared at our fuel indicator for the final hours of our journey, watching it stuck near empty, holding our breath and hoping that what God had done once before, He was willing to do again. He did, and ten minutes before reaching our destination and long after we were certain we should have exhausted our last drop, we found a gas station that still had fuel, not more than 90 minutes away from the Texas border. We could not prove that we had received a miracle of multiplication, but knowing we had driven well over 100 miles past the normal fuel rating for our model of vehicle, it was miracle enough for us.

With people dying and losing everything all around us, why, some may wonder should God take time to care about one random couple's supply of gas? Why would He even bother to extend their mileage, when matters of far greater importance were affecting hundreds of thousands of lives. I cannot claim to fully know the answer to that question. I know only that we asked, and He answered. He is a good Father. And what He has done for others, He is willing to do for you. God's pleasure in attending to the smallest details of each of our lives is not diminished by the reality of a world in chaos all around. This is precisely what distinguishes Him as God. We as humans can only handle so much chaos before we reach the point of overload. God can look upon an entire world in need, and yet take the time to bring food to your door, put gas in your tank, relieve you of your aches and pains, and soothe every individual doubt and fear. He is Almighty God, and He longs for His children to dare to believe Him for more than what we have ever imagined. Sometimes that "more" is minuscule, and sometimes that "more" is massive in its scope and imagination. The size of the need or miracle is inconsequential.

What matters is making room for Him to reveal His love and power through each one of our lives.

57 IF ONLY YOU HAD SHOWN UP THREE WEEKS SOONER

I was on the phone and not too happy with my friend David Pepper's nonchalance. He was keeping a lookout for our housing. Lenora and I had navigated America and Canada and were now just a couple days away from reaching our destination of Wasilla, Alaska. I was talking to David from the city of Whitehorse, in the Yukon Territory, asking if anything had come up in the way of rental homes. "Well, there was a great house for rent three weeks ago but someone else took it. Too bad you didn't get here sooner; but don't worry...we'll keep an eye out for you. In the meantime, you can move in with Gary & Carole Oathout!" I wasn't consoled in the least. Gary and Carole are the most wonderful people in the world, and we joke at Church on the Rock that everyone lives with Gary & Carole at least once. But I didn't want to end up camping for an undefined period in dependence on someone's hospitality. I wanted all my ducks in a row, well before arrival. But God has never catered to my need to have everything under control.

As we came nearer to Alaska, I became increasingly nervous about finding a place to live. It wasn't just the house, but it was the larger reality of having walked away from our steady salary and the security of our familiar life and culture on Long Island. Why did we have to move to Alaska anyway? Could there be any spot in America less practical for an international traveling ministry? Lenora was elated to be "going home," but I was sinking into a slough of self-pity once again.

We pulled into Wasilla and went straight to David and LaRae's home. Omar and Jonathan had both decided to move up with us, but they were set to fly in from Florida three days later. Melissa had started her Senior year at ORU in Tulsa. All that remained was to find a suitable home. As we sat in the Pepper's living room, regaling them with the tales and sights of our long road trip, the telephone rang. It was Gayle Ann, soon to become a close friend, but at that moment a stranger to us. "Have the Brakes found a home yet? My daughter's friend's grandfather has been building a home for the past three years. He is listing it tomorrow for occupancy in two weeks. It is a wonderful chalet on a wooded acre, only 2 miles from the church....private, brand new, 3 bedrooms, 2 bathrooms...it won't last 24 hours once it is listed...and he is willing to show it to them right now if they can come over!"

After driving for a month, we had now been in town for less than 60 minutes. We all piled into the car, drove over to 2101 Melanie Avenue in Wasilla, and met the owner, happy at the thought of having a clean cut preacher's family in the home he had originally built for his retirement. We were in the home for not 5 minutes when Lenora informed me of her revelation: "This is it. This is the home God was preparing for us all along." She was absolutely right, and the beauty of its setting was well beyond what we had anticipated or imagined. We informed the landlord that we would take it. He only needed 10 days to finish installing appliances and completing some of the trim work. Next thing we knew we were signing a two year lease for only $1,100 per month. We lived for nine memorable years in that home, with the rent never raised even one dollar, and a perfect landlord who lived two doors over and fixed anything and everything without hesitation. God had been preparing our home long before we even knew we were moving to Alaska. We had no need of arriving three weeks sooner after all. It was timed to the very hour of our arrival. After two quick weeks in Gary & Carole's home, we moved into our Alaskan hideaway and began hauling our 91 boxes out of church storage.

(12 years later and several of those boxes are yet to be unpacked. I will never again send books in the mail!)

58 AND WHAT EXACTLY IS AN ENCOUNTER WEEKEND?

Moments before the phone call from Gayle Ann, Pastor David threw another curve ball in my direction. "I would like you to run our Encounter Weekends. The first one is in three weeks". We had barely had time to stretch our legs, and already an unanticipated assignment was being thrust our way. "Well Dave, first you have to tell me what you mean by an "Encounter Weekend." David went on to explain that with hundreds of new people coming into the church, many did not have any frame of reference for the ministry and empowerment of the Holy Spirit in their personal lives. "We want to set up retreats for 30-35 people three times per year, during which time they can learn about the person of the Holy Spirit and conclude with an opportunity for a greater infilling in their lives." I wavered a bit, but quickly heard God whisper: **"He is not only your friend, but he is the Pastor of the church you now attend. You need to do what he is asking."** I wasn't opposed to serving, but I was concerned that if we locked into something at home it would hinder our forthcoming assignments to travel. But God knew exactly what He was doing, and David had certainly been hearing from God.

An outstanding team of Church on the Rock members joined with us and over the next eight years we experienced the ministry privilege of walking with more than 500 adults through the Encounter program of Church on the Rock. The impact was just one aspect of the revolutionary growth that came, with many emerging so on fire with what they had experienced they quickly assumed roles of service and leadership, fanning the flames of the unique type of revival that Church on the Rock was enjoying.

Hundreds and hundreds of people came to faith in Jesus Christ through the services, leadership and congregation of the COTR family. Baptisms were radically joyful and continuous. The newly built sanctuary soon required two and then three services...followed by two, three, and even four additional campuses, and church plants beyond in other states and cities. The Church on the Rock movement continues its expansive impact to this day.

Chris and Laurie Miller were just two of the many outstanding individuals who went through the Encounter Weekend. The Millers were already very seasoned leaders in church ministry, but at that particular time Chris was engaged full time in residential construction. God gave a word to them during that first Encounter that "the time is coming when you will pastor again." Some months later they were asked to help plant a new campus for COTR in Palmer, 15 miles away from Wasilla. Palmer is a small town of only 6,000, but when Chris and Laurie later became part of our Encounter team, God gave them another word, that they would ultimately have a congregation of 1,000 people in that town. It seemed a stretch to believe that such a percentage of that community could be reached by one church. As of this writing they are two months away from occupying their new facility which will have ample space for the growth God has promised, with more than 600 men, women, and children already calling the Palmer campus of Church on the Rock their home.

The Encounter Weekends not only impacted and empowered future leaders, but they impacted and transformed our lives as well. As we dug deep into the Scriptures to discover our true identity in Christ, the shackles of self-condemnation and insecurity fell freely off of everyone, ourselves included. It became one of the more personally transforming assignments we had received from God, equipping us more fully for the larger tasks overseas, and in God's gracious wisdom knitting our hearts with hundreds of other men and women whom we might never have had the opportunity to know. This became the foundation for a tremendous level of support and interest in our missions calling. The people who "encountered" God's power with us were blessed, but we also were blessed well beyond what we had ever imagined could happen in Alaska.

Our first month in Alaska a man in the church with a gift of sharing God's word prophetically approached me with a message: "You will have more resources as a missionary than you ever had as a pastor." I was glad to hear that word. We had enjoyed the privilege of seeing much go out through the missions program at Holy Spirit Church to ministries all around the world. But now we did not have a church budget to pull from...only our own faith and prayer that God would prosper and increase the potential of Brake Ministries International. When we arrived in Alaska we had one firm monthly commitment from a local church, $400 per month from Church on the Rock. We had as well a generous severance package from our church in Hicksville, but this would expire after six months. Where would all the support we needed come from, not just for living, but also for a multitude of mission projects ahead?

God does all things well. Through the relationships that developed in the Encounter Weekends, people began to love us and invest generously into our missionary work.

The prophetic promise came to pass, with many thousands of dollars annually passing through our hands from people and churches all over Alaska. Much of that went into designated projects, and much of it came in the form of honorariums for preaching, but it was still far more than we had ever imagined would come from America's Last Frontier. Long Island was an economically wealthier region, but God was wealthier still. It does not matter where He has planted you, no matter how remote or how far outside the boundaries of your expectation. He knows how to get resources to you or I in any place and at any time. He is Jehovah Jireh, the God of provision with an inexhaustible supply!

59 A PREACHER IN THE JUNGLE GETS HIS CAR

It is really true that God knows how to put resources into the hands of His people, regardless of where they have been planted. One of our friends in India, Pastor Ratna Raju, has worked for more than 35 years with Dr. K.R. Singh. This precious man has worked in a remote and hostile area all of that time. When we first met him he was walking from village to village to encourage the Pastors whom he oversaw.

Occasionally he could catch one of the dilapidated buses that chugged up and down the mountains, but most of the time he was dependent on his feet or a bicycle. His great longing was for a motorcycle, and shortly after one of our early trips to India our church was able to provide the funds for its purchase. He was delighted with that motorcycle and rode it for years until every part of that bike had long exceeded its warranty.

One day Pastor Raju had a serious accident on his motorcycle, as he came around a curve and a giant python was lying stretched out across the road. His son was on the back, and both of them tumbled to the ground as avoiding the snake was impossible.

They lay there for a few moments banged up and with the snake now eyeing a potential afternoon meal. Something about that incident greatly traumatized his boy, who became stricken with fear at the thought that they would be crushed and consumed by the python. Eventually though someone came along and they were rescued, but after several years of constant near accidents and chronic malfunctions of the motorcycle, Pastor Raju was ready for God to do something greater.

One day we traveled up into the mountains to discover him pulling up in a shiny new red car. This was an absolute impossibility for a jungle preacher, as no one in ministry in the mountains had a vehicle. A motorcycle alone was a great luxury and provision, but only folks in the cities or towns below had cars, or those who worked for the government. Pastor Raju related to us his amazing testimony:

"After my accident with the snake, I told the Lord that I needed a miracle. I was tired from the years of near misses, accidents, and constant repairs. I told the Lord that 'You are God...nothing is impossible for you...I am your servant and I am asking You to provide me with a car!'" He did not send out financial appeals or even confide with K.R. regarding his desire. It did not matter that not one other preacher in the tribal areas had a car. If no one had ever dared to ask, then Pastor Raju was going to be the first!

Shortly thereafter he was descending the mountain on his dilapidated motorcycle heading to a conference at the ministry headquarters eight hours away. For whatever reason he asked his wife, on the back of the motorcycle, if she had remembered to pack his pajamas. She had not. An unpleasant argument ensued, during which he chastised his wife for failing to plan properly. Resuming their journey Raju became very convicted by the Holy Spirit for speaking poorly to his wife. He asked her forgiveness, and as they came closer to the city decided to stop at a large store that sold women's clothing to buy her a dress as a demonstration of his love and remorse for mistreating her.

As he checked out with his purchase, the cashier handed him a slip of paper and encouraged him to fill out his name and phone number. "We are having a big drawing tomorrow for the grand prize, a brand new car. The contest has been going on for months and tomorrow is the big day. Make sure you fill your name to enter." Pastor Raju was in a hurry and didn't want to be bothered, and thousands of people had already filled out their names anyway. This was likely a foolish gimmick and he dismissed the cashier. "But sir," implored the cashier, "you never know whether or not you could win; please, take just a moment and fill it out." He hastily scribbled his name and put down Dr. Singh's phone number, not having one of his own.

The next day in the middle of the conference, K.R. received a phone call and came to speak with Pastor Raju. "Someone from such and such a clothing store is calling for you. They say you are their grand prize winner and they need you to contact them immediately." Raju could not believe his ears. Was it possible? Surely this was a scam. Racing down to the shop he discovered it was not a scam at all. Fully and legally, he was now the owner of a brand new shiny red car! He beamed with joy as he told us his story. "God can do anything! Even in the deepest part of the jungle He knows how to answer the prayers of His people. All I had to do was ask!"

To my knowledge Pastor Ratna Raju is still driving that same vehicle, afraid no longer of encountering pythons in the road. His testimony has stirred the faith of an entire generation of pastors and evangelists, emboldened in their petitions to believe that God can also equip them with those things that are needed for the fulfillment of their call. And not just the things that are needed...but perhaps even, now and then...someone might end up with a brand new shiny red car!

60 JESUS IS BETTER THAN THE INTERNET

One of the first mission teams that we led out of Church on the Rock was to the nation of Peru, where David Pepper had been born when his parents pioneered there as missionaries to the Amazon Jungle district of Loreto. We had a large team of youth, along with a worship band, and the primary aim of our trip was to minister in public schools with a concert of contemporary music followed by a short gospel presentation. The Peruvian leader of the ministry in Iquitos, our base city, had secured permission from a number of local school administrators. Though landlocked in the jungle, Iquitos was nevertheless a large city of half a million people, and there were numerous public schools with thousands of students who needed Jesus.

We had conducted several meetings in Elementary schools with real success, but the most challenging meeting was saved for last at one of the city's largest High Schools. As soon as we arrived the Principal met us and delivered the parameters of what we would be allowed. There would be time for 20-30 minutes of music, and a maximum 15 minutes of speaking. I knew in that moment that allowing for translation from English into Spanish, I would have no more than seven minutes to speak. There were well over 1,000 High School students assembled in the central courtyard of the property, along with all of the teachers, administrators, and employees. These were not children from an Evangelical context, an extraordinary chance to impact them for eternity; but I had a mere seven minutes.

I quickly whispered a prayer, as I had so many times previously in the tribal area of India: "God, you have to tell me what to do. This is too rich an opportunity to be squandered by my own reasoning. If you have ever talked to me before, please talk to me now!" I waited for just a moment, quietly shutting out the chaos of 1,000 restless high schoolers around me, but it didn't take long: **"Tell them that Jesus is better than the Internet."** I knew that more was about to follow, because that line would take up about 15 seconds of preaching. I needed an outline to know what God was thinking and where He wanted me going. And then I saw it, like a script unfolding before me, a window into the mind and desire of each of these young people. Internet access had only recently begun to sweep across the globe. Young people who were in the remotest of places now had a chance to see and experience a world that for centuries was beyond their reach. Every young person at that high school dreamed of owning their own computer, and ultimately of connecting to the world wide web.

"Tell them that Jesus is better than the Internet. He can show them things they would never otherwise be able to see, take them to places they would never otherwise be able to go, and connect them with people they would never otherwise be able to meet." That was it, in a three point sermon. God had just unfolded to me the "key" that was going to unlock their hearts. Jesus was the greatest provider of opportunity and promotion a young person could ever find. In a world of limited opportunity, His possibilities were limitless. The Internet was awesome, but Jesus far better. If they would put their trust in the One who had sacrificed His own life for their good, then an eternity of transformation, privilege, and opportunity awaited them as sons and daughters of God.

I delivered that three point sermon in seven minutes, and the Spirit of God proceeded to deliver 1,000 students, along with every single adult present, directly into the family of God. Every single hand of every single person was raised. Every student, teacher, and administrator wanted the limitless possibility brought by a relationship with Jesus. Everyone there prayed to turn away from sin, to affirm their faith in Christ's death and resurrection, and to receive the gift of eternal life. It was one of the greatest moments I have ever witnessed. And it resolutely changed my view of preaching. Sermons don't have to be 90 minutes to get a point across. God can change a generation in seven minutes if that's all He's given. Nothing is impossible for God.

61 GOLD STRIKES IN MACEDONIA

By 2007, fifteen months after moving to Wasilla, we were well settled into our new life and our mission travel was once again kicking into very high gear. All three of our kids were living in Dallas, the boys having enrolled at the Christ For the Nations Institute, and Melissa working in the neonatal unit as a nurse at a local Hospital. This was her first full time position following her graduation at ORU. With all of them in the same city we purposed to pass through frequently, spending two consecutive Christmases together and thanking God that even with a move to Alaska we were somehow managing to remain close knit as a family.

One day we attended a conference nearby in Fort Worth, where a man we trusted began to deliver a word from God's heart regarding our future ministry: *"You will receive many Macedonian Calls; you will not stay long, but God will send you from place to place with His word. When you return, you will bring the report of the great things He is doing. You will discover gold and silver wherever you go, and return home to announce 'there is gold there!'"* We knew that the gold and silver represented symbolically the moving of God in the lives of people. Many see only a desert, falsely believing that not much is really happening in the world today. They fail to see as Jesus saw, when He told His disciples to "lift up their eyes and see the fields that were white unto harvest."

World harvest had begun on a level unprecedented in history, and our task was not only to help gather it, but to report back to a sometimes skeptical or discouraged American church that "God really is pouring out His Spirit all over the world!"

We began to see the reality of that word in one Macedonian Call after another. The Macedonian Call referred to a vision recorded in the book of Acts, when the Apostle Paul saw a man beckoning him and calling for help. The man was in the region of the world still known today as Macedonia. Today the phrase is used in church circles to refer to an irresistible invitation from the Lord to travel to a part of the world to assist those in need.

Macedonian calls came from every quarter, and suddenly our mission world was no longer India, Ecuador and Peru. We traveled to Egypt, Colombia, Guatemala, Burma, Sri Lanka, Romania, Bulgaria, Laos, the Philippines, Indonesia, East Timor...and these were just the beginning. Each time we turned around it seemed that God was sending us out to a new nation filled with harvest possibility.

At Church on the Rock's Mission Conference in 2006 we met an extraordinary couple, Ron and Shirley Devore. The Devore's had spent the past 25 years pioneering an amazing work in Uganda, which had since spread to more than 100 churches over seven East African nations. They were both nearing 70 years old and still full of fire and passion for God. Lenora and I were affected powerfully by their story, seeing before us a couple who modeled precisely the kind of life of faith and mission dedication that we hoped to be living when reaching such a stage in our own journey. Our hearts were knit as we asked them to pray for us, and soon we were making plans to join them where I would speak for a Pastor's Conference in Uganda.

It turned out to be one of the most significant Divine connections we have had in our mission career. Their DNA and heart were identical to our own, and their partners in Uganda were of equal passion. Pastor Steve Mayanja preached in the opening session, and my words afterwards were these: "I did not even know that such a preaching anointing existed anywhere on earth." I experienced and heard the power of God come upon a man to a degree I had never seen or even read about before. It was undoubtedly a gifting that came directly from the Spirit of God, for no man in the natural could speak as Steve was speaking. We became equally knitted with Pastor Steve and his African team, traveling in the coming years for church planting campaigns in various Ugandan villages, and thrilling crusade style outreaches in Rwanda and Burundi.

It seemed there was "gold" every place we went. We discovered an essential principle of world mission. Jesus did not send His disciples out to fail. He told them that it was "to the Father's glory that they bear much fruit." His intent was the advancement of His kingdom, and the successful transmission of His message. Those who believed in His Name would heal the sick, resuscitate the broken, push back the powers of darkness, and set the captives free. Gospel preaching was not a gamble. The "gold" was there all along, for we all carried it within us. If we could simply believe in the ability of "Christ in us," then that same Jesus would never have a problem expressing Himself through us. This was the Spirit's purpose and power, to make each one an effective "witness" of the reality of Jesus Christ. We weren't peddling empty religion. We were proclaiming the nation transforming power of a living God, the Name above every Name, and the One who was able to deliver on every single one of His Father's promises. It was a glorious season of gold mining for His glory, but of course, the best was always still to come.

62 YOU CAN DO THAT

We were standing with Dr. Singh at his ministry center one afternoon in India as he showed us his latest project. "We want to build a place of safety for the elderly widows who have no family or home. Many of the non-Christian families simply stick their elderly out in front of the house, and wait for them to pass away. When they are widows it is even worse, for they are considered 'bad luck' for the family and are no longer allowed at birthday parties or marriage celebrations. It is as if they no longer even exist. We want to build them a place of dignity where they can pray, sleep peacefully, and be cared for until they go to be with the Lord".

No matter how many people he had already reached, K.R. and his team were always reaching for more. Our church in Hicksville had already in the past partnered in the building of several orphanages and churches, purchased ministry vehicles, and supported their medical outreaches. It was wonderful to return home from those trips in the late 90's and share the opportunities to be a blessing, to which our members always readily responded. But we were no longer pastoring a local church. It was just Lenora and I and B.M.I. - Brake Ministries International. I found it took more courage to dive into a project without the resource of an entire local church financial structure behind us. Yet God was not going to allow us to dumb down our faith simply because we were structurally on our own. It was time to learn faith at a deeper level.

"You can do that!" I heard those words clearly in my spirit, even as K.R. Singh articulated the extensive planning for the beautiful three story Widows Home that was going to cost around $50,000, half of which had already been pledged by K.R.'s friends in Germany. "You can raise the other half." God seemed quite confident in the fact that we were capable of believing Him for the provision. I was happy enough to come up with the ticket expenses for each of the many trips we were now undertaking, but a $25,000 project was not on my wish list.

"You can do that." God was not leaving me alone. I finally expressed to K.R. that God was speaking to me to commit to the project. "I don't know how, but we are going to go home and God is going to provide the funds for these widows." The money poured in almost immediately and the home was completed. A number of precious elderly widows live there now in great happiness and honor.

What does it mean when God says "you can do that?" I have heard this phrase softly repeated on multiple occasions. Most of the time God is referencing something we do not have the resources or ability to do. But we do have the gift He has given to us all, the ability to exercise faith which will always, to some degree, release the grace of God.

Faith has been given in measure to every man, woman, or child who has put their trust in Jesus Christ. We can exercise what He has given, and watch in amazement as He begins to work through our lives, or, we can bottle up what we have with a false sense of unworthiness, never realizing the miraculous things that God desires to release unto others through our obedience. When God says "you can do that," what He really means is "if you are willing to tackle this for My glory, I'll give you the courage and resources to back it up! All we have to do is say "yes" to God.

In 2010 I stood in the office of Dishan Wickramaratna, pastor of the 10,000 member People's Church in Colombo, Sri Lanka. David Pepper and I were there for a Leadership Retreat earlier in the week, and now it was after the Sunday service and we were hearing the report from Hans, a People's Church missionary to East Timor. God was moving wonderfully in East Timor, the world's newest nation at that time, but one torn terribly by a recent civil war. There had never before been a nationwide pastor's gathering for pastors from all different denominations. Hans was appealing for all of us to come and seize the window of opportunity. **"You can do that"** I heard once again. They needed literature, books in their language, and funds for the conference. "You can do that." I didn't know why God was telling me, when the other two men in the room pastored churches of 10,000 and 2,000 respectively. Why pick on little B.M.I.? And that was exactly the reason, for we needed to mature beyond having a faith proportional to our size, and develop a faith proportional to God's size. Of course He wasn't asking me to foot the bill in its entirety, or even in its majority. But he was asking me to commit myself as a partner if my friends were also willing.

Absolutely, let's do it! That was the response all around, and we embarked on what for David and I became one of our most memorable times together on the mission field. My younger brother worked as a missionary in Sulawesi, Indonesia, with access to the main printing company for Christian literature in Bahasa Indonesian. We got a rock bottom rate and were able to order multiple book titles for every pastor who would attend in East Timor, many of whom had not a single book in their library. Suddenly we were in one of the least easily accessed countries in Asia, pouring our heart and soul into men who were elated at the opportunity to attend a conference held solely for their equipping and honor. People's Church and Church on the Rock financed the costs of the conference, and B.M.I. was able to raise additional funds for the literature and some of the personal needs of the leadership. What if we had not believed God when He said "you can do it"?

One year earlier I stood in Surigao City, Philippines with Ron Devore and Steve Mayanja. We had come with the intention of conducting an unprecedented evangelistic campaign on Dinagat Island, a place controlled for years by a bizarre cult whose leader had died and been embalmed above ground. His body was on display in a mausoleum where his followers awaited his promised resurrection, bringing him elaborate meals multiple times daily. "No one has ever preached a campaign on Dinagat Island a local pastor in Surigao City now warned. You cannot go there. The spiritual warfare is too great, and the bondage too extreme. It is dangerous. You must not go. You cannot do this!"

But God had told Ron Devore that he could do it, and Ron had rounded up Steve Mayanja, Pastor Ed Pohlreich, myself and my son Omar, and several other great friends...and we were all there to do it with him. It had never been done before, but God said, "you can do this!" Never mind the skepticism of those sedentary leaders who had long since lost their fire.

God did it indeed, exploding upon Dinagat Island with the power of the Gospel such that even the mayor eventually put her faith in Jesus Christ. Scores of men and women came forward to renounce all false Gods and seek the true God alone. On Dinagat each resident wore an engraved ring to symbolize their allegiance to the deceased false Messiah they all worshipped. I will never forget one of my greatest joys in life, when a woman in her 80's who had been deceived for decades approached the altar during the altar call. She did not need that ring any longer. She had heard of the true Messiah, and wanted Jesus to enter her heart. How many more chances would that woman have had if we had not believed the word of the Lord that "we could do this?" Would she have had even one more chance? To see someone at the very end of their journey find salvation is an incomparable joy.

What is it that the Lord has asked of you? Without any doubt, you can do that.

63 HE CAN'T SIT THERE - HE'S THE WRONG GUY!

When God says "you can do that," He seldom means that you will do it alone. Team ministry is the normal method God chooses. Jesus sent His disciples out in pairs. The solo preacher or missionary will rarely go far, as we are simply not designed to succeed in isolation.

I'm not sure we will ever have a year like 2009, when our feet ended up in 32 different nations. It was a wild and crazy adventure of travel, and the success on Dinagat Island that Spring was just the beginning. Pastor Ed Pohlreich was one of our team members as we bounced along the waves on a local Philippine fishing boat, an interesting type of vessel with one narrow area for seating in a dugout hull, and two parallel stabilizing bars extending far out on each side. Eddie pastored a great church in Maple Valley, Washington, but also had worked for years alongside Papa Ron Devore in Africa. We had met once before in Uganda and were getting even more well acquainted as we headed across the open water for our cult confronting crusade. He was now slated to preach our first meeting on Dinagat and was diligently studying his open Bible when a large wave splashed over the side and soaked the pages completely. I teased him that God must be telling him he had the wrong message, but of course he delivered a great word that evening to kick off the outreach on the island. I didn't know then what a tremendous role Pastor Ed was going to play in the future of our family.

Upon returning home from the Philippines we had a strong sense that our entire family was to travel together to Uganda that September for two weeks of ministry with the Devores and Steve Mayanja. Melissa had moved to Alaska that previous Summer and was working at Providence Hospital in Anchorage, and both of our sons had graduated from Christ for the Nations and returned home. We had not been on the field all together since 1997 in India, and the prospect of traveling to Uganda as a family of five adults was like an unexpected dream come true for us as missionary parents.

Several years earlier Melissa had shared with me her heart determination that she would only marry a man who had a passion and love for the mission field. She did not meet that man during her years at Oral Robert University, but we prayed and were assured that God knows how to bring the right person into the lives of those young people who are sold out to Him. Whatever lengths it took, He had the means and method to honor her resolve.

Ron and Shirley Devore had a young man that worked at times in their ministry and they occasionally teased that they thought he was a good match for our daughter. We all knew enough though to keep silent and leave such things to the wisdom of God.

Melissa told me that there was a strong likelihood she would not be given off work for the amount of time she would need to go with us. I had a recurring thought in my heart that God intended for her to meet her husband there. I thought that perhaps it was the young man mentioned by the Devores, whom I had never met, but whether or not it was him, I was certain that Africa was a potential key for honoring Melissa's desire to have a mission minded husband. I told Melissa that God would give her favor at work, because she absolutely must go with us to Africa. Of course I was equally keen for the boys to go, but not with the same sense of what I was feeling for our daughter. I said not a word about her potentially meeting someone.

We found an amazing flight deal that allowed us a stopover in Rome for only $100 more, an irresistible adventure for our family, so Uganda was preceded by three extraordinary days of exploration, the memories of which we treasure greatly. We walked mile after mile on blazing hot 98 degree days, but we weren't complaining. We were in Rome, and the sights of the Coliseum, the Forum, the Plazas, and the Sistine Chapel at Vatican City were a dazzling foretaste of what awaited us in Africa. For myself it was an emotionally intoxicating time of reveling in the graciousness of God to our family. What were we doing eating pizza and gelato at the Pantheon? We had once foreseen nothing beyond a quiet life hidden away for decades in the Andes mountains of Ecuador. God was repeatedly granting us dreams of which we were undeserving. Yet still the greater miracle was just ahead. The greater miracle is always ahead. As is stated in the Scriptures, He moves us from glory to glory.

Ron Devore was waiting for us at the airport in Entebbe. The ministry bus was in the parking lot, and two young American men had come along with Ron to help with our luggage. I thought that one of them was the one they had mentioned previously, so naturally I gave him a bit of a closer look. A few other members of Ron's team were there as well, and after loading the luggage we all began to pile on to the small bus. I stood at the front of the bus as I normally do with a team, making sure everyone is aboard and that all is secured and in order. The two young men were the last ones to board, and with just a couple of empty spots remaining, the one in question walked right past Melissa and sat in the rear. The other young man was a very tall fellow from I didn't know where, as we had only been quickly introduced in passing while waiting for the luggage. He was quiet and appeared to be there solely as an extra pair of hands. He walked down the center aisle and spied one of the last seats remaining, an empty spot next to Melissa. And it was there that he planted himself.

Having been focused on the first young man, I was taken aback by the forwardness of this anonymous interloper who dared to sit next to my beautiful daughter. In my mind, I said very emphatically to myself: "Oh No - That's the wrong guy!"

What happened next is a moment that I refer to as "the closest I've ever come to hearing the audible voice of God." It was so loud in my head that I actually glanced back behind me. It was as if someone was shouting in a whisper. In that moment I heard the Holy Spirit speak into my mind the following words: **"I know what I'm doing!"**

I literally was startled, because my mental meandering about him "being the wrong guy" was not intended as a conversation starter with God. It was simply the pondering of a protective dad who wanted the best for his daughter. But God had entered into my train of thought forcefully to inform me that He knew exactly what He was doing.

My very next thought was that I was looking at my future son in law. God's voice was so adamant, that I could interpret it in no other way. The young man seated by my daughter had apparently not chosen that seat by his design alone. This had been the Lord's doing.

Needless to say, in the midst of a whirlwind of ministry activity over the coming weeks, I was continually focused on Derek Cladek, the man who is now in fact my son in law. And what was Derek doing there in Uganda? I soon found out that he was one of Pastor Ed Pohlreich's most faithful spiritual sons, there in Uganda with Pastor Ed for the same conference in which we were speaking, and as well having traveled previously to Africa with Ed for various outreaches. Derek was a young man with a heart sold out to foreign mission. He was a single 27 year old from Maple Valley, Washington with a genuine love for Jesus.

I kept looking for him in the services where I was preaching, but he never appeared. I calculated, very inaccurately, that if I was hearing God clearly then certainly Derek would show up in some of the meetings so as to discover what a delightful set of parents this girl Melissa had. How else would he know to pursue her? I'm speaking tongue in cheek of course, but the fact was that Melissa and Derek didn't seem to cross paths much the entire time we were in Africa. I had not spoken a word of what I had heard to Lenora, and I certainly wasn't going to tell it to Melissa. If this was God then it was going to have to be fully God. I didn't want to manipulate it in any way.

Alas, Derek skipped every single service in which I ministered. He was involved with his own activities and projects. God had said "I know what I am doing", but it was not apparent to me how He was going to work it out. We left Africa with a great time of ministry under our belts, but nothing tangible for me to grasp hold of that would give any hope of a budding relationship between Derek and Melissa. Returning home, I tucked away what I had heard in my heart, resuming our busy year of travel, but soon wondering if I had heard clearly after all. A vision delayed can often blur into a vision that is doubted. This is one reason why God told Habakkuk to "write the vision and make it plain, that he may run who reads it." We must continuously refer ourselves back to those things God has said lest we lose heart along the way and diminish the passion of our pursuit.

More than six months after our return, Melissa approached me one afternoon: "Dad, do you remember that guy in Africa that met us at the airport? His name is Derek. Well, he and I have been messaging back and forth on Facebook for a while, and he wanted to know if he can call you." Yes, I remembered "that guy" quite well! But I showed no sign of my over familiarity with the subject of Derek, and told her to pass on the message that he was welcome to call.

Fast forward through a six month courtship, a visit up to Alaska, and a wonderful time of getting to know this outstanding young man, and Derek was on the phone with me one day, nervously telling that he had a question to ask me. I already knew what the question was, and I already knew my answer. "Yes Derek, you are more than welcome to marry my daughter. I have not the slightest doubt that this was the plan and purpose of God for both of you!" Derek wanted not only her hand in marriage, but our permission to fly to Ireland where Melissa was about to travel with us for a preaching engagement in Westport, as well as a few days exploring the countryside. "Can I fly in and meet you at one of your hotels and surprise her with a proposal?" Wow, this guy was way beyond my initial assessment in Uganda! We readily agreed and Derek hatched a masterful surprise that resulted in the most romantic engagement story I've known, but that will have to be told by Derek and Melissa in their own book one day.

God so often exceeds our dreams. Six years now since their marriage in 2011, Derek and Melissa live just twenty minutes away with our two beloved grandchildren, Elijah and Emmeline. Pastor Ed Pohlreich, the man who stood with me on Dinagat Island to do what God said "we could do," went to be with the Lord in March of 2016 while serving faithfully on the field in Uganda. He has left an incredible legacy in the lives of thousands, and we will be forever grateful for the particular legacy he left in the heart of a young man who came into our lives and changed us all forever.

64 PLANES, PICK UPS, AND PAPUAN PIGLETS

Life on the edge continued to get edgier. If we had ever had any illusions about a traditional missionary life they had evaporated long ago. Every trip brought a new faith adventure. One of the greatest came when we fulfilled our college dream of ministering in one of the world's most famous mission fields, the Baliem Valley of Irian Jaya. Many of our fellow students at Nyack had connection to Irian Jaya through their missionary parents. Formerly under Dutch control, Irian Jaya was now known as the province of Papua in Eastern Indonesia. This was a different region than the independent nation of Papua New Guinea, but both of these parts of the world contained some of the least reached people groups on earth. Our childhood denomination had been one of the original organizations to pioneer missions in Irian Jaya, and we had grown up enthralled by such powerful missionary classics as Eternity In Their Hearts and Peace Child. Lenora and I had both strongly considered the possibility while in school that we might one day be full time missionaries in Irian Jaya. To reach the unreached had always been a core part of our calling and desire.

We flew into Wamena on an aircraft that seemed held together by wire and string, slipping between the narrow gap in the mountains and landing at long last in a valley that prior to World War II was hardly known to modern civilization. The Dani peoples were one of the first tribes reached by the early missionaries who went in following the war. One elderly Dani man hung around the airport wearing nothing but a gourd, the traditional attire of days gone by, but now his means of snagging a photo op with tourists for a few coins of gratitude. Wamena was a bustling town trying hard to catch up with the 21st century. We conducted some wonderful services in a local church, and had a particularly exciting outreach one evening to local teens, many of whom responded to the altar call at the end.

The greatest highlight though for Lenora and I was the invitation to preach for a Dani community outside of the city of Wamena. We visited the older pastor who shared his story, one of the first of the Dani people to go into ministry. Determined to be as cross culturally relevant as possible, we accepted his invitation to crawl through the very low entrance into the thatched hut where he lived with his wife, a number of relatives and their babies, and the mandatory complement of pigs.

The pigs slept in the same quarters as the family, and the shared life with the swine often extended beyond even cohabitation. Some Papuan women have been observed allowing the piglets to find nourishment from their own milk. This is unthinkable in our western culture, but it wasn't strange in the least to these folks who have been referred to in one book as "<u>The People That Time Forgot</u>". Time had forgotten them, but God had always kept them under His watchful eye, navigating toward that day when the many tribes that inhabited Irian Jaya would finally be reached with the liberating message of the Gospel. No longer would their women be required to hack off a finger in mourning each time a family member died. No longer would they be consigned to never ending cycles of inter-tribal warfare. Jesus had come with His message to bring peace into their world of darkness.

I regretted it immediately when I crawled into that hut, suddenly surrounded by babies and women that were all hacking their lungs out with various afflictions. The piglets lay nearby under the protective watch of the Dani pastor's wife. Later that morning we enjoyed a marvelous time of worship with the Dani congregation, celebrating afterward as they prepared a traditional pit barbecue of yams and meat smoldering underground with hot coals and stones. I took a lifetime of memories away from that morning, as well as a nagging cough and fever that was probably some Papuan version of the swine flu. If that was the risk of living on the edge, we were willing to keep risking it.

So many avoid the mission field for fear of unknown perils that may lie ahead. "Nothing ventured nothing gained" has been one of our oft repeated creeds. "But what if you lose your life one day...aren't you afraid?", we have sometimes been asked. Jesus said that "he who saves his life will lose it, but the one who would lose his life for His sake would find it." We don't expect to die during our travels, but if we one day did, we would have died while living to the fullest. Faith often pushes us out into waters that only God can navigate.

A few months later, as if we did not have enough adventure, Lenora decided that we should celebrate my 50th year by parachuting out of an airplane. I was not interested in this type of edgy living. Melissa and Lenora had long spoken of their desire to parachute and plummet miles to the earth. They are the type that seek out the wildest roller coaster at the amusement park. I prefer to park myself on a bench with some peanuts and a caramel apple. I downplayed their preoccupation with parachuting for as long as I could, arguing that it was an unnecessary danger and I did not want to be left a widower by such a calamitous means. I would crawl into the hut of a Dani tribal but I was not crawling out of the belly of a plane!

Peer pressure crushed me in the end. A place nearby my mother's home was famous for skydiving, and their plan was made during one of our family reunions in Florida. Announcing their intent at dinner, my older brother David chimed in that he too would go. Next came Nancy, David's wife. Then Nash, Nancy's son. This was now turning into a frenzy of family irresponsibility, but still I held my ground. Soon our son Omar joined the growing list of reckless relatives, leaving only Derek and I alone in our determination to resist. And then the camel's back was broken. My 75 year old mother announced her decision to join the jump. All my excuses went out the window, and shamed into submission, I feebly agreed to the inevitable.

"Think of it as a 'leap of faith' into our future!" "You are turning 50 - this is symbolic of all the great adventures that still lie ahead!" Lenora's smile and optimism were apparently intended to calm and inspire me, but it was to no avail. Strapped tightly against my skydiving guide and soaring now to three miles high, I looked at the open space where there should have been a door and pondered the insanity of falling out willingly. "You will free fall for one minute, then we will deploy the chute. You don't have to worry about a thing." I wasn't consoled by the pre-flight instructions. Always the thoughtful and supportive wife, Lenora had also prepaid for me to have an accompanying skydiver with a video camera, apparently amused at the thought of recording my terror. "It's your 50th Kelly...it will be a great birthday souvenir." I made only one request of my guide, and that was a smooth ride with no spinning or gyrations of any kind. I get sick looking at a merry go round. Being a sadist, this only inspired him to spin me wildly on our descent.

The video is a family favorite, never failing to bring endless laughs to our kids as Dad tries to avoid vomiting at 10,000 feet. Landing safely on the ground, Lenora bounded over to say "wasn't that awesome!!...we definitely have to do this again!" I promised that if we make it to our 60th anniversary when I am 80 years old, I will do it once again. I had had enough excitement to last for a while, at least until our next mission trip.

Weeks later we were bouncing along a dirt road in the back of a pick-up in rural Guatemala. Our friend Egidio Monterosso pastors a great church on Long Island, but also is very involved with church planting in his native country. After several years of invitations we finally had a window to travel with Egidio and his wife, but things were tense on the back roads that evening. Egidio and his previous team had been held at gunpoint by men who had threatened their lives. Everything was stolen, including passports and money. Now we were accompanied day and night by two policemen with automatic weapons, assigned by the tourist authority to keep us safe. Some in the village had warned Egidio that we were being watched for an opportunity, so when we set out after dark to travel to a distant village church, everyone was extra jumpy.

All of a sudden we came upon an overturned load blocking our way, the classic set up for a robbery. Just as suddenly a truck came flying up behind us and slammed on its brakes at the last moment, with headlights blinding our vision. In a flash the trained officers flew out of the back of our pick up, their firearms trained and ready to fire. Egidio sat in the back muttering "shoot first and ask questions later." Quickly the country farmer in the truck turned off his headlights, as the officer's flashlights revealed his passengers to be something other than would be assassins: a child, an elderly grandmother, and two pigs.

We laughed hysterically at our own melodrama, Egidio assuring me he had only been joking when coaxing the officers to open fire, and I knew that indeed he was. As serious as the business of the Kingdom of God may be, laughter is one of the key ingredients to long term success.

Lester wasn't laughing though as I preached that evening. Our stern guard who had leaped out of the truck ready to open fire had seen far too much of violence in his young life as an officer in Guatemala. He stared at me intently from the back of the small church, the only time I have preached with an armed guard standing directly in the doorway to screen each person that entered. I went out to talk with Lester afterward, and he gruffly told me it was a "good message." "Oh, are you a Christian" I asked? Lester was emphatic that he was not a believer. "I grew up in the home of a Pastor. I saw a lot of things, and I don't follow that way anymore." I began fervently to pray in the quiet of my heart, "Oh Lord, if we have any fruit from this time in Guatemala, let it be that Lester returns into your arms of love."

Days later we were wrapping up our time and saying our goodbyes. I could not leave without talking to Lester one more time. Egidio asked him if we could pray, and the floodgates of his heart overflowed. Sobbing now uncontrollably, Lester could no longer resist the love of God that the Holy Spirit had pursued him with all that week. "I am a sinner...I need forgiveness...I want Jesus to be in my life again." Lester was wonderfully restored to God that final day in Guatemala. And we were wonderfully renewed in our determination to continuing living on the edge. It was a good thing, for we were soon to be pushed to the precipice of our faith once again.

65 YOU ARE GOING TO MEET A MAN

"You are going to meet a man who will connect you with many new groups across the world; new streams, new relationships, new countries. God is about to open many new doors through this man whom you will soon meet." I really was not looking for a pile of new relationships. Our lives were full, and though we did sense a growing burden to mentor younger pastors and couples in leadership, our schedule was already at the outer edges of what I thought possible to manage. Yet I could not take these words lightly.

Two of my dearest friends on Long Island have been my prayer partners for years, and whenever we visited I made sure to have breakfast with Joe Lutz and Tom Carey. Joe is a widely respected church leader, now in his 80's, and Pastor Tom, also in his mid-70's, has always devoted himself to Christian unity on Long Island. Both of these men were very highly regarded by the clergy in our area. I took their words to heart, for they had been accurate in their prayers over me many times in the past. Now Joe was speaking very confidently to me the words that had come to him as we waited on the Lord. "You are going to meet a man." Tom, on the other hand, had the strangest picture come to him in prayer, and we all laughed when he shared it: "Kelly, I saw you wearing a pair of Bermuda shorts. God is sending you somewhere hot." I reminded Tom that just about everywhere we went was hot, but "I'll file the word anyway in the back of my mind to see if it has meaning down the road." This humorous picture later became a much more serious matter.

A few weeks later I sat in the annual Church on the Rock Missions conference and listened with rapt attention to a man I consider to be one of the world's foremost preachers. Dale Yerton has been preaching for nearly 60 years, beginning from the time he was a 10 year old boy. A longtime colleague of Bill Pepper, Dale too had a great calling to missionary evangelism and traveled constantly as a pastor to pastors. Thousands of pastors around the world would go out of their way to sit under his teaching ministry, and his book Foundation Truth has been translated into 26 languages. When I heard Dale preaching, I knew I was listening to a man whose fire was nowhere near going out. I did not know Dale personally, and had only heard him once prior to this meeting. He did not know me at all.

That night I received a phone call from Dale, telling me that he had spoken with David Pepper to request permission to speak with me. Would I be willing to meet him for breakfast the next morning? He had something in his heart that he wanted to share. We sat in a Wasilla restaurant as Dale began to share what God had spoken to him the day prior. "When you were on the platform, God spoke to me about you. He spoke to me about your calling and the plan He has for you to impart into the lives of pastors and leaders. I've been praying and asking God to bring someone to me who can begin to travel with me and get to know the ministry groups that I work with. I don't know exactly what God has in mind, but I felt strongly enough about it to ask you if you would be willing to pray and see if God would confirm this and then perhaps we can pray specifically about setting out on one or two trips together."

All I could think of as Dale spoke was the word Joe Lutz had spoken to me back on Long Island. "You are going to meet a man." Could this be the man? Only the night before in the service I had been approached by David Eubanks, the inspiring leader of Free Burma Rangers. David did not know me either, but he proceeded to speak the identical words about God's intent for my future as Dale was speaking to me now. I needed to pay close attention, for directive words that are identical and spoken back to back do not come on a daily basis. God was trying to drive something deep into my heart, preparing our family for a significant shift in our ministry.

Dale and I discovered we both had a great deal in common, having been baptized and beginning to share our faith at the age of 10. Our preaching styles were similar, and we both had a God instilled passion for cross cultural ministry. But Dale was known all over the world. I always joked with our children that "mom and I are famous: in jungles, dusty villages, and obscure countries that no one has ever heard of. Outside of that we are quite anonymous". Dale was not anonymous, and it was a great honor to be asked to pray about traveling with him.

That breakfast with Dale opened up an entirely new direction in our lives. Dale worked with the key national church leaders in almost every nation he traveled to, and that number was not a few. With all of the places Lenora and I ministered in, it seemed that almost none of them overlapped with the places Dale ministered. It was as if we had been working in one quarter of the nations while he worked in another quarter. Our sphere was about to increase dramatically, just at a time when we felt we had enough to keep us contentedly busy for life. But scheduling in the ministry is not about what makes us happy or content. It is all about what best serves the purposes of God. And what best serves the purposes of God is always the swiftest path to contentment.

Dale and I made our first trip that following year to Armenia, and we have been collaborating and networking ever since. Through Western Asia, Eastern Europe, Mexico and Central America, we have enjoyed our fellowship as a God arranged team. I have enjoyed learning from a man who loves people with an even greater intensity than that with which he preaches. He walks in a unique humility for a man who preaches with such power. I am so glad for the word in 2012 from Joe Lutz, and that God saw fit to prepare me with that word, "you are going to meet a man." The new priority of traveling with Dale would bring some logic to another one of those strange and unexpected twists in our journey. We were about to discover the meaning of the Bermuda shorts, and would need every confirmation from heaven that we could get.

66 THE EAGLE FLAPS ITS WINGS

Around the same time that I was meeting Dale Yerton I began to be distracted by a recurring thought that our time in Alaska would not be permanent. It seemed that each time we had settled on the idea of permanence, God would send us out into another assignment and phase of ministry. But Alaska was a wonderful situation in so many ways. We were part of an amazing body of believers. We were generously supported with both finances and prayer. We had precious friends, and even Derek and Melissa had purchased a home only a mile away. We had been looking at homes ourselves in 2012 in the Matanuska Valley around Wasilla, but nothing clicked.

By now we were traveling out of Alaska a least a dozen times per year. This added 9 full hours of flying round trip each time, and that was just to get to the lower 48 in Western Washington state. If we needed to get to the East coast before heading to Europe or Africa, another 18 hours round trip was added in the air, not counting layovers and boarding times. Over the course of the year it was adding up to more than 140-150 extra hours of flight time. With the upcoming assignments to accompany Dale Yerton, that looked to only increase. Basing out of Alaska would become a greater challenge.

Our youngest son Jonathan was in a relationship with Lynn Olson, one of 13 children born to Dan and Allouiz. The Olson's oldest son Alan, twenty years Lynn's senior, was coincidentally one of my good friends. We had met on a previous excursion to some remote villages in Peru's Amazon. Shared adventures on the mission field have been the source of most of my closest friendships, and Alan and I have a great camaraderie. Dan Olson was also the first member of Church on the Rock to bring over a gift of food when we moved into Wasilla, some ground moose meat for burgers, and frozen halibut from his Summer fishing.

Alaskans are wonderful about sharing nature's bounty with one another, and our New York taste buds would need some rapid adjustment to an entirely different cuisine.

Jonny and Lynn began dating at the same time as our family trip to Uganda, so by 2012 they had already been together for three years. They were not engaged, but we thought they might likely be married one day. I recall a distinct thought that Fall that "if we were to move, it would likely coincide with their wedding." "Two years from September" flitted across my mind, but there was no clear word to move yet, just the sense that change was coming. Some things God communicates with undeniable clarity, and other things come by an impression or recurring thought that must be pursued in prayer. Lenora and I began to talk about the possibility of an eventual relocation, even though neither of us were overjoyed at the prospect of pulling up stakes once again.

When we had first driven up to Alaska, I asked the Lord in real sincerity "why do we have to move all the way to Alaska?" He gave me only one clear answer, and repeatedly reaffirmed it to me over the years we were there: "I am sending you to be a friend to David and LaRae." There were many wonderful things that came out of our time in Alaska, not the least of which were a lifetime of friendships, open doors of ministry, amazing lessons of faith, and the list goes on and on. We could itemize a hundred different blessings, including at the top a husband for Melissa and a wife for Jonathan. God is an expert at making many things happen at once, and causing "all things to work together for good." The friendship with the Peppers was obviously about more than sentiment and good times however, for God is not likely to uproot a family and send them 5,000 miles just for the sake of warm feelings. There was a great responsibility that the Peppers would carry, and Church on the Rock would eventually influence multitudes of people all over the world. The leaders of such a movement always have a need for trustworthy friends. We were honored that God had called us to Alaska for this purpose.

The preacher Charles Carrin had been ministering in Alaska a year or so earlier, and he felt prompted to give me a word which would have bearing on our future: "You came into Alaska by following the cloud of the Holy Spirit's leading, and you are only to leave Alaska by following that same cloud; don't get ahead of the cloud." I certainly at the time had no intentions of leaving, so I wasn't too worried about getting ahead of the cloud. Yet the Lord knew that the time would come when I would be tempted to move faster than what He had in mind.

In 2013 the time came for Bill Pepper to hand over the reigns of Amazon Outreach, the ministry he had founded more than 50 years prior. His son David was the logical person to take on the responsibility. David had in fact for some time been thinking of turning the Wasilla campus over to another staff member for the purpose of stepping more fully into international ministry. Now it was the Peppers who would be moving out of state, and the flash thoughts six months earlier about relocation suddenly began to make sense. If we had been sent by God primarily to stand with David and LaRae, and if they were now relocating, was that in God's mind the completion of our assignment? It made sense, but where were we to go, and when? And why when we had such a strong support base for our mission calling did we have to put it all on the line. It was much easier to step out on the ledge when we were barely 30, but now nearing our mid 50's risky ventures did not have quite the same glitter. But such are the ways of God. We never retire from living by faith. Just ask Caleb, who at 85 was contending for his mountain. God never caters to the pleas of the soul for a reprieve from faith's demand.

With the church facing transition, I now wanted to speed up our own transition. I did not want to hang around for the long and convoluted process of installing a new lead pastor, helping a church through the emotions of change, and lingering over the thoughts of how it could have been different. If it was time for change, then let's get on with the change. But God wasn't just thinking of our change, or only of our friendship with David and LaRae. We were friends as well with so many families and staff members at Church on the Rock. From God's point of view, we had a debt of gratitude that we needed to repay by walking with the leadership through the transition process. That was best for David and LaRae, and that was best for the hundreds of other families at COTR. Yet it wasn't only about the present. God was also thinking about the future, for we did not know then that I would soon be asked to serve as an overseer for the Church on the Rock community. If we had cut and run early, racing ahead of the cloud simply to selfishly save ourselves from the task of navigating change, we might have missed an important opportunity to continue to support and strengthen the body of Christ in Alaska, even if from afar. We were keener than ever to hear clearly and stay focused on the cloud.

By Summer of 2013 I decided to take into confidence one of my most trusted friends in Wasilla. He was one of my prayer partners, and a great source of solid counsel. I shared my conviction that a relocation would come, but admitted that I did not yet have a timeline from the Lord. What my friend did next was something he had never previously done. He bowed his head at our table in Starbucks, sat quietly for a moment, then looked up at me directly and stated quite firmly: "your move will coincide with Jonathan's wedding." I was impacted greatly, for I had never told a soul about my previous impression that there would be a connection between Jonathan & Lynn getting married, and Lenora and I moving. This seemed a tremendous confirmation from the Lord, with the exception of one small hiccup: Jonny & Lynn were not yet even engaged.

That was July, but in August things changed. We were out of state when Jonathan called me to announce the good news that Lynn had said "yes!" They wanted to know if November of 2014 was a good time for us with our travel schedule. I told my son that anytime he wanted was a good time; we would alter our travel schedule accordingly as their wedding was top priority. When I hung up the phone I thought briefly about my impression almost a year earlier regarding "two years from September," but just as briefly dismissed it. I thought I had been right but it's not unusual to get these things wrong. We all see in part; no one sees perfectly. My bigger concern was the thought of relocating and driving out after a November wedding during Alaska's Winter. It would have been much easier to move in the early Fall.

A few weeks later and Jonathan was on the phone again: "Dad, would it be a big problem if we move the wedding from November back to September? Will that be a conflict with any of the plans you have made?" "No son, no conflict in the least!" What a wonderful confirmation from the Lord that He was fully behind our move. I didn't need seven confirmations like when we had first moved up in 2005, but I sure did not want to blow it on the way out. Being in Alaska at Church on the Rock was a dream come true situation for any traveling missionary. We would be fools to leave without God's authorization and command. Now we only needed to figure out where we were moving. We had been here before, but that part never seems to get easy.

As Lenora and I prayed over the coming months, no instruction or revelation came. We considered all our options, usually involving a church we knew well where we could fit in seamlessly and resume our ministry without having to break completely new ground. It wasn't going to be that simple. Florida was repeatedly the only place where we seemed to have a peace. It was true that there was much to endear us to the idea of moving to the Gulf Coast area of Tampa, Florida. We had vacationed there at my mother's home almost every year since 2000. My older brother was there, as well as our much loved Aunt Hannie, Uncle Omar's widow. The Tampa Airport was rated #1 in the nation in several categories, and an excellent gateway to Atlanta or New York.

But Florida was one of the states we had never preached in a single time. If we moved to Florida, where were we going to attend church? And why would we move to a place where no one but family knew us? This was a conundrum that pushed us repeatedly back to the drawing board to consider all our options. One by one each other option was eliminated, due to a lack of peace. God wasn't writing Florida in the sky, and we had no dreams or visions compelling us to go there. It was simply the one place for which the light always seemed green. There was no command to go to Tampa, but there was no heaviness, weight, or prohibition either. We had the desire for it, we could see some of the logic of it, and if God wasn't saying no, then to Florida we would go unless he stepped in and said otherwise.

God is not obligated to spell everything out for our doubts, but I'm so thankful for His goodness to give us confirming words once we have made up our minds. We were attending a meeting in Canada in the Spring of 2014, and a preacher was speaking who I had only met once previously. He did not know our story, and he did not know of our plans, though he did know we lived in Alaska. Calling me up to the front, he began to relay a picture that God had shown him earlier:

"When you walked into the room, I saw you and your wife standing in Alaska. Suddenly a large eagle was hovering over you, and then it mightily whooshed its wings. When it flapped it's wings, you both went tumbling forward, and I watched as you tumbled over and over all the way down to the Southeastern portion of the United States."

Suddenly it was "Florida, here we come!" We were elated at this comforting confirmation from the Lord. We were heading in the right direction and we were not heading there on our own. A hovering eagle in the Andes mountains had confirmed God's care before we drove up to Alaska, and a wind whipping eagle in a vision was now confirming God's direction before we would drive back out. How grateful we were for the kindness of God in giving us strength for the challenge of pioneering once again in a brand new land. It might not be easy, but He would still be with us. And that was all that mattered; that has always been the only thing that mattered. "I will never leave your or forsake, for Lo, I am with you, even unto the end of the Age."

67 A HOUSE AND A CHURCH OF GOD'S OWN CHOOSING

With our travel schedule, Jonathan and Lynn's impending wedding, and the transition at Church on the Rock, I felt overwhelmed by the additional prospect of locating a new residence in Florida. We wanted to be somewhere in the vicinity of my mother's home, but aside from that we weren't sure about much of anything. We were traveling in Asia late in 2013 and the weight of starting over hit me like a wave. I said to the Lord, "I have no idea which town, what house, or where I even will be going to church." I'll admit that it was another moment of self-pity, but God did not hesitate to lend me His perspective:

"You know that you are going to Florida and you know that you will be in the Tampa area; that's way more information than Abraham had when he had to move."

Case closed, but once again there would be no time for a scouting trip in advance. I told God sincerely that with everything else on our plate, I needed Him to find for us a place of His choosing. I woke up one night after Midnight in Wasilla and did something I absolutely never do. I don't work at night, snack at night, or walk around in my sleep at night. Once in bed I stay there until it is time to begin a new day. But something was strongly pushing me to get up and open my laptop. I was sitting in the chair where I studied and a thought came to me almost like dictation: "Craig's List Dunedin Florida Home Rentals."

There are several reasons why this was strange, first of which was that I had looked only once in my entire life at Craig's List for anything. It was when we were looking for a black Labrador puppy, and for those who follow us on Facebook, you are well acquainted with Max, our now six year old Lab. Aside from puppy hunting, I had never had need of Craig's List. In fact, I did not know that people even listed their real estate by that means. I had no frame of reference for thinking to look for a home rental in this way. I can only conclude that God spoke this to my mind, just after Midnight, and compelled me to enter that terminology into the Google search engine.

Dunedin is the town where my Mom lives. She had been looking for homes, other family members had been looking for homes, and we had looked a few times on sights like Zillow, but nothing had popped up that looked right. Now at 12:20 AM Alaska time I was looking down at a listing that had just been listed 20 minutes prior...at around 4:00 AM in Florida. Who posts a listing at 4:00 AM?

Quality home rentals last a few days at best in Florida. The competition in this crowded area to snag a decent home at a reasonable price is fairly fierce. One has to be vigilant constantly or at the very least have a realtor working on their behalf. We did not have a realtor, but we did have the One who owns all of the real estate. He had just pushed me out of bed to be the first person to see a listing that was exactly what we had been thinking we would need.

It was one mile from my mom's, fully furnished, in a golf community, and allowed for pets. Pets were the biggest issue, as most rentals had a strict "no pets" policy. We weren't just asking God for a place for us, but we needed one as well for Max the dog and Lucy the cat. I immediately emailed the owners to inquire, telling them a bit about our occupation and reason for moving to Florida from Alaska. I asked if my family members in Florida could come over for a look if it was still available. First thing in the morning I had a response:

"You are the very first person to respond to our advertisement. Yes, your mom is welcome to come by this afternoon. And how wonderful if this turns out to be the right home for you. We are also Christians. Perhaps you can visit our church when you arrive here to Florida."

My mom and aunt headed over there pronto later that day, reported back that the home was suitable for our needs, and later I was on the phone with the landlord. They had already had a slew of phone calls, some offering to pay more than the listing price, and even people at the door with cash in hand. But we had responded <u>first</u>, and their ethic was that the first to respond has first right of refusal. If we wanted it we could have it.

Lenora and I had already been praying, but we took one more step to clarify to ourselves that I had indeed been awakened by God to find this particular home: I asked them for a 15 month lease at $100 less per month than their listing price...and they accepted it! They emailed us a lease, which we signed and returned with our deposit, and just like that, sight unseen, we knew our next address in Florida. With my own imagination I could never have come up with searching for "Craig's List Dunedin Florida Home Rentals." That might be a common sense approach to some, but I did not have the experience to know that one could find a home in this manner. I would never have thought to search at 12:20 AM Alaska time, twenty minutes after the ad had posted in Florida at 4:00 AM. No one was awake and searching yet in Florida, but we serve a God who never sleeps. Just as He guided Abraham each step of the way toward Canaan, so He was ordering our steps as well.

The plan was for Omar and Derek to drive a U-Haul down at the end of July to move the possessions of our two families, then fly back to Alaska. Derek and Melissa had decided to move to Florida as well and would store their things with us until they found a place of their own. Lenora and I were heading to Uganda and Burundi in August, and after three weeks in Africa would return to Wasilla to pack up the house in time for the whole family to fly to Hawaii for Jonathan and Lynn's wedding. We would fly back from the wedding and 24 hours later close up our rental home of nine years and set out in a two car caravan, Melissa and Derek with baby Elijah in their vehicle, and Lenora and I in our own. Omar, Jonathan's best man in the wedding, would fly from Hawaii to Florida as our advance team, we would take three weeks to drive down preaching along the way, Max & Lucy would sit in a kennel in Wasilla until October when we came back for Missions Conference and could fly them back to Florida with us, and then we would all live happily ever after!

We declared it the most madcap and audacious sequence of events we had ever concocted, and one completely impossible without some miraculous grace from God. We would need a multitude of flights and road trips and mission outreaches to all come off without a hitch, not to mention the most important event of all, Jonathan and Lynn's wedding. Everything was timed down to the day and hour, and everything unfolded with perfection. We were peaceful and joyfully exhausted, but so amazed by His grace. True to the timing He had whispered two years prior, it was now the Fall of 2014 and on October 1st we crossed over the Florida state line.

The challenge of our residence resolved, we now faced the challenge of discerning our new place of worship. Just as God steered us clearly to our home we were also asking that He steer us clearly to our church. We did not want to shop around like consumers.

We knew that if God had sent us to Florida, He was also sending us to a particular community of believers. But the Tampa area seemed to have a few thousand places of worship. Where in the world to begin?

Only two weeks after arrival we were back on a plane to Alaska for the annual Missions Conference and to retrieve our pets. One of the speakers at the conference was our friend Dominic Russo, one of the leaders of Missions.Me. When Dominic heard that we had moved to the Tampa area he enthusiastically recommended a church he had once visited: "You ought to go to Citylife! Great church, great leadership, and a great heart for missions." I had been praying for God's direction, but to my discredit I did not take Dominic's recommendation seriously. For one thing Citylife Church was over in Tampa, almost an hour from our new home in Dunedin. And Dominic was 30 years old.

Perhaps I didn't like the idea of such a young guy being God's means of showing us where we should go to church. Sometimes we are stuck on a roof and praying for rescue, then after refusing the helicopter and boat we accuse God of not keeping His promise. Too often we are looking for dramatic fireworks, when God is trying to speak to us and help us by the simplest of means. Sometimes the answer is staring us right in the face. We should not miss God by insisting on everything being so profound. It might feel awesome to have a fiery prophet wave a finger of revelation at us while pronouncing "thus saith the Lord;" but more often than not, the greatest messages of life come to us through the usher quietly stacking chairs, or the sweet older lady who has faithfully served in the nursery or cleaned up in the church kitchen.

It is critical that the older generation have an ear to hear the word of the Lord through the Samuels being raised up in this hour. I filed away what Dominic had spoken, and Lenora and I returned to Florida to begin searching on our own. After a couple of disappointing Sundays, we realized we ought to give Dominic's suggestion a try. Lo and behold, Dominic's friendly suggestion a month prior had been the answer from God after all. When we moved away from Church on the Rock we wondered how and where we could find a place so spiritually rich and fulfilling. Once again, God took us from one glory to another glory.

Citylife Church has been to us for the past 2.5 years an oasis of life and a well of living water. Every service is an absolute delight. The preaching by Pastor Tony Stewart is some of the best we have ever heard, and there is always a powerful presence of God in worship. It is a move of God that far surpasses anything we have been a part of previously in North America.

Our Father God really does know best. He chooses well and wisely for every season of our life. As our mission work now exponentially increases, we are so grateful for a location that gives us easy access for travel, and a home church that refuels us with a steady stream of fresh oil each time we return. As an added bonus we even get to go home to Alaska twice a year to minister and celebrate among our precious Church on the Rock family, and to see our daughter in law and son. We go home every year to Long Island, Canada, Washington and see families that He has given us all over the world. It truly is a wonderful life when Jesus is the One leading the journey.

68 IT IS NIGH UNTO THE TIME THAT MY WORD COME TO PASS

"The time will come when this church will give more than $1,000,000 to world missions." I wanted to cup my hand right over my mouth. I was in Alaska preaching about God's provision back in 2002, less than two years after Church on the Rock began.

The congregation was still under 200 people and they were meeting now in a storefront building. I was not anticipating that the inspiration to speak something prophetic was going to come while I exhorted, but it happened, and now I was speaking out what seemed foolish. How would this small group of believers ever give that much money to the Great Commission? My friend David Pepper gave me one of his bemused looks that said "you've really gone and done it this time Brake."

Missions Conferences came and went, the church growing in its size and generosity and at times surpassing $500,000 or $600,000 in mission giving. These were tremendous amounts, but still far from what had been spoken in those beginning years.

Now it was 2014, and Lenora and I were just back from our move to Florida. I was slated to give a seven minute spotlight testimony of our missions work on the night of the missions banquet. The closing banquet was the highlight each year, a night when the church members would bring their mission pledges and offerings and the sum would be totaled. By now there were many mission organizations from every region represented, and some of the world's best speakers would be in attendance for the COTR annual event. A handful gave spotlights in each service over the four day conference, and one would also preach. It was important for all of us to keep to our allotted time.

I was in prayer that banquet morning, seeking God's thoughts on how best to fill my seven minutes, when I heard once again a word that was totally out of left field: **"It is nigh unto the time that My word come to pass."** This did not come to me as a vague whisper, but was once again one of those emphatic directives from God. Immediately He flashed my thoughts back to the prophetic statement 12 years earlier about the church giving more than one million dollars to missions. I began to feel uneasy with the implications of what I was hearing. "What does that mean God that it is 'nigh unto the time that Your Word come to pass'?" "What am I supposed to do?" God then told me what I was to do with my time that night: "You are to get up and remind people of what I have spoken. And then you are to declare what I have just declared to you: 'It is nigh unto the time that My Word come to pass'."

I began to wrestle just a bit, because if I was going to get up and say those words, then there was no out - the word would have to necessarily come to pass. Otherwise my wife and I might be slipping out of town in the dark of night. We are firm believers that if something is declared it ought to be followed by a demonstration of what was spoken. It would be no problem if I simply stood up and said "God wants to see this church give over $1,000,000 tonight!" That was not however what He told me to say. He was being very explicit, telling me to declare the original word, and then to follow it up by making the declaration that the time for fulfillment was upon us. That meant that anything less than $1,000,000 coming from gifts and pledges would be a miss.

I called the office and made an appointment with the pastor. I had experienced the privilege of praying over Jonathan Walker when he was installed as Lead Pastor the first week of January in 2014. Jonathan is an excellent teacher and a no nonsense leader, not one with a penchant for flaky prophecies or theatrics. If I was going to deviate from the path of an assigned seven minute spotlight, I did not want to do so without securing his permission. A guest speaker's plan and program should not supersede the authority of local leadership.

I went in and shared with him that God had given me a prophetic word that I believed I needed to share that evening. I asked if he would give me a full ten minutes, because I didn't think I could do it in seven. I then asked if I could speak as the last speaker, right before the pledges were to be taken. Jonathan agreed to everything, and I went about the business of working up my courage for the remainder of the afternoon. The service that night was going to be live streamed all over the world. I reminded God that it would not help our ministry reputation if I made a fool and spectacle of myself publicly. "Just do what I have asked you", He said, "and leave the rest to Me." There was no squeaking out of it.

That night the banquet proceeded as usual, and my time came to speak. All of my nerves evaporated as the calming authority of God's presence began to rest upon me. I related the story of the prophetic word from 12 years earlier. The majority of the people there that night had no knowledge of those previous events. I then delivered God's message for that night, announcing it with every ounce of conviction I could muster: "God is declaring to all of us here that 'it is nigh unto the time that His word come to pass'!" I resumed my place on the platform with all of the other guest missionaries, watching as the greatest spirit of giving I have seen swept over that room. The only thing I've seen comparable was the spirit of giving that came upon the lepers on that long ago day back in India.

The first to pull the trigger was Pastor Jonathan himself, who stepped right up following the pronouncement, and pledged that he and his wife Kitri would give an amount far above what they had intended. People were exultant with the joy of supernatural giving. The missionaries themselves were giving away thousands of dollars. The staff and pastors of the church were giving extraordinary sums. Everyone was compelled by joy to go far above and beyond what they had ever given before. The tally as checks were totaled was ticking higher on the projection screens over the sanctuary and the applause became louder as the numbers went higher. There was no manipulation from the pastor or from any other speaker. There was no pre-planned method for what unfolded. It was spontaneous and Spirit inspired. It was a manifestation of grace, and an explosion of joy.

As the numbers shot over the $1,000,000 mark, one of the missionaries walked over and whispered to me: "I'll bet you were standing here sweating - you must be relieved." "Relieved" would be the understatement of the year. Yet the moment those words were spoken, I felt a peace that the outcome was set into motion. Would we have had the same outcome if the words had not been spoken? Would the outcome have changed if Pastor Jonathan had not embraced God's intent? That is a deep and important question. I do believe that there are many things God wants to do that only are accomplished through the conduit of individual obedience. There are people He wants to heal, souls He wants to save, families He wants to feed, and destinies He wants to release. But someone has to be the trigger. God isn't bound by our action or inaction, for He is God, and He can do whatever He pleases. But as God, He has chosen to work through the vehicle of faith and obedience in the lives of His people. He can work around that, but He most often works through that. We may not like such a responsibility resting on our shoulders, but whether we want it or not, it is this to which we have all been called.

What is it that will be released by your response to His command? What soul is waiting for you to step up and speak what He has spoken? Will we deprive others of seeing His glory and encountering His love, only for the sake of saving our reputations or sparing ourselves the rejections that may come? I was approached that same evening by several men after the service, all asking if the $1,000,000 had been staged and pre- planned. I was surprised by their question, yet I understand that this is representative of where many people are at. We simply find it hard to believe God speaks in this way. We are perplexed by a God of miracles, a God for whom the working of wonders is business as usual. May God steadily continue to convert our minds in this 21st century age of skepticism, back toward a 1st century faith in the simplicity of the power of Jesus Christ. May the miraculous become Believable once again. For He is, and He will always be, a God Who works wonders. Nothing is impossible for those who believe.

BRAKE MINISTRIES INTERNATIONAL

69 I DON'T WANT TO GO BACK TO
THE DOMINICAN REPUBLIC

The only country that I had ever left and determined never to return was the Dominican Republic. It's a wonderful nation of people, but my experience with feuding church leaders there in 1994 had spoiled my perspective. Here we were now in 2014 and Pastor Jeremy Cotton, one of my prayer partners, was proposing that I join the One Nation One Day series of crusades being planned by Dominic Russo and his Missions.Me team. "I could see you doing one of the stadium crusades bro.", he appealed to me after our time of prayer. Jeremy was planning to lead a large team out of Church on the Rock and thought it would be great if I joined them. The twenty one largest stadiums in the nation had been reserved across twenty one states for the culminating night after a week of evangelism and relief work. It was to be an historic and epic event in world mission history on July 25th, 2015. The President and Congress of the Dominican Republic had given their full backing and declared the crusade day as a national day for dedicating the nation to God. Hundreds of thousands would be reached with the gospel.

I wasn't interested, or so I told Jeremy. I explained that we really didn't focus much anymore on large scale events of that type, preferring to invest our effort into training and supporting pastors. I appreciated his zeal to have me join the effort, but it just wasn't on my radar for 2015. We would be moving soon anyway to Florida, and the last thing I wanted was to add another major project to our plate. We were already scheduled in 2015 for Peru, South Africa, Armenia and Eastern Europe. The Dominican Republic would have to wait.

God had other plans. The very same morning that He spoke to me about resurrecting the million dollar prophecy, He also began to speak to me about the Dominican Republic. I had an insistent conviction that Jeremy may have been right. I sincerely did not want to commit myself to such a large endeavor, but I prayed and asked God to give me a very specific sign: "Lord, if this is you, and if this is something you are assigning to me, then let me know by causing Dominic Russo to walk straight up to me tonight to ask me directly if I would be willing to join their team as one of the stadium preachers." Dominic and I had shared very limited conversation in the past at Mission Conferences, and we had certainly never spoken about my partnering with Missions.Me. If he did in fact approach me that night in such a manner, it would be an irrefutable sign from God.

As the banquet concluded and people were milling about, Dominic made a beeline in my direction. "Pastor Kelly, I would like to ask if you would pray about something. Would you consider being one of our stadium speakers for the Dominican Republic? We have 18 of the 21 stadiums sponsored, but we are asking God to direct us regarding the other three. I felt that I should ask you."

There could have been no clearer confirmation from God than this. I answered Dominic immediately, "Yes, I'll be glad to do that." "Oh that's great" he replied, "thank you for praying about it." "Actually Dominic I don't have to pray about it" I explained. "I meant 'yes' I will do it." Dominic looked at be surprised, not expecting such an immediate answer. "Are you aware of the cost for one of our preachers to sponsor a stadium event?" Most of their speakers were the pastors of mega churches, men far more well-known than myself. "No Dominic, I am not aware, but it doesn't matter. God already told me that I was to speak for one of the events, so He will have that taken care of as well." "Wonderful" Dominic replied. "I'll call you as soon as I get home and we can discuss the details."

I didn't think I needed more confirmation, but God knew that I would as this project was going to require of us way more than I had imagined. The next morning as we were leaving for the airport I received a call from Laurie Miller over at the Palmer campus of Church on the Rock. Laurie has always had an exceptional ear for hearing from God. "Pastor Kelly, this may sound really strange, and if it means nothing please just discard it. But as I was praying for you I had the strongest sense that you were supposed to speak for one of the stadium events with Dominic in the Dominican Republic. I felt I should tell you that before you leave". Neither Dominic or I had told anyone of our conversation only 12 hours earlier. (Other than my discussing it of course with Lenora both before and after the banquet that evening). "Laurie, thank you so much - you have no idea what those words means to me!" I let Laurie know how timely and profound her words had been.

Lenora and I flew back to our new life in Florida, where we would shortly discover that Dominic's word about Citylife had been accurate, and I awaited his phone call. There were two levels remaining of stadium sponsorship, one requiring $40,000 and one requiring $65,000. These were small figures relative to the overall costs of the outreach for which Missions.Me raised and spent millions. If the organizations and churches represented by the stadium preachers could cover the costs of the outreach night itself, that would enable everyone to share more equitably the faith responsibility for changing a nation in a day. It was a wise structure and a reasonable request. "Well Dominic, for us there is no difference between $40,000 or $65,000; either one requires a miracle. If we are going to believe for 40, we can just as well believe for 65; but let me consult with Lenora first, and I'll get back to you by the end of the day." Lenora, the greatest faith partner on the planet, did not even blink. "Of course we should commit to the $65,000! What difference does it make. God said clearly we should do this, so let's take the high road of faith and watch Him do the impossible."

I am so thankful for the privilege of living such a life of faith. We did not see the assignment as a burden, but as a wonderful challenge to believe God for more. Dominic and his team are outstanding leaders, and we considered it exceptionally good ground into which to sow our resources, time, and gifting. We began to share the project with our friends and supporters, and within a couple months half of the funds had come in.

And then donations ground to a halt. We were committed to paying in full by the month of May, but May was now upon us and we were still $30,000 short. Setting off on a preaching trip to Washington and Alaska, I was somewhat stressed over the amount of money that was still outstanding. We did not want to cause a problem for Missions.Me as they also had bills to pay. The 1Nation1Day event was now only two months away. I sent an email to their office and promised that within 21 days, we would meet our obligation in full. There are times when you have to put God's promise and your own word on the line.

God is so wonderful. At the first church we visited, the Pastor shared his burden from the Lord to help raise any remaining funds we needed. At the next church we visited, they held a dessert auction, something they had never done before. We ended up surpassing what we needed for the Dominican Republic and joyfully fired off our check for the remaining $30,000. When you are giving to God, there is a great joy in releasing money for His kingdom. There are always a thousand and one things we could do with $65,000, but "seek first the Kingdom of God." This has always been our guiding principle. We knew that in sowing at that level there would be a reaping in the days to come. It is impossible to out-give God.

That July 25th was the greater reward, far greater than any sum of money that could ever come into our hands. More than 400,000 souls in the Dominican Republic were touched by the gospel of Jesus Christ across 21 stadiums and seven days of outreach by an army of more than 2,000 missionaries, mostly young people. A new generation has arisen that is going to reach more people than have ever been reached. They are out of the box thinkers, anointed by God's Spirit, and called to bring in the greatest harvest the world has ever seen. Are we who have been around a while willing to believe in them, support them, and applaud their success, even if their methods are different than our own? Dominic Russo and thousands of young men and women like him have been born for such a time as this. Let us run along beside them as they write the final chapters of missions history, celebrating together when the harvest comes.

70 WHAT WILL YOU DO ABOUT THE U.S.A?

Our first full year in Florida, the year 2015, was another year packed with foreign mission. The Dominican Stadium would have been enough, but God had so much more in store. In January we camped with Pastor David Pepper among the Candoshi Tribe in one of the most unreached parts of the Amazon. The Candoshi were a severely marginalized people group with a lot of suffering and broken promises from the government. The atmosphere in our first night's meeting was tense and skeptical, but by the end of the three day event the tribe was rejoicing in a visitation from God. One chief stood up to testify that he had just received Jesus, would like to become a Pastor, and would also like to be baptized the next morning. Lenora and I were full of aches and pains after camping in the open on mats that were too thin. We groaned a few times, but still had the time of our life. The revival among the Candoshi is still going on with multiple teams returning to build churches and provide medical care. We did decide however we were getting past the stage of sleeping in the jungle...at least that is until the next time God might send us.

In February we were in Mexico, South Africa in May, and the Fall season was filled with some of the best pastor's conferences and church meetings we've ever experienced in Armenia, Bulgaria, and Romania. In between all of that was sandwiched the 1N1D campaign in the Dominican Republic.

Half way through the year the American Presidential Election for 2016 was in full swing, and most everyone was demoralized about the prospects for a happy outcome. Many pastors I spoke with bemoaned the state of our country, and it looked like things were only going to get worse.

One day in prayer I was thinking on these things when the Holy Spirit asked me a question: **"Your country is in trouble; what are you going to do about it?"** I certainly did not know what I was supposed to do about the mess in Washington so I just sat silent and continued to listen as the Lord proceeded: **"Are you going to sit on the sidelines and watch things go down the tubes like so many others, or are you going to do something about it?"** This time I responded with my own question, "Lord, what can I do?" His reply stirred up a seven year old memory from a meeting in Fort Worth where I had received a very particular word from the same man who had once prophesied to us about "Macedonian calls." He had spoken on another occasion that **"a time will come when you will be called upon to go to State Capitols with the Word of the Lord. People will call you seeking counsel from the Lord."** I had sensed that this was a true word from God's heart, but I had filed it away, occasionally thinking and praying about it but concluding it was not my responsibility to see that it happened.

The memory of that moment now fresh in my mind, I heard the Lord ask specifically, **"what are you doing about that word."** I objected mildly that "I hadn't exactly been getting phone calls lately from the Governors of any states." Our conversation in prayer continued, with God challenging my faith: **"Faith always** steps out. Faith doesn't sit and wait. If you really believe that this word was from Me, you should be doing something with it." We were back to square one, with my mind again perplexed as to what I could possibly do to have any effect on such a huge issue as the future well-being of America.

Things turned in that moment from a conversation to a command: "I have an assignment for you and your wife. Beginning with the New Year you are to travel to all 50 State Capitol cities and Capitol buildings in America. You are to pray and declare my word over each state house, each state and it's leaders, over My pastors and My people, over the outcome of the election and over the future of the United States...and you are to complete this prior to the election in November."

My brain started spinning on several levels, for though administratively inclined, this was beyond the logistics of anything we had done before. This also meant suspending almost all of our international outreach in 2016. People supported us as foreign missionaries, not as stay at home evangelists. I had a flash thought that such a project would put our funding into a death spiral. It is amazing how shortsighted we can be sometimes. God was giving us a dream assignment, asking that we play our part as millions of others would in the spiritual reformation of a morally wounded nation. I was worried about my pocketbook.

At the end of 2015 I took two full weeks to hammer out the logistics of traveling and spending at least one night if not several in all 50 capital cities. This included determining the opening times for each capitol building, preaching locations on weekends, meetings for prayer with pastors or friends at each stop, and access if possible to each of the legislative and senate chambers. It would require numerous flights and 20,000 miles of driving, and yes, it would include Honolulu, Hawaii and Juneau, Alaska. I sat with my calendar and said one word to God: Help! I could not do this without His help in charting out a master plan.

God does all things well. He has a grace for every assignment. The year unfolded as one of the smoothest, most peaceful, and most stress free years we have ever had. During the 50 specific days when we actually were at each State House, there were 50 days of sunshine. We have a photograph in every city of a bright blue sky over the capitol buildings. It did not rain on us even once. In three states the buildings were under renovation, Alaska, Wyoming, and Minnesota. Those were the only places where we could not gain physical access, but we fulfilled our mission while standing on the lawns outside. (In Juneau's case, the small patch of flowers around the flagpole).

We did what God had sent us to do, and our understanding of His plans and purposes for the United States were enlarged far beyond any burden or insight we had previously carried. He gave us His word for each of the 50 states. I won't go here into all that we gleaned and heard and experienced of God's heart for this nation, but it will likely be an upcoming 50 chapter book to tell the story. We learned that God deeply loves the people of this land and has a desire and game plan for revival. **"If My people, who are called by My name, humble themselves, pray, seek My face, and turn from their wicked ways, then I will hear from heaven and heal their land."** It is an ancient promise that God gave to King Solomon, and it is just as true today. Jesus is still a Savior. He is not finished with bringing in the harvest, and He is not finished with this nation of America that many of us call home. God is looking for someone who will stand in the gap and call for mercy. Even as we continue to run forward internationally, there will always be a new affection and calling in our hearts to give ourselves to the dream of revival in America.

POSTSCRIPT

It is the Spring of 2017 now. Dale Yerton and I just recently returned from the Middle East, where we stood in a swimming pool with seven Iranian pastors as nearly 200 new Iranian believers publicly professed their faith in Jesus Christ and followed in His example of baptism. It is a time of worldwide harvest, unprecedented in history. Thousands of laborers around the world are reaping the greatest number of souls into the Kingdom of God that earth has ever seen. Jesus is winning on every front. Radical religions and radical secularism will never bring down the church of Jesus Christ. Every knee will one day bow, and every tongue will one day confess, that Jesus Christ is Lord.

Dale Yerton, David Pepper, Dominic Russo, K.R. Singh, Steve Mayanja; each of these and others like them are simply a component of a much larger global army. It takes millions, all doing their part. Where is God calling you? What is He saying to you? Do you have an ear to hear what the Spirit of God is speaking in this hour?

Lenora and I count ourselves blessed to find ourselves on any given day in some small corner somewhere on the planet. Each day that we wake up with health and strength is another day where we get to do what we do. Time and health and grace and unfolding eschatology permitting, we hope to do it well into our 80's. We look forward and keep pressing ahead. We also make sure to live one day at a time. We revel in our grandchildren, honor our parents, laugh with our kids, stay in touch with our friends, and go to church on Sundays. It is in the repetition of simpler things where true success is found. It is in loving God and loving people, the greatest of the commandments, where the foundation for a Believable life is firmly laid. If we fathom all mysteries, prophesy with great accuracy, move mountains with our faith, and speak in the most eloquent of tongues...but have not love...we have accomplished nothing

FOR MORE INFORMATION ABOUT
BRAKE MINISTRIES INTERNATIONAL

We hope that God has encouraged you through the testimonies in BELIEVABLE. Prayer support from people around the world is the foundation for all that we do and the key to any success we may have had. Please pray and believe with us for continued harvest at this critical time in history. The fields are ripe and ready!

website at **www.brakeministries.com**.

For more information about our ministry, or to connect with us personally, you can contact us by the following means:

BRAKE MINISTRIES INTERNATIONAL
KELLY & LENORA BRAKE
3034 SAVANNAH OAKS CIRCLE
TARPON SPRINGS, FL 34688
kelly@brakeministries.com (email)

Facebook: R.k.Brake
Facebook: Lenora Brake
Facebook: Brake Ministries International

ABOUT THE AUTHOR

Kelly and Lenora Brake have been married since 1983, working together in Christian ministry since first meeting on an evangelism team in the lower East side of Manhattan in 1980 while students at Nyack College. The majority of each year they are active in missionary endeavors around the world, teaching and pastoring national church leaders in numerous countries. They also travel regularly across North America to share God's message with church congregations, speaking in conferences on mission or family, and encouraging people everywhere to stand strong in their faith.

Made in the USA
Columbia, SC
27 August 2019